HIMMLER'S CHILDREN

Himmler with his favourite daughter Gudrun, the only child he had with his wife Marga. He fathered two more children with his secretary. This book is not about them. (*Public domain*)

HIMMLER'S CHILDREN

LEBENSBORN AND RACIAL POLITICS

GUUS DE VRIES

Pen & Sword
MILITARY
AN IMPRINT OF PEN & SWORD BOOKS LTD.
YORKSHIRE – PHILADELPHIA

First published in the Netherlands in 2023 by S.I. Publicaties BV as *Himmlers kinderen: Lebensborn en de rassenpolitiek*

First published in Great Britain in 2024 by
Pen & Sword Military
An imprint of
Pen & Sword Books Ltd
Yorkshire - Philadelphia

ISBN 978 1 39908 055 2

A CIP catalogue record for this book is available from the British Library.

Typeset by SJmagic DESIGN SERVICES, India.

Printed and bound in the UK by CPI Group (UK) Ltd.

Pen & Sword Books Limited incorporates the imprints of Archaeology, Atlas, Aviation, Battleground, Digital, Discovery, Family History, Fiction, History, Local, Local History, Maritime, Military, Military Classics, Politics, Select, Transport, True Crime, After the Battle, Air World, Claymore Press, Frontline Publishing, Leo Cooper, Remember When, Seaforth Publishing, The Praetorian Press, Wharncliffe Books, Wharncliffe Local History, Wharncliffe Transport, Wharncliffe True Crime and White Owl.

For a complete list of Pen & Sword titles please contact

PEN & SWORD BOOKS LIMITED
George House, Units 12 & 13, Beevor Street, Off Pontefract Road, Barnsley, S71 1HN, UK
E-mail: enquiries@pen-and-sword.co.uk
Website: www.pen-and-sword.co.uk

or

PEN AND SWORD BOOKS
1950 Lawrence Rd, Havertown, PA 19083, USA
E-mail: uspen-and-sword@casematepublishers.com
Website: www.penandswordbooks.com

FSC
www.fsc.org
MIX
Paper | Supporting responsible forestry
FSC® C013604

Contents

FOREWORD

The name 'Lebensborn' is shrouded in secrecy and evokes special associations. This is mainly due to the way the organization became known to the general public, when novels and a film in the late 1950s associated it with the commercially successful mixture of sex (brothels) and violence (SS). Subsequently, a number of more and less serious publications about Lebensborn appeared, but it was not until 1985 that the German historian Georg Lilienthal published a book still regarded as the standard work.[1] In the English language, only two books on Lebensborn were published: *Of Pure Blood* (1978), translated from French and written by Marc Hillel and Clarrisa Henry, and *Master Race: The Lebensborn Experiment in Nazi Germany* (1995) by Catrine Clay and Michael Leapman. Despite their merits, both publications described only a small part of the organization and its activities.

This book attempts to provide as complete an overview as possible of Lebensborn and its activities, in connection with and as part of German racial politics. First, the spiritual and political climate in which racial politics arose is discussed, followed by a description of the organization, the position of women and the people behind Lebensborn. Then the clinics and homes are described, and the activities of Lebensborn in Eastern and Western Europe, which were of a very different nature because of the racial ideology. The last chapter describes the end of the organization, followed by the fate of the perpetrators and victims.

It is a difficult book. Because of the suffering inflicted on the victims, and because it is hardly possible to enter into the minds of the perpetrators to understand why. It is also difficult because of the language used, because with this subject it is impossible to avoid the typical Nazi terminology: Germanic blood, Germanic race, Germanize, good blood, blood mixing, Nordic blood, Nordic race, purebred, racial elite, racial division, racial value, racial quality, inferior race, racial undesirable, racial value, race group, racial hygiene, race theory, race poisoning, race mixing, racial purity… to name the most common.

As for all the words and word combinations mentioned above that contain the word 'race' and 'racial', they have, as far as humans are concerned, no factual meaning whatsoever. There is only one human race. There are as many differences among the individuals within a given 'race' as there are among men of different 'races' and it is therefore not possible to divide humanity into clearly distinct racial types. (It follows that the word 'racism' is really an empty concept, and should more accurately be called 'discrimination based on outward physical characteristics', but that aside).

The Nazis interpreted the concept of race in different ways. It was variously used for people with certain physical characteristics, adherents of a specific religion, people of the same ethnic origin, inhabitants of a certain area or people belonging to the same language group – just as it was convenient.

Then there is the way other existing terms were used. For example, the term Aryan, which actually refers to a group of people that are difficult to define precisely and who lived thousands of years ago in the area that roughly coincides with present-day Iran, were used in the Nazi era for the blonde, blue-eyed 'Germanic' (the ideal image of the race fanatic), who, according to the race ideologists, had 'Nordic blood' or 'good blood' running through their veins, who belonged to a superior 'race' and were presented as the proto-German.

Thus, many words and concepts used or described in this book have no actual meaning or have been contaminated by the interpretations given to them by the Nazis. However, the story of Lebensborn and race politics cannot be told without using these terms frequently. To prevent the text from becoming illegible, quotation marks indicating self-invented terms, meaningless words or irony have been kept to an absolute minimum.

Readability has been further enhanced by the people who struggled through the manuscript, made many helpful suggestions, saved me from mistakes, and thereby made it a better book. Therefore, many thanks to Pauline and Richard Oonk and Flip Witte.

Guus de Vries, Oosterbeek, The Netherlands, December 2022

INTRODUCTION

Lebensborn was founded by Heinrich Himmler, the Reichsführer-SS, to increase the number of births of 'racially pure' babies. Himmler was obsessed with birth rates and racial purity; two factors he believed would determine the future of Germany and the 'Aryan' (or 'Nordic') race. Like Hitler, he was convinced that the course of history was determined by the struggle between different races. Those races would have a different 'value' and possess innate, hereditary physical and mental characteristics. It is no coincidence that the Nordic or Germanic race, the greater part of which would live in Germany, was the most 'valuable'. But that race would be seriously threatened by low birth rates and the danger of 'miscegenation', especially with Jews. (According to Hitler and many other Nazis, Jews were not a religious group but a race.) Only population growth of 'racially pure' people and expansion of territory, making the chosen race completely self-sufficient, would offer salvation in the long run.

These ideas had not been developed by the Nazi leaders themselves, but were adopted from a varied group of scientists, writers and fantasists, who brought their ideas to the attention of the public from the second half of the nineteenth century. Although not typically German – it was also commonplace in Europe and the United States at the time to regard the 'white race' as superior – such views gained more ground in Germany than elsewhere. In that country, after the First World War, pre-existing social and political antagonisms and tensions were magnified by the unexpected defeat, followed by the humiliating peace treaty and the disastrous economic misery of the late 1920s. The Nazis blamed the Jews for all German disasters. Hitler explained in *Mein Kampf* the causes of and the solutions to all problems and was allowed to repeat this in detail during his trial following the failed Putsch (coup) attempt in 1923.

After the seizure of power, Nazi ideology could be converted into race politics and its theory put into practice. This first led to legislation aimed at 'racial hygiene' and 'forced euthanasia', and after the outbreak of the war and the occupation of Poland to ethnic cleansing and later mass murder. The expulsion and extermination of the 'racially inferior' were countered by measures aimed at gathering the 'Aryan' population in their own territory and increasing the birth rate of 'racially valuable' babies. Himmler played a leading role in both extremes of race politics. His SS was responsible for the racial selection and the deportation and death of millions of people, but at the same time he did everything in his power to accelerate the population growth of 'racially desired' as much as possible.

One of Himmler's measures was the establishment of Lebensborn, an organization that opened several dozen maternity hospitals, children's homes and boarding houses from 1936, especially for pregnant 'Aryan' women and their new-born children. This was where the leading class of the coming Greater Germanic Empire had to come from. The first branches were in Germany and annexed Austria, but later the organization also became active in the occupied countries. In Western Europe, Lebensborn performed more or less the same activities as in the German Empire, but in Eastern and Central Europe, Lebensborn participated in the abduction and 'Germanization' of foreign children. Himmler attached such credence to the idea of inheritable race characteristics that he thought by stealing foreign children, he would not only strengthen his own 'race', but also prevent the emergence of a new leadership class in the subject country.

I

RACIAL DELUSION

Lebensborn and Race Politics

'I regard Henry Ford as my inspiration.'
Adolf Hitler

Race Politics

In the summer of 1936, more than three years after the Nazis seized power, Lebensborn opened its first branch. It was a maternity clinic called Heim Hochland in the village of Steinhöring, about 30 kilometres east of Munich. In the following years, several dozen more clinics and children's homes would follow. First in the territory of the Third Reich and later also in the occupied countries in Northern and Western Europe.

Lebensborn has been shrouded in secrecy from its inception. Almost immediately after the first branch opened its doors, stories began to circulate that the organization was intended to have specially selected men and women father children. Such rumours easily arose in the countryside where the institutions of Lebensborn were established, and the inhabitants of nearby villages soon saw pregnant women or young mothers with babies pass by. The clinics were located on estates closed off from the outside world and housed in large, luxurious buildings. While it was no secret to anyone that they were guarded and run by the SS, it was not clear what went on inside the walls. Pregnant women, young mothers and the SS. This mysterious combination stimulated the imagination of local residents at the time and, after the war, also that of writers and film producers, who understood that such a subject – sex and violence – guaranteed considerable sales figures.[1]

However, the American military court in Nuremberg, before which a number of staff members of the organization had to answer after the war, came to a very different conclusion. According to the judgment of the tribunal, Lebensborn was nothing more or less than a charitable institution, which had done everything in its power to care for the children entrusted to it.

FORSCHUNGEN ZUR NEUEREN MEDIZIN- UND BIOLOGIEGESCHICHTE 1
Herausgegeben von
GUNTER MANN und WERNER F. KÜMMEL

Georg Lilienthal
Der "Lebensborn e.V."
Ein Instrument nationalsozialistischer Rassenpolitik

SEMPER BONIS ARTIBUS
AKADEMIE DER WISSENSCHAFTEN UND DER LITERATUR · MAINZ
GUSTAV FISCHER VERLAG · STUTTGART · NEW YORK

Above left, above right and left: Lebensborn only became known to the general public in 1958 through a novel that was falsely presented as if the story was based on facts. However, because sex and violence sell well, the book was filmed as *Lebensborn: Liebe auf Staatsbefehl* (translated as Ordered to Love and *Les fiancées d'Hitler*). The German historian Georg Lilienthal's book, *Der Lebensborn e.V. Ein Instrument nationalsozialistischer Rassenpolitik* (2003), is still the standard work on the subject. (*Public domain*)

Both views were wrong. Lebensborn was not an organization that operated luxury brothels or breeding establishments, but it was not a charity either. Lebensborn was an instrument of Heinrich Himmler, the Reichsführer-SS, who had founded the organization to operate maternity hospitals and children's homes to increase the birth rate of Aryan babies.[2] Lebensborn was a small part of the many organizations involved in so-called race politics of the Nazi regime. This policy was based on the racial theory that there were different races whose members shared not only physical but also mental characteristics, which were also considered to be hereditary. The adherents of these ideas were also convinced that these different races had a different value or quality. At the very top were the Aryans (also described as the 'Nordic race' or the 'Germanic people'), all the way down to the Jews.

Although it goes without saying that these views had no factual basis and were completely unscientific, the racial doctrine and the politics based on it formed the central element of Nazi ideology. The idea that humanity could be divided into 'good' and 'bad' races dominated both the domestic and foreign policies of the Third Reich. Racial policy measures and actions were often implemented, even if they were detrimental to the warfare.

The ultimate goal of the Nazis was a Greater Germanic Empire, inhabited by a 'racially pure' Germanic people who were not only completely self-sufficient, but would dominate first Europe and later the whole world. Hitler had written down both his views on racialism and the ultimate goal of his movement years before taking power in *Mein Kampf*, and megalomaniacal and bizarre as they were, nothing would change, as Germany first and later much of Europe would experience.

Immediately after taking power, the Nazis embarked on a radical racial policy characterized by two extremes: on the one hand protecting the 'good blood' against the influence of all 'inferiors' and on the other hand increasing the number of Aryans. In practice, the first aspect led to sterilization and the 'forced euthanasia' of people with physical and/or mental disabilities, massive ethnic cleansing, and finally to the mass murder of Jews, Slavs, Roma and Sinti. On the other hand, there were large-scale operations to transfer as many *Volksdeutsche* (ethnic Germans) and other settlers with 'good blood' as possible to the territory of the planned Greater Germanic state, the abduction of foreign children with the desired racial characteristics, and all kinds of measures to increase the birth rate of Aryans.

Naturally, the murderous side of race politics has received much more attention than the seemingly opposite actions. Yet the other side of Nazi racial politics also deserves attention. Not only because this provides a better insight into the motives and ideas of the perpetrators, but also because the measures to collect as much 'good blood' as possible on German soil have caused untold suffering and many victims, especially in Eastern Europe.

The Nazis' war aims and 'racial' attitudes meant that there were huge differences in the way the population of the occupied territories was treated. In Eastern Europe, the so-called *Volkstumspolitik* was put into practice. This concept, which is difficult to translate, has different meanings depending on time and place, but during the Third Reich it stood for the subjugation, exploitation and elimination of peoples considered inferior, and the conquest of *Lebensraum*. In Northwestern Europe, the occupation initially had a completely different character, because a policy was pursued there that the Nazis called *Germanische Politik*. Its ultimate goal was the merging of the Germanic countries into one Greater Germanic Empire, which, according to the Nazi ideologues, would automatically lead to the 'rebirth of the Germanic race'. In order to win over the (Germanic) population of northwest Europe to this aim, they were treated much less brutally.

Race politics and the foundations for Lebensborn were based on a number of beliefs that formed the basis of Nazi ideology: a potentially very evil mixture of which race doctrine, anti-Semitism and ideas about Lebensraum (living space) and Blut und Boden (blood and soil) were the main ingredients. Developed mainly in the nineteenth century, these ideas originated with publicists and scientists from a variety of disciplines (anthropologists, physicians, philosophers, historians, botanists and zoologists) who brought their pseudoscientific ideas to the public's attention through brochures, books and lectures. Interest in such subjects was great. This was evident not only from the number of publications, but also from the often high circulations. Subjects such as Lebensraum and the inequality of races and peoples were of great interest to a significant part of the conservative German middle and upper classes. Discourses on the danger of miscegenation, Jews and Freemasons also attracted great interest.

Social Darwinism and Eugenics

One of the main sources of inspiration for the racial theory, the central idea of Nazi ideology, was Social Darwinism. This pseudoscientific movement within social science applied Charles Darwin's (1809-1882) theory of evolution and natural selection to human society. The English sociologist and philosopher Herbert Spencer (1820-1903), then a world-renowned writer and one of the founders of Social Darwinism, introduced the idea of 'survival of the fittest'. This notion was then used as an argument to claim that while modern medicine allowed unhealthy individuals to survive, humanity as a whole would weaken as a result. The Nazis went even further. They explained it as the 'right of the strongest': as in nature, the strongest would have the moral right to act as he/she sees fit. Social Darwinism also led to the idea that Judaism was not a religion, but that the Jews were a race.

The view that there were heritable differences between individuals and human populations led to the idea that the population could be improved through artificial selection. The English anthropologist and statistician Francis Galton (1822-1911), a cousin of Darwin, was the founder of this doctrine, eugenics, and was imitated in Germany by Wilhelm Schallmayer (1857-1919) among others. Unlike Galton, who propagated the dissemination of good qualities – the so-called positive eugenics – Schallmayer emphasized the limitation of offspring with bad hereditary qualities; negative eugenics. In 1903 he received a prize from the Krupp Foundation for a book that would become the standard reference for eugenics in Germany in the following decades, including the racial experts of the SS.[3] Schallmayer was a democrat and pacifist, and thus

Above left and above right: Francis Galton (left), a cousin of Charles Darwin, was the founder of eugenics; the teaching that human populations can be improved through artificial selection. The physician Alfred Ploetz (right) was one of the founders of German race politics and introduced the term 'racial hygiene'. (*Public domain*)

certainly not an early Nazi ideologue, but like many of his contemporaries he believed that modern medicine was weakening the human race. He therefore advocated legislation to prevent the reproduction of people with bad hereditary characteristics. Furthermore, Schallmayer propagated early marriages, the highest possible number of children and a cult around motherhood, of course from people with good hereditary characteristics, and all this in the context of a population policy under the permanent control of the state.

Schallmayer received support for his views from several compatriots, including the zoologist Ernst Haeckel (1834-1919), who argued for a strong state led by a biological elite, and the physician Alfred Ploetz (1860-1940), who introduced the term 'racial hygiene' – the prevention of miscegenation. Through a magazine and an organization he founded,[4] Ploetz became widely known and exerted a great deal of influence on the racial politics of the Third Reich. As early as 1895 he suggested that a baby who had been born too weak or deformed should be given a gentle death with a dose of morphine.

The botanist and geneticist Erwin Baur (1875-1933), the anthropologist Eugen Fischer (1874-1967) and the physician Fritz Lenz (1877-1976) published the two-volume *Grundriss der Menschliche Erblichkeitslehre und*

Eugen Fischer was a physician, anthropologist and Nazi, and co-authored the most important book on heredity and eugenics with Erwin Bauer and Fritz Lenz. He was already involved in racial hygiene before the First World War and was appointed rector of the University of Berlin by Hitler in 1933. Here he stands a year later between the leader of the Nazi student union (left) and Professor Bacher, the prominent NSDAP member and veteran of the right-wing Kapp-Putsch. (*Bundesarchiv 183-1998-0817-502*)

Rassenhygiene (Basics of Human Heredity and Racial Hygiene) in 1921. This edition, of which four new editions appeared until 1941, was the most influential work in the field of heredity and eugenics, both in Germany and abroad. This book not only explains how and why the German population shrank and 'degenerated', but also what could be done to reverse these trends. The scholarly writers also advocated ancestry research to gather knowledge about the racial composition of individuals and populations as a basis for racial hygiene legislation and population policy. The University of Munich established a department for racial hygiene in 1923, with Lenz at its head. It was the first of the more than forty academic institutions in this field that existed in Germany until 1945, the first of which were thus founded well before the Nazi era.

Racial Doctrine

In addition to the view that the human population had to be improved, theories were also formulated in the nineteenth century about the value and qualification of the different human races; the so-called 'race theory'. A pioneer in this field was the French nobleman, diplomat and writer Arthur de Gobineau (1816-1882), who published a treatise in which he argued that humanity consists of three races: 'the Caucasian or white, the negroid or black and the mongoloid or yellow race.' According to Gobineau, the Caucasian race was superior – for he believed it was responsible for the origin of culture and civilization – and the current mixing of races led to chaos, degeneration and ultimately the downfall of Europe. He also argued that the basis for European civilization was rooted in the ancient Indo-European culture, which he believed coincided with the people of the Aryans and that the Germans, and thus by extension the Germans, had the most in common with that people.

The English-born author Houston Stewart Chamberlain (1855-1927) was strongly influenced by Gobineau's ideas and published *Die Grundlagen des neunzehnten Jahrhunderts* (The Foundations of the Nineteenth Century) in 1899, in which an argument about the superiority of the Germans was combined with outspoken anti-Semitic views. History, in his view, was a battle of the races, with the German race representing the good and the Jewish race representing the bad. (Like many of his kindred spirits, he used the concept of race as he saw fit, and for the population of a country and adherents of a religion respectively.) Despite its size – Chamberlain managed to fill no less than 2,100 pages – the book became a great commercial success and a standard reference for

Houston Stewart Chamberlain, who viewed history as a struggle between different races, exerted great influence with his publications on the followers of racialism and counted the German Kaiser and Hitler among his admirers. (*Public domain*)

racialists. He was a welcome guest at the court of the German emperor, who saw to it that the book was included in German libraries and in the teaching materials of schools. In 1908 Chamberlain married Eva Wagner, the youngest daughter of Richard Wagner. This was probably at least partly due to his boundless admiration for the composer. He was visited once or twice in the 1920s by Hitler, who not only knew his work well, but was also a great admirer of Richard Wagner's work. Both Chamberlain and the would-be dictator wallowed in in his old Germanic musical dramas, while the composer was also an outspoken anti-Semite.

A third non-German racialist pioneer was the American Madison Grant (1865-1937). A graduate of Yale and Columbia University in law and zoology, he published a book in 1916 that followed Chamberlain's course, entitled *The Passing of the Great Race or The Racial Basis of European History*. This work, which was later published in German, also made a deep impression on the future dictator. Like Chamberlain, Grant viewed history as a battle of races. In his book he described the 'racial history' of Europe and identified the Nordic race as the most important group for human development. He also advocated segregation and sterilization of 'undesirables', weaklings and 'worthless races', to prevent the 'good blood' from becoming further diluted. Like Chamberlain, Grant's view of the essential process of history – the struggle between different races – exerted great influence on Hitler's ideas and worldview.

Many publications appeared in Germany with the same purport as those of Gobineau, Chamberlain and Grant. For example, enthusiasts of this kind of

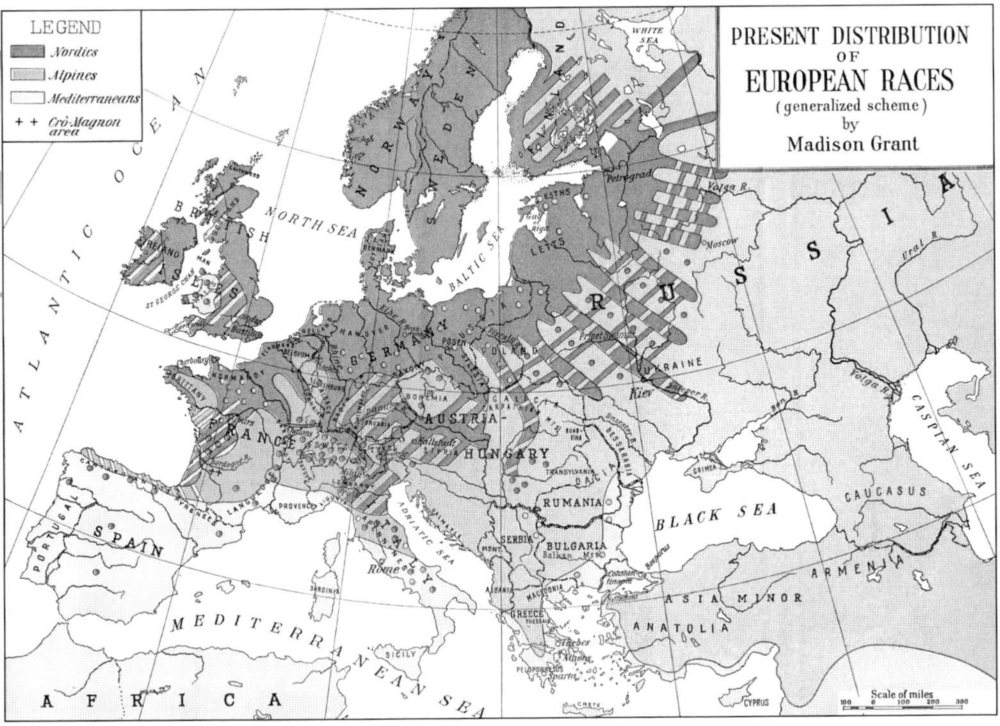

A map from *The Passing of the Great Race* by the American Madison Grant. Like Chamberlain, he saw history as a racial struggle, considered the 'Nordic race' to be the most important, and was one of the Nazi Party's inspirations. (*Private collection*)

views could turn to *Rassenkunde des deutschen Volkes* (Racial Science of the German People), which was published in 1922 by Hans F.K. Günther (1891-1968). It was published by F.J. Lehman's publishing house, which specialized in racist and right-wing extremist publications. The book was a huge success and reached a total circulation of about half a million copies. It was one of the first, but certainly not the last, publications by Günther, who developed into the most important and best-known propagandist of race doctrine after the First World War. In the Germany of that time, where racial science was not a dirty word, he was nicknamed 'Rassegünther' and 'Race Pope'. According to Günther, the European population consisted of six different races, each of which possessed specific, race-related and hereditary external and internal characteristics. He considered the Nordic race superior in physical and mental terms, and Germany, he believed, harboured the greater part of the 'Nordic blood'. In order to prevent the degeneration and downfall predicted by Gobineau, according to Günther, a population policy had to be pursued aimed

Hans F.K. Günther's *Rassenkunde des Deutschen Volkes* reached a total circulation of 500,000 copies between 1922 and 1944, making it the best-known and most influential publication in this field. (*Private collection*)

at strengthening and multiplying the Nordic race, which he equated with the Aryan race. According to him, this so-called *Aufnordung* ('northern') would be a lengthy process that would take hundreds of years.

Racial theory and eugenics were by no means exclusively German obsessions. All over the western world, and especially in the United Kingdom, France and the United States, these issues were the subject of discussion, publications and pseudoscientific research from the second half of the nineteenth century. It was not limited to theoretical treatises, for not only was the notion of the inferiority of other 'races' the starting point and excuse for colonialism, but it was also used in a large number of western countries from the end of the nineteenth century to practice a form of racial politics and eugenics well into the twentieth century (and beyond).

For example, in the United States, as early as 1896 laws were passed that prohibited people with intellectual disabilities or epilepsy from getting married; later enforced sterilizations and legislation restricting the immigration of certain non-white populations followed. As a lobbyist, the aforementioned Madison Grant played an important role in the passage of the Immigration Act of 1924, which prevented Asians from settling in America. In addition, sterilization programmes also existed in many European and South American countries to limit the reproduction of certain undesirable population groups.

Eugenics was mainly practiced by preventing the reproduction (through marriage bans and sterilization) of members of the own population deemed inferior, while racial politics was practised by legislation that discriminated against non-white populations, as was the case with the subordination of the inhabitants of the colonized countries, the segregation in the United States and the Apartheid in South Africa, to name only the best known examples.

Anti-Semitism

Although manifestations of Jew-hatred already occurred some 2,000 years ago, the pogroms in several German cities in 1096 – prior to the First Crusade – are considered the beginning of European anti-Semitism. Initially it was mainly based on religious motives, but later anti-Semitism acquired more and more social and economic motives. In the second half of the nineteenth and early twentieth centuries, when Judaism was viewed by many not as a religion but as a race under the influence of Social Darwinism, anti-Semitism also took on biological and political motives. In Europe at that time, hatred of Jews played a role mainly in Austria-Hungary, France, Poland and Russia – in the latter country thousands of people were murdered in pogroms in 1905 – but it was not completely absent in any country, as the Briton Chamberlain and the American Grant proved.

In Germany, the last two decades of the nineteenth century were particularly fruitful for anti-Semitic authors and agitators. For example, in 1879 the unemployed journalist Wilhelm Marr published the pamphlet *Der Weg zum Siege des Germanenthum über das Judenthums* (The Road to Victory of Germanism Over Judaism) in which he argued that the Jewish and Germanic races were engaged in a battle that the first group threatened to win. In the same year he also

Der Weg

zum

Siege des Germanenthums über

das Judenthum.

Von

Wilhelm Marr.

(Verfasser von: Der Sieg des Judenthums über das Germanenthum; Vom jüdischen Kriegsschauplatz.)

Vierte Auflage von „Wählet keinen Juden".

Berlin N., 1880.

Otto Hentze's Verlag.

106a Friedrich-Straße.

Der Weg zum Siege des Germanenthum über das Judenthums (1879) by Wilhelm Marr is one of the earliest German anti-Semitic lampoons that began to appear from the last decades of the nineteenth century. (*Private collection*) founded the *Antisemiten-Liga*, the first German organization to fight the 'threat' of the Jews by expelling them from the country.

In 1887 no less than three publications were published that would have a major influence on the development of German anti-Semitism: Theodor Fritsch's *Handbuch der Judenfrage* (The Handbook on the Jewish Question), which was reprinted no less than twenty-four times in seven years; Adolf Wahrmund's *Das Gesetz des Nomadenthums und die heutige Judenherrschaft* (The Law of the Nomad and Today's Jewish Dominion), which argued that the 'notoriously rapacious Jews' should be expelled from Europe; and Paul de Lagarde's *Juden und Indogermanen* (Jews and Indo-Germanics). De Lagarde, who was appointed professor at the University of Göttingen in 1869, combined fanatical anti-Semitism with a plea for German territorial expansion to the east.

However, anti-Semitism, as mentioned, was by no means a typical German obsession. One of the most influential activists in this field was the world-famous American car manufacturer Henry Ford. In 1920 he published a book written by several authors with the revealing title *The International Jew: The World's Foremost Problem*. This release, which would eventually consist of four volumes, became a huge commercial success. The American version reached 500,000 copies and the book was translated into sixteen languages. In terms of content, the book consisted of no more than a collection of malicious lies and myths that had in common that they put the Jews in a bad light: Jews were allegedly forging an international plot to seize world power; the press and film industry would be wholly in their hands and misused for their purposes; behind the scenes they were the real rulers in the Soviet Union; they poisoned the world with ('black') jazz music; were responsible for the American Civil War, the First World War and the Russian Revolution etc.

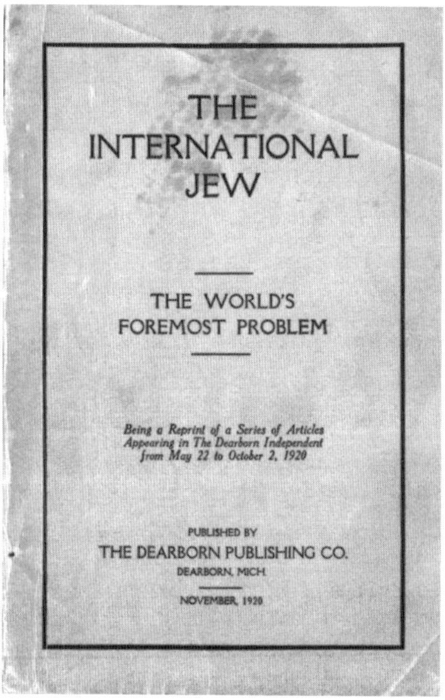

Henry Ford, famous for his T-Ford, was a fanatical anti-Semite. On his initiative, this book was published in 1920. Entitled *The International Jew: The World's Foremost Problem*, it was to exert great influence on Hitler and his future followers. (*Private collection*)

The German edition, which appeared in 1922 under the title *Der internationale Jude*, sold about 100,000 copies. It was also read by Hitler, Himmler and Baldur von Schirach (the leader of the Hitlerjugend) and made a deep impression on them. The latter stated in the dock at the Nuremberg trial that this was the most important anti-Semitic book he read at the time and had a great influence on him: 'I read it and became an anti-Semitic.'[5] Himmler called Ford one of the most valuable, most important and brilliant champions and Hitler's office in the NSDAP headquarters in Munich even displayed a portrait of Ford. When a journalist asked Hitler what Ford meant to him, he replied 'I consider Henry Ford to be my inspiration'.[6]

Henry Ford's lampoon fell on fertile soil because anti-Semitism in Germany experienced a strong growth in the years after the First World War. This was partly due to statements by Hitler and Ludendorff who, during the trial after their failed coup d'état, accused the Jewish population of having been on the side of the enemy during the war. Such ideas were increasingly accepted as in the early 1920s, several important conservative political parties spread outspoken anti-Semitic propaganda. It was also received with approval by a large part of the population because of the large Jewish refugee flow from Eastern Europe in the previous years.

One of the best-known German anti-Semitic works from the interwar period was Alfred Rosenberg's *Der Mythus des 20. Jahrhunderts* (The Myth of the Twentieth Century), which was published in 1930 and sold more than 1.2 million copies. This was not the first, but certainly the most important book by Rosenberg, the high circulation of which was at least partly explained by his position within the NSDAP. Rosenberg was an early supporter of Nazi ideology, writing for the *Völkischer Beobachter* since the early 1920s,

Alfred Rosenberg is often regarded as the main party ideologue of the NSDAP. He wrote the fiercely anti-Semitic *Der Mythus des 20. Jahrhunderts*, which, with 1.2 million copies sold, is probably the best-selling Nazi work after *Mein Kampf*. (*Bundesarchiv Bild 183-1985-0723-500*)

becoming editor-in-chief of this Nazi Party newspaper in 1923 and taking part in the failed Hitler putsch. After the seizure of power in 1933, he held various senior positions within the party and the state, including (from 1941) that of *Reichsminister für die besetzten Ostgebiete* (Reich Minister for the Occupied Eastern Territories). In this position, Rosenberg, who was often regarded as the party ideologue of the Nazis, was able to put his anti-Semitic ideas into practice.

In *Der Mythus des 20. Jahrhunderts*, which was influenced by the works of Arthur de Gobineau and Chamberlain, among others, Rosenberg attempted to formulate a Nazi ideology based on his own interpretation of history. Like Chamberlain, he distinguished between different races, which, according to Rosenberg, were characterized by a soul or spirit of their own, one of which was far more valuable to human history than the other. Naturally, he placed the Aryan race at the top of the ladder and the Jews at the bottom. An essential part of his argument was that from the 'racial soul' would arise the will, to which morality would be subordinate. The consequence, according to Rosenberg, was that all acts of the will – when ordered by a strong leader – were legitimate.

Lebensraum and Blut und Boden

Alfred Rosenberg, Paul de Lagarde and many other anti-Semitic activists combined the propagation of Aryan superiority and Jew-hatred in one effort with a plea for expansion of the territory, generally eastward, to give the German people more space to live. The expansionist plans were often followed by a plea to populate the newly conquered territory with farmers, because this population group would be closest to the original Nordic race.

One of the best-known representatives of these views was Richard Walther Darré (1895-1953), who, in his books *Das Bauerntum als Lebensquell der nordischen Rasse* (The Peasantry as Life Source of the Nordic Race) and *Neuadel aus Blut und Boden* (New Nobility from Blood and Soil), copied a large part of Rassegünther's ideas about the Nordic or Aryan race, but also added a new dimension to it. Indeed, following Otto Ammon (1842-1916), Darré argued that the peasantry constituted the most valuable part of the people from a racial point of view, and that industrialization and urbanization weakened the Nordic race. According to Darré's Blut und Boden doctrine, the peasantry formed the cultural and racial heart of the German nation and the Germanic traditions. This had been pushed into the background by Christianity and had to be restored. After the necessary Lebensraum would have been conquered

Richard Walther Darré advocated the conquest of Lebensraum and populating that area with 'racially pure' Nordic farmers. Like Himmler, he was a member of the Artamanen and was the first leader of the Rasseamt der SS, where he and Himmler drew up the racial selection criteria. (*Bundesarchiv Bild 183-H1215-503-009*)

in the East, an elite of pure-bred Nordic gentleman farmers was to rule that area. These views also formed the core of the ideology of the *Artamanen-Gesellschaft* (Artaman League), founded in 1923, whose members, including Himmler, called themselves Artamanen.

Darré was introduced to Hitler in 1930 and soon after began his career with the NSDAP and the SS. At Hitler's request he set up a party department dealing with agriculture and a few years later was appointed Reichsbauernführer (Reich Farmers Leader) and minister for food and agriculture. Himmler, who would become friends with Darré and shared his views on the peasantry as a new German nobility, also appealed to his qualities and 'expertise'. At his request, Darré helped build the SS as a 'racial elite' and in 1931 was put in charge of the Rasseamt der SS (Race Department of the SS).

Darré was inspired, among others, by Friedrich Ratzel (1844-1904), who had published a book in 1901 with the revealing title *Lebensraum*. It advocated, among other things, an expansion of the German territory and the establishment of agricultural settlements in the annexed area. With this publication, Ratzel established himself as one of the founders of geopolitics (the influence of geographic conditions on political issues), considering the state as an organism that must grow. The conflicts between countries for territory were, according to Ratzel, a natural selection process according to the Social Darwinist principle of survival of the fittest; the strongest country would eventually survive. The Swedish scientist Rudolf Kjellén (1864-1922) further developed Ratzel's ideas. According to him, it was the ambition of the state to be 'organically' connected to the territory. He too assumed that large states would flourish and the smaller ones would eventually disappear.

The ideas about and the desire for more Lebensraum were not only propagated by (pseudo)scientists but were also spread among broader layers of the population through more accessible publications. The most famous example was Hans Grimm's novel *Volk ohne Raum* (People without Space) which was published in 1926. The central idea of the book, which sold more than half a million copies, was that Germany's problems were caused by too small a territory, which prevented both the individual and the nation from developing fully. The title of Grimm's book quickly became an important slogan of the Nazi movement.

Incidentally, the ideas about territorial expansion sounded much less unworldly and virtually impracticable at the time than in a later period, because at the peace of Brest-Litovsk in December 1917, the eastern border of the German Empire had actually moved hundreds of kilometres to the east. (Not much later, after the country was defeated by the western Allies, the territorial gains were cancelled out again.)

Karl Haushofer (1869-1946) was the best-known and most influential German geopolitician who argued for territorial expansion on a 'scientific' basis. Haushofer served as a brigadier general in the German army during the First World War and was appointed professor of geography at the University

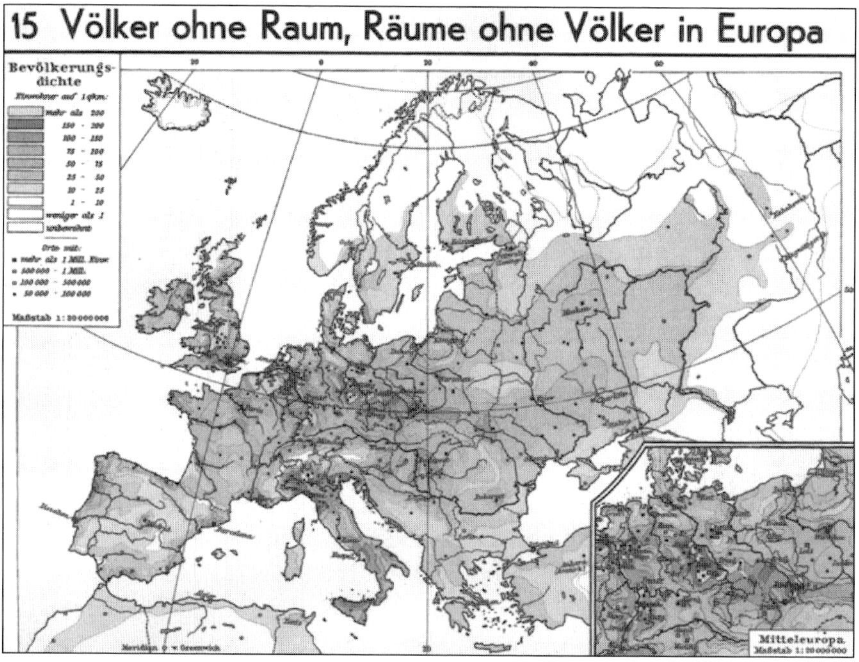

A map from *Velhagen & Klasings grosser Volksatlas* with a title that refers to the famous novel by Hans Grimm, *People without Space*. (*Private collection*)

of Munich in 1919. He soon enjoyed great prestige in science and politics and sought rapprochement with far-right parties. His followers included such men as Darré, Rosenberg and Hess. According to Haushofer's views, which were also disseminated by a scientific institute, a magazine, countless lectures and even a monthly radio talk, a state only had sufficient Lebensraum if it could be completely self-sufficient. He argued densely populated Germany therefore had a 'geopolitical natural right' to expand its territory at the expense of less densely populated countries in order to safeguard autarky. In addition, a larger territory was considered necessary due to the military-geographical circumstances.

The ideas of Haushofer and his colleagues found a great response and were therefore of essential importance for the political education of the German people in general and that of Hitler and his followers in particular. Haushofer had come into contact with Hitler in 1921 through his student Rudolph Hess. He visited him during his imprisonment after the failed Putsch and brought him books on geopolitics. In addition, he also exerted influence on the future dictator through Hess, who assisted Hitler in writing *Mein Kampf*. Those passages in the book in which Hitler writes about geopolitics and German foreign policy are largely based on Haushofer's views.

Anti-Semitic ideas, ethnic nationalism and imperialist notions of the concept of Lebensraum had thus become commonplace in Germany long before the Nazi era. This was also apparent from the enormous size of the so-called *völkische* movement. Its adherents, all very nationalistic, regarded the German people as an organic unity, said to have sprung from common Germanic ancestors. In Germany there were dozens of different völkische associations and organizations with objectives ranging from territorial expansion within or outside Europe, a stronger fleet, or anti-Jewish measures to bring all Germans together in one empire. Membership of these organizations ranged from about 1,500 in the *Reichshammerbund* to 2.5 million in *Verein für das Deutschtum im Ausland*. However, they all pursued some form of ethnic nationalism and often shared the ideal of a 'blood and racially pure' organic people's community in a strong, autarkic state.

That such ideals were more alive in Germany than elsewhere can be partly explained by the country's relatively late unification and fierce nationalist propaganda, the unexpected defeat in the First World War, the humiliations following the Treaty of Versailles, and the economic and social disaster at the end of the 1920s. However, a lesser known but important factor was the question of the so-called Volksdeutsche in Eastern and Southeastern Europe. These ethnic Germans were a very diverse group, from the descendants of people who had left Germany in the twelfth century to the German speakers

Hitler gained great popularity when he succeeded in annexing the Czech Sudetenland without a fight and brought the Volksdeutsche living there 'Heim ins Reich'. This postcard, made shortly after that event, shows Hitler with Konrad Henlein, the leader of the Sudeten Germans. (*Private collection*)

who, due to the breakup of the Austro-Hungarian dual monarchy and the provisions of the Treaty of Versailles, became a minority in another country. In total, this concerned about 10 million people, some of whom were often discriminated against because of their origin, language and culture. The fate of the Volksdeutsche was already an important theme during the Weimar Republic, and Hitler immediately took advantage of this after the takeover of power. He acted as their advocate and used the Volksdeutsche as a means of blackmail against other countries. After the annexation of the Czech Sudetenland, he subsequently achieved great popularity as the man who 'liberated' the resident Volksdeutsche from their 'foreign oppressors'.

Lebensborn: Himmler's Children

After the seizure of power, Himmler was singled out by Hitler as the chief executor of race politics. He was by all accounts the most suitable man for the task: doggedly loyal to his Führer, utterly ruthless, and – probably even more so than Hitler and the other leading Nazis – obsessed with racial ideology. While the SS, at his command, became the main executor of the terror and mass murder that fell victim to countless 'undesirables', he simultaneously tried to increase the birth rate of Aryan babies.

One of the methods to achieve that goal was the establishment of Lebensborn. Between 1936 and 1944, this organization founded several dozen clinics, homes and boarding houses in Germany and the occupied countries. Pregnant women could give birth in the maternity hospitals, provided that both parents met the criteria set by the SS. The organization was initially set up to give unmarried Aryan pregnant women the opportunity to give birth to their child in peace and to prevent them from choosing an abortion, but married women could also give birth there.

For those children born at Lebensborn, Himmler wanted to lay the foundations for a 'new nobility', made up of families of men and women who

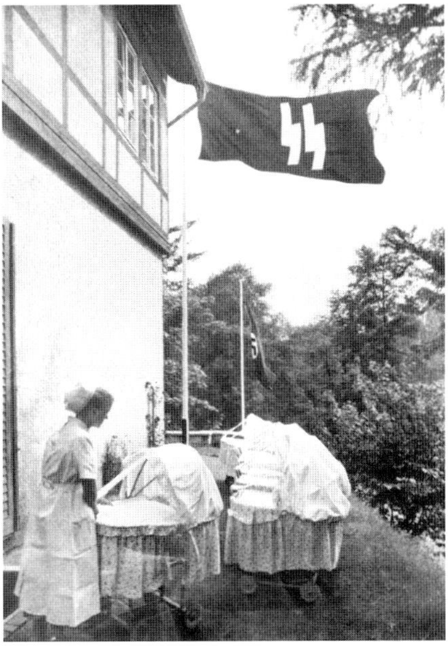

Above left: A greater contrast seems difficult to achieve. The chief perpetrator of large-scale ethnic cleansing and mass murder founded an organization that operated maternity hospitals. In his bizarre worldview, this all served the same purpose; an autarkic Greater Germanic Empire, inhabited by a pure-bred, Aryan population. (*Public domain*)

Above right: This photograph of a nurse with several cradles in front of the Lebensborn settlement Heim Harz was printed with an article about the organization in the *SS-Leitheft* No.3, 1943. (*Bundesarchiv Bild 146-1973-010-11*)

met the highest racial, hereditary and ideological requirements of the SS. His ultimate goal was to create, through selection and education, a new type of human who would be able to overcome all the great challenges ahead and become the leading class of the future Greater Germanic Empire.

In addition to operating maternity hospitals and children's homes, Lebensborn was involved in the kidnapping and 'Germanization' of approximately 1,000 foreign children in Central and Eastern Europe who had the desired 'Nordic' characteristics. According to Himmler's views, characterized by racial delusion, he cut the knife both ways. He thought that by kidnapping these children he would both strengthen the German people and weaken the countries involved by taking away the 'most valuable' children and 'thus robbing them of the future leaders'.

In the almost ten years that the organization existed, about 16,000 children were born under Lebensborn's care, including approximately 8,000 in the German Empire and around 7,600 in Norway. The vast majority of those babies (probably about three-quarters) were born in normal hospitals or clinics and then ended up in public or private children's homes because their own facilities were almost always fully occupied. However, the children all remained under Lebensborn's supervision and control. A private nurse who cared for some of these children described them in her records as 'Himmler's Kinder' (Himmler's children).

The title page of Lebensborn's brochure from late 1939, early 1940, showing the *elhaz* rune and swastika. The rune was the symbol of the organization and has traditionally had several meanings, including protection and the tree of life. (*Private collection*)

II

HIMMLER'S OBSESSIONS

Racial Purity and Population Growth

> '*The goal for me ... since I became Reichsführer-SS has always remained the same: to create an order of good blood that can serve Germany.*'
>
> Heinrich Himmler

Youth

Heinrich Himmler was born in Munich on 7 October 1900. As the child of a middle-class professor, he had a carefree childhood, at least materially. He got on well with his brothers, Gebhard two years his senior and Ernst five years his junior, and loved his parents. Modelling the average middle-class citizen of the time, his father was authoritarian, conservative, and a fanatical patriot, which is also how he raised his children. He set high standards for them and the young Heinrich apparently had no problem with this. He was an obedient boy and a very diligent student who excelled in practically every subject. The big exception was sports and gymnastics. Heinrich was physically weak, absolutely unathletic and wore glasses from quite a young age. His physical shortcomings must have frustrated him greatly. Not only did the Prussian ideal of the exceptionally masculine and ascetic Spartan warrior prevail in the Germany of his youth, he also had no chance of a career as an officer in the Imperial Navy; something he dreamed of from an early age.

Due to his upbringing and environment, he wanted nothing more than a military career. Such a career offered the opportunity for prestige, respect and perhaps even heroic deeds for the greater honour and glory of the fatherland, something that probably counted even more heavily in Germany at the time than in other countries. During Himmler's early years, tensions at home and abroad had risen, largely due to German domestic developments.

From the second half of the nineteenth century, rapid and far-reaching changes had taken place in the western world. Industrialization, urbanization and the rise of socialism had major consequences. In most European countries, these developments went hand in hand with a process of democratization. This gave the growing working class a form of participation and kept social tensions manageable. But in Germany, the upper class successfully resisted the democratic movement. The nobility, together with senior officials, the military leadership and the industrialists, managed to maintain an authoritarian form of government.

In Germany, therefore, state power was not only reserved for a small upper class, but it also differed from most other European countries in other respects. The German Empire was only created in 1871, when the many counties, principalities and duchies were united under the leadership of Prussia after the Franco-Prussian war had been won. This brought about political unity, but great divisions in the areas of politics, religion, social classes and regional sentiments remained. Moreover, the transition from a predominantly agrarian society to an industrial society took place more quickly in Germany than in the rest of Europe, so that the consequences for living conditions and social relations were much more far-reaching. The population centres grew rapidly, mainly due to the mass migration from the countryside to the cities, and huge slums were created where the industrial workers lived in very poor conditions.

In order to reduce divisions and rising tensions between the various population groups, the conservative upper class began to encourage nationalistic sentiments. This nationalistic propaganda mainly focused on foreign policy and the military situation – the country had hardly any colonies and was 'surrounded' in Europe – but often also had strong racist and anti-Semitic components, in which the perceived superiority of the German people and 'threat' of the Jews played a leading role. The propaganda was partly fed and spread through the so-called völkische movement, a broad nationalist movement characterized by the emphasis on a common origin, the so-called *Deutschtum* (Germanness).

Heinrich Himmler aged around 12 years old. He was an obedient child and a diligent student. (*Public domain*)

The goals of the dozens of different völkische organizations and associations varied widely, but they all sought an organic *Volksgemeinschaft* (people's community) in a strong, self-sufficient state, independent of foreign countries.

At the outbreak of the First World War, the divisions between the various German political and social groups temporarily faded into the background and the vast majority of the population rallied behind the government. In a speech on 4 August 1914, Kaiser Wilhelm II declared that there were no longer any parties, only Germans. From a military point of view, the battle was not unfavourable for Germany. After a rapid advance in the West, in which Belgian neutrality was ignored and the German army committed massacres of innocent civilians, an 800-kilometre front line was formed in November 1914, stretching from the Belgian coast through northern France to the Swiss border.

On the Eastern Front, the Germans were initially taken by surprise by the unexpectedly rapid attack of the Russian army that invaded Prussia shortly after the declaration of war, but by the end of the year the Russians had been pushed back to the east. In the years that followed, that process continued gradually, and in December 1917 an armistice was signed on the Eastern Front, followed four months later by the Treaty of Brest-Litovsk. As a consequence, Russia

A German postcard from the First World War depicting a German soldier with a Pickelhaube who, while smoking his pipe, is easily disabling his three main opponents: Russia, the UK and France. Until the spring of 1918, a German victory did indeed seem possible. (*Private collection*)

A peace treaty between the Central Powers (Germany, Austria-Hungary, Bulgaria and the Ottoman Empire) and Ukraine was part of the Treaty of Brest-Litovsk, and officially ended the First World War on the Eastern Front. (*Public domain*)

lost a large part of its territory and the German eastern border shifted many hundreds of kilometres to the east: the followers of the Lebensraum doctrine saw their dreams come true.

Heinrich Himmler was almost 14 when the war started. He followed events closely and not only meticulously recorded the military operations in his diary, but also commented on them. His longing for the moment when he would be allowed to enlist became more and more intense and that became even stronger in 1916, when his brother Gebhard left school to start officers' training.

Despite endless fighting that claimed millions of victims, the front line in the West had hardly changed in more than three years. But from the end of 1917, when the German army had won the battle on the Eastern Front, a large part of that force was transferred to the West in preparation for the spring offensive that had to decide the war in Germany's favour.

In the same period, Heinrich Himmler had managed with great difficulty to be placed with the 11th Bavarian Infantry Regiment, where he had reported for officer training on 1 January 1918. The experience was particularly difficult for him and he initially suffered from intense homesickness, but he persevered to achieve his great goal; participation in the war.

The ultimate German attack in the West started on 21 March 1918. After a successful start, in which the Allied lines were broken and a rapid advance followed, the German offensive slowed down. This was partly a result of the ever-growing American force, which was reinforced by 60,000 men every week from the spring of that year. After the German advance had finally been halted in July, the Allies launched the decisive counter-attack in late September, and just as Himmler's much-desired transfer to the front seemed imminent, the German High Command recognized that the battle was lost and an armistice was concluded. The guns fell silent and Kaiser Wilhelm II fled to the Netherlands.

Disillusions

For the majority of the Germans, the defeat came completely unexpectedly. Although millions of German soldiers had been killed, wounded, captured or were missing, and the civilian population had suffered greatly from hunger and cold as a result of the war effort and the Allied naval blockade (it is estimated 1 million civilians had died), the majority of the German population continued to believe in victory under the influence of government propaganda. It was therefore not difficult for the military leadership to create the 'stab in the back myth', which blamed the defeat on internal enemies, especially the social democrats, the communists and the Jews.

Himmler was told in December 1918, after some uncertain months, that he was being discharged from the army. It was a great disappointment that he never had the opportunity to join the battle and prove himself to both himself and others, and he proved very receptive to the propaganda that defeat was the result of internal enemies. He was not alone in that.

An Austrian postcard from 1919 showing a caricatured Jew stabbing a German soldier in the back with a dagger, suggesting the defeat of the Central Powers was due to domestic enemies, especially the Jews. (*Public domain*)

Armed civilians and soldiers on the streets of Berlin during the communist inspired Spartacist uprising in January 1919. The revolt was crushed by the army, assisted by right-wing Freikorps. (*Public domain*)

The first years after the First World War in Germany were characterized by chaos and violence. Political and social antagonisms became increasingly sharp and the new social democratic government of the Weimar Republic had to put down left and right coup attempts. The Treaty of Versailles, which placed the full blame for the war on Germany, caused the country to lose about 15% of its territory and to pay very high reparations. The frustrations and bitterness that had arisen among a large part of the German population after the armistice flared even higher.

After his discharge from the army, Himmler joined the far-right paramilitary *Freikorps Oberland*, [Highlands Free Corps] which in the spring of 1919 contributed to the overthrow of the *Bayerische Räterepublik*, a short-lived, far-left regime. His company did not take part in the actual battle, but the events left a deep impression and had a major influence on the formation of his worldview. Not only were the main organizers of this coup d'état Jewish anarchists and communists – some of them even sent by the Russian Soviet government – they also acted mercilessly against their opponents. Just before the revolution was crushed, they executed a number of hostages, including seven members of

This propaganda poster by the Freikorps Oberland shows the intentions of this extreme right-wing group against the Poles in the controversial Upper Silesia, where the bloodshed only came to a (temporary) end in 1922. Himmler was a member of this Freikorps for some time but never took part in any action. (*Private collection*)

the *Thule-Gesellschaft*, an exclusive right-wing extremist society that would make an important contribution to the formation and rise of the Nazi movement.

When the Freikorps Oberland was disbanded shortly after the failed Putsch, Himmler's hopes of joining the regular army as a member of this organization were dashed and he decided to concentrate on agriculture instead. At first glance, this choice seemed to have nothing in common with his military ambitions and political views, but that was indeed the case. In reactionary circles, people cherished an ideal image of the pure countryside as a counterpart to the pernicious city life, and the peasantry was considered to be the racially most 'valuable' part of the population. Such ideas particularly appealed to the young Himmler, which is why he also joined the Artaman League. This was a reactionary and racist society that wanted to conquer Lebensraum in the East and then populate that area with pure-bred Nordic gentlemen farmers. Himmler would continue to cherish and pursue the ideals of this company to the very end. At the Artamanen he also met the like-minded Richard Walther Darré, whom he later engaged in the SS selection.

Himmler, however, turned out to be completely unsuited to the harsh reality of peasant life. His intention was to work first as a farmhand for a year in order to gain experience before starting agricultural training, but he had to give up after barely four weeks due to exhaustion. However, he successfully completed the theoretical side, at the technical college in Munich, followed by an internship on a farm.

Meanwhile, the power struggle between left and right in Germany continued in full force. Himmler and his brother had joined a section of the right-wing

The logo of the Artamanen, a society to which Heinrich Himmler and Richard Walther Darré belonged. They wanted to conquer Lebensraum in the East and then populate that area with purebred Nordic gentlemen farmers. The elhaz rune, a vertical line with two branches at an angle of 45 degrees, later became the symbol of Lebensborn. (*Private collection*)

paramilitary *Einwonerwehr*, an official army reserve unit that could be called upon to provide military assistance in an emergency. Here he met Ernst Röhm, an officer of the Reichswehr, the post-war German army, who secretly supported the Einwonerwehr and other right-wing and extreme-right movements with money and weapons, and who would later become leader of the *Sturmabteilung* (SA), the NSDAP's paramilitary squad. Under the influence of events at home and abroad, the circles in which he moved and the books he read during that period, the young Himmler became increasingly radicalized.

A fanatical German patriot also apparently had every reason to be upset about the decline and belittling his beloved homeland had to endure. The humiliations of Versailles, which had already made a deep impression, were followed up a few years later when French and Belgian troops occupied the Ruhr area due to delays in reparations. The workers who went on strike against the occupation were paid by the German government, resulting in hyperinflation. Pensions and savings became worthless and the middle class was particularly hard hit. Right-wing groups and movements pointed to communists and socialists as the main scapegoats, and anti-Semitic sentiment reached new heights. The anti-Jewish mood was boosted by the immigration of Eastern European Jews, who had moved to Germany after the end of the First World War, and influences from Austria, where anti-Semitism was even more deeply rooted.

The NSDAP

Himmler briefly worked at a fertilizer factory but soon resigned to devote himself entirely to his political and paramilitary activities. On the advice of Röhm, whom he had come to regard as a sort of mentor, he joined a new extreme nationalist paramilitary group, and when this group split up a short time later, he followed Röhm to its new faction, the *Reichskriegsflagge*. Subsequently, in August 1923, again through Röhm's intercession, he became a member of the *Nationalsozialistische Deutsche Arbeiterpartei* (National Socialist German Workers' Party; NSDAP).

The NSDAP was founded in 1919 as one of the many southern German right-wing extremist parties and was led by Hitler from 1921 onwards. Thanks to his rhetorical qualities and – among the extreme right – popular views, the membership grew rapidly and two years later already amounted to about 50,000 members. During the chaotic period of hyperinflation, the NSDAP attempted to seize power in Bavaria in November 1923 through a coup d'état in Munich. Since Himmler had followed Röhm, he played a small part in that too. While Hitler was proclaiming the revolution in the Bürgerbräukeller, Röhm led his men to the building of the Bavarian Ministry of War. Himmler was in the front ranks, carrying the Reichskriegsflagge (Imperial War Flag). The coup failed completely. The army and police remained loyal to the government, a dozen insurgents were killed, a number were injured and others, including Hitler, were arrested.

Although the NSDAP was now banned, this did not mean the end of the Nazi movement. On the contrary, Hitler managed to turn the trial against him into a propaganda manifestation and thus acquired great national fame. The very conservative judges, who, like most of their colleagues, disapproved of the republic, gave Hitler every opportunity to make propaganda for his cause. In addition, they sentenced him to only five years in prison for a crime (high treason) for which he could have been sentenced to death. He was finally released after just thirteen months, a period he used to write the first part of *Mein Kampf*.

Himmler had also been arrested following the Putsch. However, his role was insignificant and he was released after questioning. While the leaders of the Nazi movement were in prison and the party was banned, he continued his political activities for the völkische parties. In 1920 he had bought a motorcycle and with it he now criss-crossed the Bavarian countryside, giving speeches everywhere on topics such as the 'Jewish question', the associated power of big business and the misery and poverty they caused. According to his brother Gebhard, he believed completely in what he proclaimed, while his world view took on increasingly fixed and extreme forms.

Himmler cherished the relationship with the leaders of the movement; felt valued as a fellow fighter for the common cause and was able to confirm his prejudices time and time again. He studied books on racial inequality and the

During Hitler's failed Putsch in November 1923, Himmler (fourth from left) carried the so-called Reichskriegsflagge as he marched under Röhm to the Bavarian Ministry of War. (*Private collection*)

imminent danger of Jews, communists, Jesuits and Freemasons, and he read the memoirs of German commanders in the First World War defending the stab-in-the-back legend. He also immersed himself in literature on astrology, spirituality, homeopathy and books in which the Nordic man was idealized.

These were not the easiest years for the Nazi movement. In the course of 1924, political tensions eased and a new German government, with American help, managed to bring inflation under control. A year later, relations with other countries also eased when, in the Treaty of Locarno, Germany recognized its western borders – but not those in the East – and was guaranteed that France and Belgium would not invade the country again. Moreover, a year later, in 1926, Germany was allowed to join the League of Nations. The five years between 1924 and 1929 were therefore a period of relative relaxation and prosperity, and the far-right parties lost a large part of their following. However, the seeds for the SS were sown in that same period.

The Nazi movement had had the SA since 1920, which had started as a hall guard, order service and thug squad and would later grow into a mass movement with millions of members. But although indispensable to the Nazi Party, Hitler repeatedly doubted the loyalty of the SA's leaders and therefore, in

1923, ordered his chauffeur-cum-bodyguard Julius Schreck to set up a personal bodyguard. This unit was first called the *Stabswache* and then renamed the *Stosstrupp Adolf Hitler*, but the group soon became unemployed when the object to be protected was imprisoned after the failed Putsch. When Hitler was released again, Schreck was ordered to re-establish the bodyguard, which was now baptized the *Schutzstaffel* (SS).

In the same period, Röhm was busy reorganizing the SA after it had been banned for several years following the failed Putsch. But when Röhm refused to subordinate the organization to Hitler's political leadership, the latter decided to expand the SS and branches were also established in other cities. In addition to protecting Hitler, the SS was given the task of recruiting party members, protecting party meetings, and recruiting advertisements and subscribers for the National Socialist newspaper the *Völkischer Beobachter*. From the very beginning, the SS – unlike the SA – was emphasized as an elite unit and potential candidates were rigorously selected.

In July 1926 the leadership of the SS was taken over by Joseph Berchtold, the publisher of the *Völkischer Beobachter* and a former member of the Stosstrupp Adolf Hitler. Not much later, the SS received open recognition of Hitler as his elite organization when, on the second party day, he handed over

The members of the Stosstrupp Adolf Hitler in Bayreuth on 'Deutscher Tag' in September 1923. The company was disbanded when Hitler was imprisoned but was later re-established after his release under the name Schutzstaffel. (*Private collection*)

Heinrich Himmler, aged around 25 years old, with the NSDAP pin on the lapel of his jacket. (*USHMM*)

the 'blood flag', the flag that had been carried on the day of the coup attempt, to the SS. Despite this, the SS remained subservient to the leadership of the SA, which is why Berchtold, who was the first to bear the title of Reichsführer-SS, gave it up a year later. He was succeeded by his second in command, Erhard Heiden, who took Himmler as his assistant in September 1927. When Heiden was relieved of his position for unclear reasons, he was succeeded on 6 January 1929 by Heinrich Himmler.

Five years earlier, in June 1924, Himmler had become the secretary to Gregor Strasser, an early and influential member of the Nazi Party. Although he could barely make ends meet on his meagre salary and lived in a tiny room above Strasser's pharmacy, this appointment was the real beginning of Himmler's career within the movement. After all, when Strasser was appointed the first leader of the Gau (NSDAP district) of Lower Bavaria after Hitler's release and the re-establishment of the NSDAP, Strasser had taken Himmler on as his assistant. And because Strasser was often absent for party building in Northern and Western Germany, Himmler was effectively the party leader in one of the most important Gau. He was literally and figuratively close to the centre of the party in Munich, got to know important figures in the movement and impressed them with his great commitment and organizational skills.

Himmler no longer felt like a fish out of water and, after years of doubting and searching, had finally found his 'home'. He was a valued member of the Nazi Party, as nationalistic as he was anti-Semitic, and was firmly convinced that Germany had to be saved by securing the future of the 'Nordic race'. He was finally 'someone' and at last he had a mission. Not much later, he would recognize in Hitler the man whom Providence had sent to lead him to his goal. Around the same time, in the first months of 1924, he also broke with his faith and the Roman Catholic Church; National Socialism became his new religion and Hitler his new god.

The fact that the NSDAP was still in its infancy at that time and the prospects for the right-wing extremists were bleak did not prevent Himmler from continuing to devote all his energy to his ideals and to the party. He was rewarded with a new step in his career after his boss, Strasser, was appointed head of the propaganda department of the NSDAP in 1926, making Himmler assistant chief of propaganda. He also continued his work for the Gau, contributed to the local völkische newspaper and held a position with the Artaman League.

In 1928, aged 27, Himmler married Marga (Margarete) Boden, a divorced nurse seven years his senior with blonde hair and blue eyes. A strong, independent woman, she ran a clinic that she had opened with money from her father, a large landowner in the East. She was clearly unconcerned by his social position or prospects and everything indicates that it was a genuine love match. However, it does seem that Marga Boden seduced him and that it was probably Himmler's first relationship, also sexually. Presumably she shared his political views and, like him, was drawn to rural life. With her money they bought a small farm just to the east of Munich, where Lebensborn's roots would also lie, where they planned to make money from chicken eggs and herbs. In practice, Marga did the work there while Himmler spent almost all his time in Munich on his political activities.

Himmler (centre), Hess (left) and other NSDAP leaders listen to a speech by Hitler at the Third Party Congress in Nuremberg, August 1927. (*USHMM*)

Reichsführer-SS

In the first week of 1929 Himmler became even busier when he was promoted to Reichsführer-SS. However, although the title sounded impressive, it meant little in practice. In January 1929 the entire organization consisted of no more than 280 men and the SS was also still subordinate to the SA. However, Himmler was the right man in the right place. He was extremely driven, a good organizer and completely devoted to the Nazi movement in general and Hitler in particular: 'I would do anything for him. Believe me, if Hitler told me to shoot my mother, I would do it and be proud of his confidence',[1] he said at the time.

He also had the time on his side, because at the end of the 1920s foreign competition first broke out into a major agricultural crisis and in October 1929, the great Wall Street Crash followed. Within a few years, a large part of the population, including the peasantry and middle classes, fell into poverty. On top of the disastrous consequences of the war and the unexpected defeat, the revolution(s), the financial and moral consequences of the 'dictate' of Versailles, the failed coups d'état, the humiliation of the occupation of the Ruhr and the subsequent hyperinflation, there now came a deep economic recession. Within a few years, unemployment and bankruptcies tripled. Conditions could hardly have been more favourable to the Nazi Party.

Himmler travelled all over the country recruiting members and quickly expanded his organization. At the end of 1929 there were almost 1,000 members; by the end of 1930 this had already risen to over 2,700. Although this was still a small number compared to Röhm's SA, which at that time was several hundred thousand men strong, the SS had been a factor to be reckoned with since 7 November 1930. Hitler, who had quickly realized that Himmler would always and unconditionally obey him, had decreed on that date that the main

Heinrich Himmler in uniform shortly after his appointment as Reichsführer-SS. The photograph was probably taken in 1931. (*Public domain*)

task of the SS was to carry out police services within the party and that SA commanders were no longer allowed to give orders to the SS. Furthermore, the SS now got its own uniform – with black shirts instead of the SA's brown – and a new structure. With this, Hitler would henceforth have a completely reliable personal bodyguard and an intelligence service, while Himmler would have the opportunity to further expand his organization and position of power without interference from Röhm and the powerful SA.

The expansion of the tasks and powers of the SS was not an isolated event, but a result of the division and unrest within the Nazi movement, with the SA appearing to be a threat to Hitler's leadership in the early 1930s. So, in order to stay ahead of potential competitors and ensure his personal safety, he relied on Himmler, 'the faithful Heinrich', who would prove time and time again that he was completely devoted to his leader.

In addition to protecting Hitler, racial politics and espionage were the core tasks of the SS. Therefore, in the early 1930s, Himmler founded two departments that, despite various name changes and task expansions, would continue to form the core of the SS until the end of the war: the Rasseamt der SS and the Ic-Dienst.

The Rasseamt was primarily used for the racial examination of potential SS members and their future wives. It was led by fellow Artaman Richard Walther Darré, known for his publications on Blut und Boden and the peasantry as a source of life for the Nordic race. The Rasseamt was gradually given more and more tasks and was later renamed the *Rasse- und Siedlungshauptamt* (Race and Settlement Main Office; RuSHA).

The second department set up during this period was initially called the Ic-Dienst, but was shortly afterwards renamed the *Sicherheitsdienst* (the Nazi intelligence service; SD), and was primarily intended to spy on political opponents and dissidents within the party. Its leader was the former naval officer Reinhard Heydrich and in his hands, this department would develop into a very extensive, powerful and feared organization that was later called the *Reichssicherheitshauptamt* (Reich Security Main Office; RSHA).

In the same period when Himmler was working almost day and night to build up the SS, parliamentary elections were held four times in an impoverished and deeply divided Germany. Campaigning was incessant for nearly three years, from the summer of 1930 to the spring of 1933. The contradictions became even sharper now and the political crisis manifested itself again in full force on the streets, where bloody fights constantly took place between thugs and paramilitary groups from the left and right. The average citizen could gradually no longer escape the impression that the government had lost all control, both

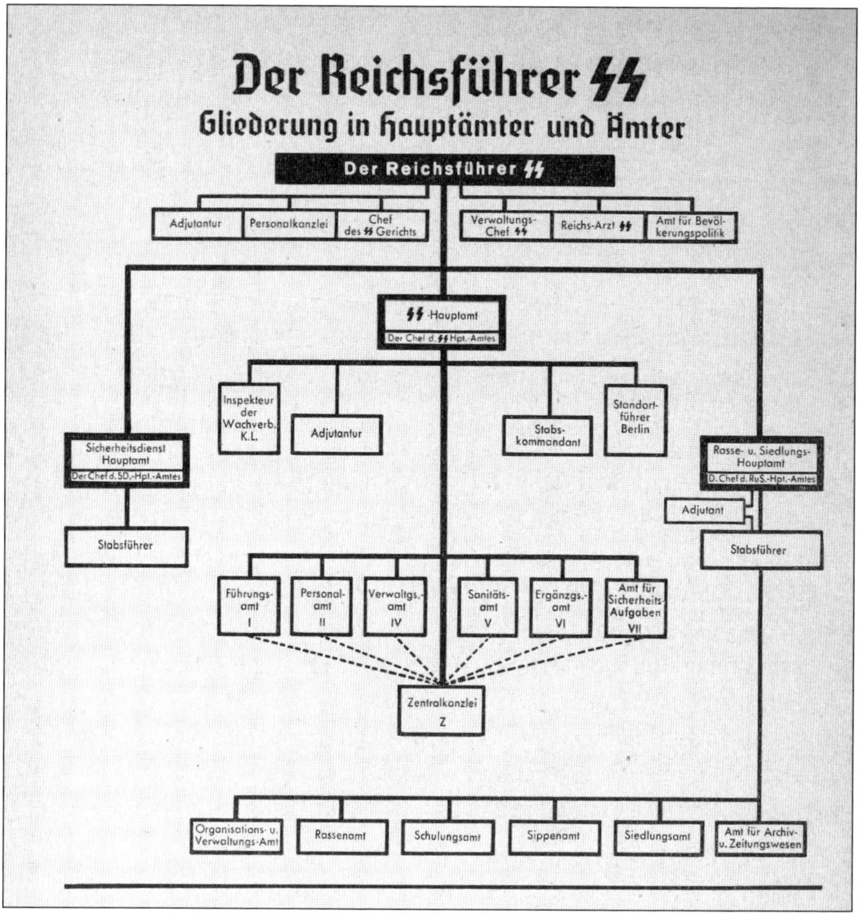

A diagram showing the organization of the SS in the mid 1930s. It had three main departments: the *SS-Hauptamt;* the *Sicherheitshauptamt* (the former Ic-Dienst and later Reichssicherheitshauptamt) and the *Rasse- und Siedlungshauptamt* (the former Rasseamt). (*USHMM*)

Reinhard Heydrich was the head of the SS department which developed into the Reichssicherheitshauptamt (RHSA). Until his death following an assassination attempt, he was one of the most powerful and feared leaders of the Third Reich. (*Bundesarchiv Bild 152-50-10*)

economically and politically, and that a coup d'état or revolution could take place at any moment. Many therefore sought refuge with parties on the extreme left or right wings of the political spectrum.

The NSDAP pointed to all kinds of scapegoats for Germany's misery: democracy, the Weimar Republic, the Treaty of Versailles, Marxists, socialists, communists, big business, war profiteers, land speculators, France and, of course, Jews, while at the same time being the main instigator of the chaos and street violence that was seen. But their promises about restoring order and peace and combating the left-wing threat, combined with visions of a united community of people in a resurrected, proud nation that had regained its rightful place in Europe, appealed to a large section of the population. Consequently, Hitler's party won more than a third of the vote in the 1932 elections, making it the largest faction in the Reichstag.

With the support of right-wing, nationalist and anti-republican groups who thought they could use Hitler as a middleman, on 30 January 1933 Hitler was appointed chancellor by President von Hindenburg. In the last free elections, in March 1933, the Nazi Party received 44% of the vote, but with the support of other nationalist parties, Hitler secured a majority on 23 March to pass a law granting him dictatorial powers for a period of four years. This was the beginning of the end. The Nazis immediately banned other political parties and trade unions, imprisoned their political opponents and made a start with the Nazification of society. Race politics played a central role in this. Within a few years, a number of laws were passed that made Jews second-class citizens and gave the state the power to require sterilization of people with hereditary diseases.

Nevertheless, for Himmler, the period immediately following the Nazi takeover must have been a disappointing one. While many of Hitler's followers ended up in high-ranking posts in the national government, he was 'only' appointed chief of police in Munich. But Himmler was a cunning, patient tactician who slowly built up his position of power. At Hitler's request, for example, he supplied 120 specially selected SS men as personal bodyguards, who were shortly afterwards given the official name *Leibstandarte-SS Adolf Hitler*, an action that once again showed the great confidence that Hitler placed in him.

To further strengthen his position of power in the new Reich, Himmler mainly concentrated his efforts on the police, all in close cooperation with Reinhard Heydrich. In the spring of 1933, he founded the so-called SS-Sonderkommandos, which were deployed all over Germany to 'support' the local police, especially in fighting political opponents. In March 1933, in order

The *Leibstandarte-SS Adolf Hitler,* Hitler's bodyguard, pictured in 1934 in front of the Munich Feldherrnhalle. This picture was to be placed in a special album depicting the rise and reign of the Nazis, published in the second half of the 1930s. (*Private collection*)

to imprison those opponents, he had a facility called a *Konzentrationslager* opened especially for this purpose in the southern German town of Dachau, making it the first large-scale concentration camp in the Third Reich. In this and the camps established later, the normal rules no longer applied and the guards of the SS, who from 1936 organized in the so-called *SS-Totenkopfverbände*, literally ruled life and death.

Although Himmler had risen to great esteem within the party thanks to the build-up of the SS in the early 1930s, his quest for absolute control of the German police force was seriously hampered by Hitler's close confidant, Hermann Göring. The latter had collected the positions of Reich Minister of Aviation, President of the Reichstag and Reich Master of the Hunt, and was also Prime Minister and Chief of the Police of Prussia, the most important German state. In the end, Göring proved willing to hand over control of the Gestapo (Secret State Police) to Himmler, if in return he would eliminate the leader of the SA, Ernst Röhm.

The SA had grown from a small gang into a paramilitary mass organization with eventually some 4 million members. Until 1933, the SA had served Hitler

An SS guard unit in KZ Lager Dachau, the first large scale concentration camp, 30 kilometres north of Munich. This picture was taken in May 1933, two months after the opening of the camp. (*Bundesarchiv Bild 152-01-16*)

The 'Tag der Deutschen Kunst 1933', 15 October, Munich. In the foreground is Adolf Hitler with Adolf Wagner, and Gauleiter Munich-Upper Bavaria. Behind them (from left to right) Hess, Himmler and Röhm. In the summer of the following year, Himmler would have his mentor and friend Ernst Röhm murdered. (*Private collection*)

well on several occasions and although there had been conflicts over direction and control before, after the takeover of power in 1933 the organization caused the Führer more and more problems. Within the SA there were not only calls for a socialist revolution and the replacement of the regular army, the Reichswehr, by the 'revolutionary people's army', i.e. the SA, but Hitler also regarded its leader Ernst Röhm as a threat to his position of an autocratic ruler. Despite Röhm's great merits for the National Socialist cause, he was murdered by the SS during the Night of the Long Knives (30 June – 2 July 1934), along with dozens of SA members and other potential opponents.

Although Himmler regarded Röhm as a friend and mentor, having known him for some twelve years, and much of his political career had been determined by his advice, he seemed to have no doubts or hesitations whatsoever in his efforts to remove him. When it came down to it, he had his men kill the SA leader in cold blood. With this action, Himmler proved that he could carry out every one of Hitler's orders and seized the opportunity to eliminate an important competitor with both hands. Another prominent victim, who together with Röhm was responsible for Himmler's career within the Nazi Party, was Gregor Strasser. He too was murdered by Himmler's men, who once again showed himself to be the perfect follower of the Führer: as loyal as he was ruthless.

The rewards soon followed. After Hitler had already officially made the SD the intelligence and counterintelligence service of the NSDAP at the beginning of June 1934, he promoted the SS on 20 July to an independent body of the party, no longer subordinate to the (new leadership of) the SA. A few months later, on 24 September, it was also officially established that an *SS-Verfügungstruppe* the size of three regiments would be trained in a military manner. This unit would form the core of the later Waffen-SS, which would eventually develop into a force consisting of nearly forty divisions.

From the mid-1930s, the SS grew rapidly. Himmler's ambitions knew no bounds and he continued to expand the organization. Police, armed forces, politics, education, science, economics, race and population politics; there was hardly an aspect of society in which the SS did not interfere. But the organization was also a product of chance and improvisation and would eventually grow into what could best be compared to a many-headed monster, on the understanding that the heads not only sought the life of outsiders but also constantly fought among themselves. There was constant power struggle and rivalry on many levels caused by self-interest, opposing views, differing interpretations and personal feuds, all compounded by theft, corruption and self-enrichment.

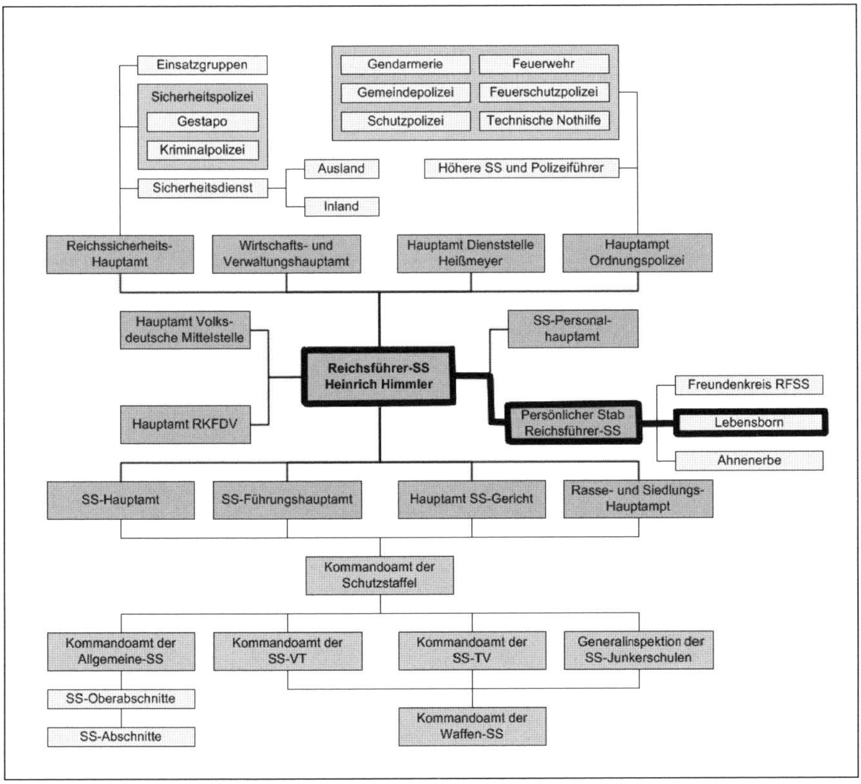

A diagram showing the organization of the SS around 1941. Due to its continuous development, this had changed practically every year. From 1938, Lebensborn fell under Himmler's personal staff (see also image on p.36 and p.48). (*Public domain*)

Racial Selection and Population Growth

The SS had started mainly with members of the bourgeois middle class, but Himmler's ideas about good blood, racial selection and the idea of a new elite increasingly appealed to people from other backgrounds. These included war veterans and Freikorps members – often as uprooted as they were violent – members of the old nobility who had lost their privileged positions under the republic and businessmen and shopkeepers who had gone bankrupt due to the economic malaise. After the First World War, the radical right had established a link between democracy and what was termed the 'rule of the inferior'. Supporters of these views proclaimed that the 'racially superior' had died in the war, and that a purge was now necessary. Many of them had been through the trenches and were scarred by their experiences. They were accustomed to strife and bloodshed.

However, it was not just people who wanted to somehow take revenge on the past or get ahead in society who joined the SS. Many ambitious and intelligent students, scientists, doctors and lawyers were also attracted to Himmler's views on racial selection and the call for more Lebensraum, all for the greater honour and glory of Germany and the future of the race, which was variously called Germanic, Nordic or Aryan. Hitler, Himmler and many of their followers were convinced that the achievements of people are determined by the quality of their race. The German people would be better than all the others because there the proportion of the Nordic race – in their opinion superior to all others – was the greatest. But that race would now be threatened by low birth rates and by mixing with other races, and these dangers determined Himmler's thinking and actions. The core of his obsession was that the best race – and with it the German people – should be saved by keeping it as pure as possible and expanding it as much and as quickly as possible.

Himmler proceeded according to the same principles in the construction and expansion of the SS. Unlike the SA, he was not concerned with quantity, but with quality, especially racial quality. He regarded the SS as a modern order of chivalry; an elite whose purpose was to unite and multiply the Nordic blood inside and outside Germany in order to form a new nobility that would lead the future Germanic Empire and its provinces. In his first year as Reichsführer-SS, when the entire organization consisted of less than 1,000 men, he therefore introduced racial selection criteria (*rassische Auslesebestimmungen*) for the SS. (An exception was made for First World War veterans who were already members of the SS.)

Himmler was ultimately concerned with the formation of a pure-bred community made up of *sippen* (lineages) of 'good blood', who, with their descendants, were to secure the future of the Nordic race. The suitors of his selected men were therefore equally important and consequently these women also had to meet the racial selection criteria. Both the SS man and his future bride had to undergo an examination of their racial characteristics and health and be able to prove with official documents that they had no Jewish ancestors. This was laid down at the end of 1931 in the so-called betrothal and marriage order of the SS (*Verlobungs- und Heiratsbefehl der SS*). In the first three of this ten-point order – presumably by analogy with the Ten Commandments – Himmler summarized the nature and purpose of the SS:

1. The SS is an association of German-Nordic men selected on special criteria;
2. In accordance with the National Socialist worldview and recognizing that the future of our people depends on the selection and maintenance of racially and hereditarily healthy blood, from 1 January 1932, I am issuing marriage authorizations for all unmarried members of the SS;
3. The goal to be pursued is the hereditary healthy, valuable sippe of German-Nordic nature.

The 'racial research' was carried out by a special officer of the *Rasse- und Siedlungshauptamt* (RuSHA), the racial expert. Of all the functions, tasks, professions and pseudosciences that were exercised within the many departments of the SS, from camp guard to professor of Germanic history, that of the so-called race expert has received very little attention. Wrongly so, in fact, because their judgment was so decisive for the fate of many.[2]

The SS race experts formed a group of around 500 people in total who belonged to the RuSHA. They were responsible for the racial selection from the criteria developed by Himmler and Darré and were initially concerned with the selection of SS men and their future brides. The racial examination had far-reaching consequences. In the first instance for the SS men themselves, who, because of the selection, came to regard themselves as members of an elite and on this basis believed they had the right to judge others on their racial characteristics as well. This would happen on a large scale during the war, when the

An SS-Unterscharführer with his bride, Stuttgart 1938. To obtain permission for their marriage, they both had to meet the requirements of the Verlobungs- und Heiratsbefehl der SS. (*Private collection*)

procedure of pedigree testing and selection was applied to the population of the occupied countries. It played a central role in the occupation policy. The 'racial value' determined by the experts of RuSHA was decisive for everyone's future, because for Himmler, racial science was the basis of population policy and had priority over all other criteria and interests.

Himmler's racial experts belonged to a relatively homogeneous group of committed ideologues and followers of Nazi racial doctrine. Most of them were born between 1900 and 1909 and had a university education. After registering with the SS and passing the selection, they had undertaken internal 'training' to become a racial expert. Most were then deployed as *SS-Eignungsprüfer*: an official who conducted the racial examinations and then passed judgment on someone's racial value. While there was some variation over time and place in how 'racial value' was determined, it consisted mainly of an examination of around twenty external characteristics (skin, eye and hair colour, shape of nose etc.), as well as health and information about their ancestors. The answers to these questions formed the basis of how one was classified in a certain 'race group'.

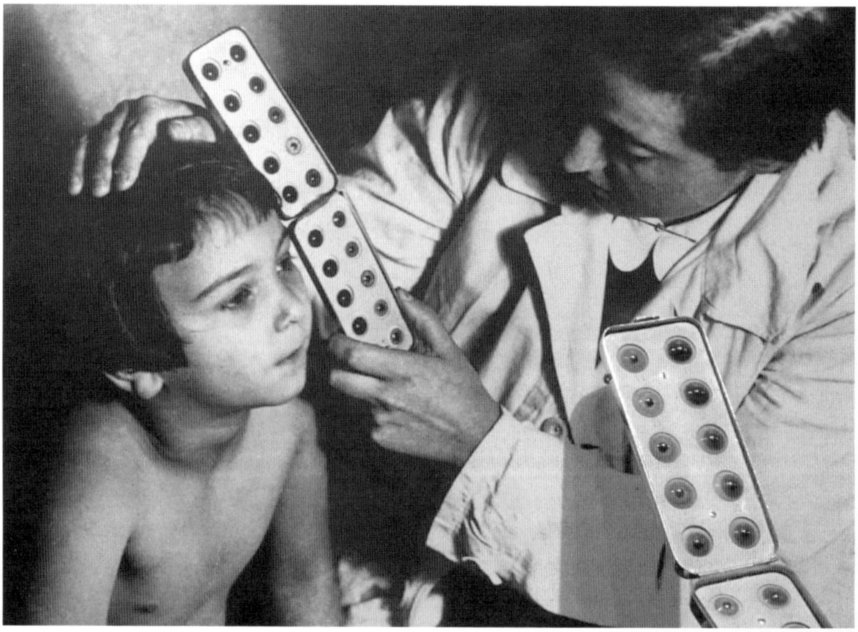

A person's 'racial value' was determined on the basis of around twenty external characteristics. One of these was eye colour, which is being examined here by a 'breed' expert, an SS-*Eignungsprüfer*. (*Private collection*)

Further, in each HSSPF district (*Höhere SS- und Polizeiführer*, the commanding SS officer in a certain area directly under Himmler), a so-called *SS-Führer im Rasse- und Siedlungswesen* (RuS-Führer) was assigned. This officer was responsible for the racial politics in his district, organized education, information and propaganda and also carried out racial investigations himself, all in the service of the 'good blood' and racial politics.

The SS race experts were both theorists and implementers of a ruthless racial policy that contributed in two ways to the ethnic cleansing and the genocide carried out by the Nazis. They provided the German policy of conquest, extermination and Germanization with a seemingly rational basis and actively assisted in the decimation of those races deemed to be inferior.[3] Fear and terror, arrests, deportations, ethnic cleansing, mass executions and industrial mass murder were the core tasks of Himmler's SS, and they were legitimized by the race experts of the RuSHA.

Racial purity and population growth were, in Himmler's eyes, the necessary conditions for the survival of the Nordic race, and these obsessions dominated his thinking and determined his actions. In addition to the racial

Above left and above right: *Sieg der Waffen – Sieg des Kindes* (Victory of Arms – Victory of the Children) was a propaganda book commissioned by Himmler to urge the German people to have as many children as possible. 'In the struggle for the survival of our people we have two weapons at our disposal', he wrote in the preface, 'strength and natural fertility'. (*Private collection*)

purity, which was investigated first on his own people and later on the population of the occupied territories, birth rates were naturally a constant concern for him.

According to Himmler's reading list, which has largely been preserved, in January 1926 he read a book by a Professor Thomsen on the rise and fall of people, and it seem to have made a deep and lasting impression on him. This publication in particular, and the low German birth rates – a logical consequence of the First World War – were at the root of his belief that Germany was doomed to go under unless the tide was turned drastically. More children had to be born, as many and as quickly as possible, and all, naturally, from 'good blood'. Once he became Reichsführer-SS, Himmler put all his resources into achieving this, with orders, appeals, and speeches, and returned to the theme at practically every opportunity. The outbreak of war and the need for future soldiers only increased that need.

On 28 October 1939, eight weeks after the invasion of Poland and the start of the Second World War, he issued the infamous *Befehl für die gesamte SS und Polizei* (Order for the entire SS and Police). In it he called on the members of the SS and the police to father a child before they potentially died in the war. The worst part was not that the best men died in battle, Himmler said, but the children who would never be born as a result. The Reichsführer-SS, however, did not limit himself to this general exhortation, but went on to say that 'beyond marriage for German women and girls it might be a lofty task' to become the mother of a soldier's child who went into the field. If necessary, Lebensborn would take on the guardianship and care of 'all conjugal and illegitimate children of good blood whose father has fallen in the war'. This call for the conception of children out of wedlock went down extremely badly in conservative German society. A storm of indignation arose, including among many Nazi organizations and prominent figures, but Himmler did not retract his words.

Three years later, on 15 August 1942, his *Befehl an die letzte Söhne* (Order for the Last Sons) followed. To those SS soldiers who had been given a short leave it declared:

> You have been withdrawn from the front by order of the Führer. This measure has been carried out because it is in the interest of the state and the government that your families do not die out.
>
> It is your duty, by begetting and bringing forth children of good blood as soon as possible, to ensure that you are no longer the last sons.

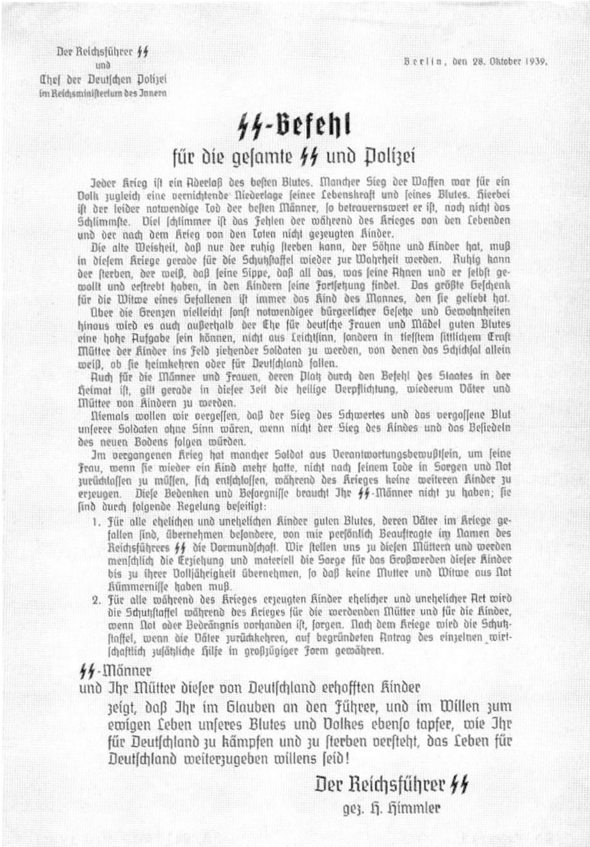

Der Reichsführer SS
und
Chef der Deutschen Polizei
im Reichsministerium des Innern

Berlin, den 28. Oktober 1939.

SS-Befehl

für die gesamte SS und Polizei

Jeder Krieg ist ein Aderlaß des besten Blutes. Mancher Sieg der Waffen war für ein Volk zugleich eine vernichtende Niederlage seiner Lebenskraft und seines Blutes. Hierbei ist der leider notwendige Tod der besten Männer, so betrauernswert er ist, noch nicht das Schlimmste. Viel schlimmer ist das Fehlen der während des Krieges von den Lebenden und der nach dem Krieg von den Toten nicht gezeugten Kinder.

Die alte Weisheit, daß nur der ruhig sterben kann, der Söhne und Kinder hat, muß in diesem Kriege gerade für die Schutzstaffel wieder zur Wahrheit werden. Ruhig kann der sterben, der weiß, daß seine Sippe, daß all das, was seine Ahnen und er selbst gewollt und erstrebt haben, in den Kindern seine Fortsetzung findet. Das größte Geschenk für die Witwe eines Gefallenen ist immer das Kind des Mannes, den sie geliebt hat.

Über die Grenzen vielleicht sonst notwendiger bürgerlicher Gesetze und Gewohnheiten hinaus wird es auch außerhalb der Ehe für deutsche Frauen und Mädel guten Blutes eine hohe Aufgabe sein können, nicht aus Leichtsinn, sondern in tiefstem sittlichem Ernst Mütter der Kinder ins Feld ziehender Soldaten zu werden, von denen das Schicksal allein weiß, ob sie heimkehren oder für Deutschland fallen.

Auch für die Männer und Frauen, deren Platz durch den Befehl des Staates in der Heimat ist, gilt gerade in dieser Zeit die heilige Verpflichtung, wiederum Väter und Mütter von Kindern zu werden.

Niemals wollen wir vergessen, daß der Sieg des Schwertes und das vergossene Blut unserer Soldaten ohne Sinn wären, wenn nicht der Sieg des Kindes und das Besiedeln des neuen Bodens folgen würden.

Im vergangenen Krieg hat mancher Soldat aus Verantwortungsbewußtsein, um seine Frau, wenn sie wieder ein Kind mehr hatte, nicht nach seinem Tode in Sorgen und Not zurücklassen zu müssen, sich entschlossen, während des Krieges keine weiteren Kinder zu erzeugen. Diese Bedenken und Besorgnisse braucht Ihr SS-Männer nicht zu haben; sie sind durch folgende Regelung beseitigt:

1. Für alle ehelichen und unehelichen Kinder guten Blutes, deren Väter im Kriege gefallen sind, übernehmen besondere, von mir persönlich Beauftragte im Namen des Reichsführers SS die Vormundschaft. Wir stellen uns zu diesen Müttern und werden menschlich die Erziehung und materiell die Sorge für das Großwerden dieser Kinder bis zu ihrer Volljährigkeit übernehmen, so daß keine Mutter und Witwe aus Not Kümmernisse haben muß.
2. Für alle während des Krieges erzeugten Kinder ehelicher und unehelicher Art wird die Schutzstaffel während des Krieges für die werdenden Mütter und für die Kinder, wenn Not oder Bedrängnis vorhanden ist, sorgen. Nach dem Kriege wird die Schutzstaffel, wenn die Väter zurückkehren, auf begründeten Antrag des einzelnen wirtschaftlich zusätzliche Hilfe in großzügiger Form gewähren.

SS-Männer
und Ihr Mütter dieser von Deutschland erhofften Kinder
zeigt, daß Ihr im Glauben an den Führer, und im Willen zum ewigen Leben unseres Blutes und Volkes ebenso tapfer, wie Ihr für Deutschland zu kämpfen und zu sterben versteht, das Leben für Deutschland weiterzugeben willens seid!

Der Reichsführer SS
gez. H. Himmler

Himmler's SS-Befehl für die gesamte SS und Polizei (Order for the entire SS and Police) caused a storm of protest and indignation after it called for the fathering of children out of wedlock. (*Public domain*)

He initially demanded four children from his subordinates, but later increased this to at least four sons. He preferred, however, that the women of his SS order had a child every year. As a result, Himmler therefore urged his commanders to give their men leave at the right time, if the women were of the right age, in order to make it possible for as many children as possible to be fathered. 'The number of cradles must be much greater than the number of coffins', was one of his statements.

In October 1939, shortly after the occupation of Poland, having gained even more influence over population and race politics, Hitler next put Himmler in charge of a new organization, the *Reichskommissariat für die Festigung deutschen Volkstums* (Reich Commissariat for the Consolidation of German Nationhood; RKF or RKFDV). He was thereby instructed to bring back the so-called Reichs- and Volksdeutsche from abroad and settle them in territory annexed by Germany. The goal was to gather the entire Germanic population in the territory of Nazi Germany. Furthermore, Himmler was to eliminate all 'harmful influences' of 'foreign parts of the population', which gave him a license to deport and murder 'undesirables'. Himmler assumed the title of *Reichskommissar für die Festigung deutschen Volkstums* (Reich Commissioner for the Consolidation of German Nationhood) for himself and was overjoyed with this assignment, which considerably expanded his power.

Shortly afterwards he was also given authority over the *Volksdeutsche Mittelstelle* (Repatriation Office for Ethnic Germans; VoMi). This organization had been set up three years earlier to provide political and financial support to Volksdeutsche people living outside the Third Reich, but from the end of 1939 it was mainly aimed at resettling ethnic Germans in the newly conquered areas in the East. The activities of the RKF and the VoMi, which thus partly overlapped, led to a large-scale, forced and violent repopulation of Eastern Europe, of which many millions of people – the vast majority of them Poles – would fall victim.

The activities of Himmler's instruments of power were later summarized by the Nuremberg prosecutor as follows:

> Generally speaking, VoMi was to deal in deportations, forced evacuations, kidnaping, and slave labour; RuSHA was to

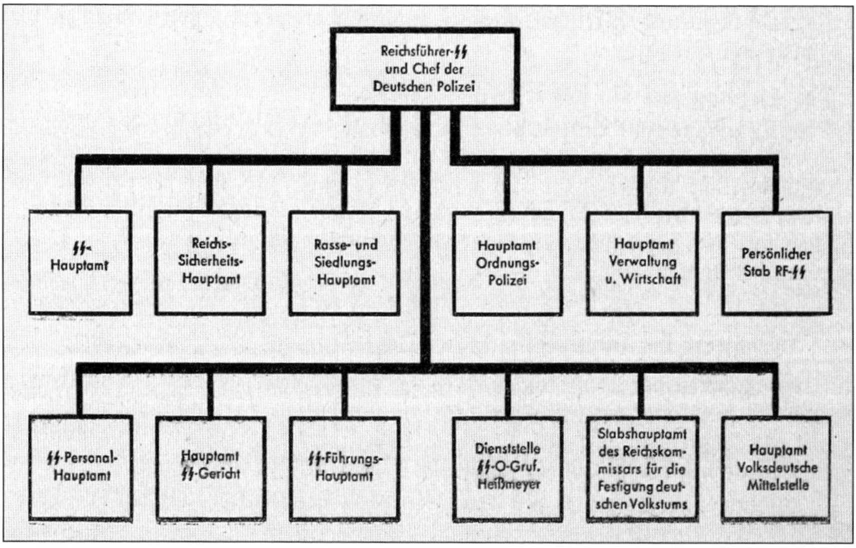

The main departments of the SS in 1943. In the bottom right are the RKFDV and VoMi, in the top right, Himmler's personal staff, which included Lebensborn. (*Public domain*)

> conduct racial examinations, decide who went to concentration camps, who were to be sterilized, on whom abortions were to be performed, which children were to be kidnaped and which were to be exterminated; the Security Police and SD, including the Higher SS and Police Leaders, were to 'take care' of foreign elements dangerous to the German people, or, in plainer language, to exterminate the Jews and undesirable Poles and Russians; Lebensborn was to handle the abduction of children and their Germanization; and over all of these, and other agencies, was the Staff Main Office [*Stabshauptamt* of the RKFDV] – the office that planned, directed, and coordinated the whole gigantic effort.

From early 1940 Himmler could thus consider himself the most important implementer of population and race politics, but he did not reign supreme in the snake pit that formed the top of the Third Reich. All sorts of individuals close to Hitler constantly vied for the favour of the untouchable Führer. He carefully curated that no one in his entourage amassed too much power. And while Himmler finally succeeded in establishing himself in a more powerful position than most of his fellow aspirants, he would never succeed in rising above Martin Bormann; the Reich leader of the NSDAP (*Parteikanzlei*). Bormann had been Hitler's deputy from the end of 1942 and from April 1943, was also officially his secretary. His unassailable position of power and ambitions would often hinder Himmler, including in the development of Lebensborn, the organization founded by Himmler in 1935 to play a role in population and race politics; two subjects that formed the core of his philosophy of life.

Lebensborn's main goal was to increase the birth rate of Aryan babies by preventing abortions among unmarried women. But in addition to Himmler and the SS, the NSDAP was also very active in racial and population politics, including through the *Nationalsozialistische Volkswohlfahrt*, (National Socialist Public Welfare Association; NSV), a party organization led by Erich Hilgenfeldt, which, with the support of Bormann, was able to gain increasing control in this matter. The NSV supplied a large proportion of the nurses needed at Lebensborn and was initially sympathetic to Himmler's project. For example, in 1937 the NSV donated a number of buildings to Lebensborn to establish a maternity hospital, and until 1939 Lebensborn was subsidized with hundreds of thousands of Reichsmarks per year. But this attitude changed from 1940 onwards and Bormann began to use the NSV to weaken Himmler's position – and therefore also that of Lebensborn. Not because Lebensborn's size was a threat to the NSV, but to limit the growing power of the Reichsführer-SS. In the

Above left: Following Hess' flight to England, Martin Bormann was the most powerful man after Hitler and thus one of the few Himmler needed to be wary of. There followed a secret but increasingly fierce battle over who had the most influence over Hitler: Bormann and the NSDAP or Himmler and the SS. (*Bundesarchiv Bild 183-R14128A*)

Above right: Erich Hilgenfeldt was the leader of the NSDAP organization NSV, from which Lebensborn initially received support. Bormann later used Hilgenfeldt and the NSV to limit Himmler's ambitions in the field of population policy. (*Private collection*)

end, the battle was about who had the most influence on Hitler: Bormann and the NSDAP or Himmler and the SS.

During the course of the war, several more rounds of this power struggle were played, without a clear victor emerging. In early 1942, Hilgenfeldt went so far as to question Lebensborn's right to exist. As far as he was concerned, because the NSV had been instructed by the party leadership to ensure, through its daughter organization *Hilfswerk Mutter und Kind* (Welfare Organization Mother and Child), that the birth rate would rise as much as possible after the war, his organization was now responsible for the entire birth policy and that as a result, Lebensborn, as a separate institution, was subsequently superfluous. Therefore, he continued, Lebensborn had to be taken over by the NSV or, if Himmler preferred, would only exist on a small scale for the women and children of the SS and police. Himmler reacted quickly, writing that he 'would only give something from Lebensborn on the express order of Hitler. Otherwise,

I will defend it to the very last bit.'[4] On the one hand he was not going to give up anything about Lebensborn, but on the other he was also so insecure that he quoted Hitler. High talks on the birth policy between Hitler, Himmler and Hilgenfeldt, in September 1942, did not bring a final solution to the conflicts, presumably because of Hitler's divide and rule policy. The struggle between Himmler and Bormann, who used Hilgenfeldt as a pawn, therefore continued until the end of the war and was one of the reasons that Lebensborn remained smaller than the Reichsführer-SS had always intended.

Romantic and Fantasist

Not only was Himmler a tireless organizer, a cunningly patient tactician and a ruthless killer, the Reichsführer-SS also had a completely different side. He was a romantic and a dreamer who lived in both the real world and a fantasy world at the same time. For example, he dreamed of a future that resembled his idealized past, of a great and powerful empire stretching far to the East, inhabited by Germans led by an elite of purebred peasant warriors and noblewomen: tall, slender, blonde and with blue eyes. 'I work because it is my duty, because I find peace in my work, and I work for my ideal of the German woman with whom I will one day live my life in the East and fight like a German far from beautiful Germany.' That ideal, which he wrote down in his diary as a 19-year-old student, never changed. And when in 1940 Hitler approved his plans for the repopulation and colonization of the conquered territories in Eastern Europe by an armed peasantry, Himmler declared that it was the happiest day of his life. He was not deterred by the fact that the realization of his dreams and fantasies would cost an unimaginable number of people their lives.

The Reichsführer-SS was also particularly interested in astrology, spiritualism and occultism and was convinced that it was possible to contact the spirits of dead people. For example, he himself claimed, on the border between waking and sleeping, to receive regular visits from the German King Heinrich (876-936), who would provide him with advice. There is little doubt that he saw himself as the reincarnation of this king, although the name must have played some kind of role in this.

This mystical side formed an important part of his world of thought, and after renouncing his Catholic faith, Himmler devoted much of his time to the creation of an alternative religion in which he combined Hitler worship, old Germanic customs and fantasies from the Middle Ages. For example, he acquired the Wewelsburg, a castle southwest of Paderborn, which dated from

Above: Every year on 1 July, the anniversary of King Henry I's death, Himmler laid a wreath on his grave in Quedlinburg, a town in the northeast of the Harz. He probably saw himself as the reincarnation of the (eponymous) king who, he claimed, regularly visited him on the border between waking and sleeping. (*Private collection*)

Left: Himmler wanted to establish the mystical seat of his knights at Wewelsburg (seen in the background), where he could meet with twelve senior SS men. The legend of King Arthur served as an example. (*Private collection*)

the early seventeenth century but had since fallen into ruins. It was rented for the symbolic sum of 1 Reichsmark for a period of 100 years, after which he built a concentration camp (KZ Niederhagen) to house forced labourers who worked on the castle. According to the official plans, they converted the castle into a special SS school, but in reality, Himmler had something else in mind.

The Wewelsburg was to become the mystical seat of his order of knighthood where, by analogy with King Arthur and the Knights of the Round Table, he could meet with twelve chosen SS-Gruppenführer.

In 1935 he founded the *Forschungsgemeinschaft Deutsches Ahnenerbe e.V.* (Research Community German Ancestral Heritage). Initially, this organization served to research early Germanic history and to locate, collect and propagate scientific evidence demonstrating the superiority of the Aryans as the foundation of the new Germanic Empire. Over the years, however, the areas of interest and activities expanded considerably, and the group gradually developed into the scientific centre of the National Socialist ideology, to which scientists from all kinds of fields were affiliated. In practice, however, many of the activities had little to do with science and research results were modified to conform to Nazi ideology. It happened more than once that a researcher who presented undesirable results was told by Himmler that he lacked the will and the right attitude; a reproach with potentially life-threatening consequences.

One of Ahnenerbe's teachings was the so-called world ice doctrine, a completely unscientific theory in which the whole cosmos is said to be based on the battle between fire and ice, which was nevertheless adhered to and fanatically defended by Himmler (and Hitler). During the war, a sub-division of Ahnenerbe, the *Institut für Wehrwissenschaftliche Zweckforschung* (Institute for Applied Military Scientific Research), carried out gruesome, often deadly, and completely pointless medical experiments on concentration camp prisoners

In the same period that Himmler got his hands on the Wewelsburg and founded Ahnenerbe, the foundations for Lebensborn were laid. From the second half of the 1920s he had become increasingly convinced that the Nordic race had to be saved from impending doom. To this end he had propagandized tirelessly and then, when he was put in charge of the SS, first established the racial selection procedure for the members, and soon after extended it to their future wives. The goal was to ensure that as many purebred children as possible were born. Lebensborn served the same purpose, and would offer unmarried, pregnant Aryan women a discreet opportunity to give birth in one of its maternity hospitals.

Lebensborn was in all respects an instrument of Himmler, not only of his imagination but also of his means of power and authority. He founded the organization to increase the birth rate of Aryan babies, spurred on by his obsessions about Germany's low birth rates and racial purity. With Lebensborn he wanted to lay the foundations for the 'new nobility' that would provide the leaders of the coming Greater Germanic Empire, something in which he firmly believed. Of all the activities that Himmler would develop in the field of racial politics, Lebensborn

The activities carried out by Forschungsgemeinschaft Deutsches Ahnenerbe e.V. (Research Community German Ancestral Heritage) were initially relatively innocent. Here SS-Hauptsturmführer Bruno Beger conducts 'scientific' research during an expedition to Tibet on behalf of Himmler in search of the origins of the Aryans. Later, gruesome and often deadly experiments on prisoners were also carried out. (*Bundesarchiv Bild 135-KB-15-089*)

was his favourite project. He himself became chairman of the association, placed the leadership of the organization in the hands of people he knew personally and visited the clinics and children's homes regularly. He interfered in the smallest details in the running of the clinics, drafted prescriptions and recommendations, became godfather to children born on his birthday and sent them gifts. He made sure that the women and infants lacked nothing, studied and commented on the reports on the young mothers and regularly kept himself informed about the ups and downs of individual children. He used his private plane to transport Lebensborn mothers and children and had the clinics and homes supplied with the best foods. He ensured that the organization was given a legal exceptional position in order to avoid government interference and defended Lebensborn to the utmost against the claims of the NSV. And even in the later phases of the war, when the tide had long since turned and the Allies were advancing from all sides, he never lost interest in Lebensborn and always made time for his Aryan mothers and their children.

Throughout his career, Himmler devoted so much attention to issues of marriage, children, and racial purity that it was almost certainly an unconscious response to the relationships and sexual frustrations he had experienced as a young adult. The resulting insecurity and presumed feelings of inferiority were suppressed and masked by an exterior designed to exude an extreme form of masculinity and self-confidence. His outward appearance did not make this

Himmler seen taking a fitness test at the SS officer school in Bad Tölz. From an early age he was anything but an athlete and looked nothing like his ideal Teutonic, the athletically built, purebred peasant warrior. (*USHMM*)

any easier, for he was anything but the example of his 'ideal Germanic'. '… if I looked like Himmler, I wouldn't be talking about races at all', remarked SS-Obergruppenführer Albert Forster, a senior Nazi official in the annexed Polish territory and no friend of Himmler in 1943.

In addition, Himmler suffered from chronic stomach pain. It was probably caused by tensions arising from an inner conflict about following Hitler's orders on racial politics and an innate aversion to the carnage that inevitably followed. Only his masseur Felix Kersten could offer him relief from the recurring hellish pains.

Consciously or unconsciously, perhaps his involvement with the women and children of Lebensborn counterbalanced the mass murders and unending misery that were perpetrated at his behest. Another possible explanation, which could also apply to more aspects of his personality, is that with Lebensborn he wanted others to become something that he himself was not; a representative of the new nobility who was not only a leader of his people, but also met – in his eyes at least – the highest racial requirements.

III

THE RACIALLY PURE GREATER-GERMAN REICH

War Aims and Race Politics

'The race question holds the key not only to world history, but also to all human culture.'

Adolf Hitler

Mein Kampf

Hitler's ultimate goal, and that of his followers, was a pure-bred Greater Germanic Empire that was completely autarkic and strong enough to win the struggle for world domination. Nazi Germany, therefore, went to war to seize territory and introduced increasingly extreme and ruthless measures to 'cleanse' the population of its own country as well as the occupied and annexed territories.

The views and sentiments on which the Nazi actions were based were present long before the dawn of that era, and not only among the adherents of the extreme right. Racist ideas about anti-Semitism and the alleged inequality of races, the need for Lebensraum, and the ideas about a German national community also found great support among many conservative Germans.

In that respect, there was therefore nothing new in Hitler's *Mein Kampf*, but because the author also set out his goals and less than eight years later was willing, and able, to put even the most extreme of his ideas into practice,

The cover of an early edition of *Mein Kampf*. (*Private collection*)

also and especially in the field of race politics, a closer look at the contents of the book is essential.

Mein Kampf (My Struggle) is a political-ideological writing that consists of two parts. In the first part of the book, the author gave a rarely truthful description of his youth and political-ideological formation, his opinion on the First World War and the German revolution, and also set out his views on races and nations. The second part, 'The National Socialist Movement', was mainly devoted to his worldview and vision of the future, and the aims and means of the state and the Nazi Party. Even before Hitler's appointment as Chancellor in 1933, nearly 250,000 copies of the book had been sold; by the end of 1933 that number had risen to over a million and by 1945 the total circulation in Germany was almost 11 million copies.

From beginning to end, *Mein Kampf* is imbued with an obsessive anti-Semitism and further with a vehement hatred of everything (in alphabetical order) democratic, French, liberal, Marxist, pacifist, socialist or weak. But it is more than a muddled and completely unscientific discourse about races and cultures, interspersed with tirades at Jews, people of colour, politicians, trades union and other alleged domestic and foreign enemies. The book also presents the reader with simple solutions to Germany's misery and paints a vision of a resurrected, united and internationally respected nation where camaraderie and patriotism reign supreme, and unemployment and poverty have been eradicated. Furthermore, it contains long passages about the use of propaganda and the methods of demagoguery that Hitler used with great success. (In that respect, too, it is a remarkable piece of writing. The future dictator explained exactly how he played his people and his audience and in doing so revealed an important part of his political strategy.)

Also, and this is the main point here, Hitler set out his worldview and vision of the future in the writing and presented his goals in *Mein Kampf*, which would remain constant from then on. Central to his worldview was the belief that the course of history was determined by the struggle between different races – 'The race question holds the key not only to world history, but also to all human culture' – and that the Aryan race, whose Germany was to be the heartland, was in all respects superior to all other races, for that he regarded as the 'carrier of human cultural development'. The Aryan, according to Hitler, stood above the others because of his idealism, his willingness to work for the community and even to sacrifice himself if necessary.

According to him, the Jews were not a religious group but a race that used a religion as a cover. They were, for many different, often contradictory, and without exception nonsensical arguments, 'the utmost opposition' to the

Aryans, and would be bent only on enslaving and oppressing others. According to Hitler, they had already succeeded in this in some countries. 'The worst example in this regard is the Soviet Union ...'. The German defeat at the end of the First World War, the revolution after it and all subsequent humiliations and miseries were explained in *Mein Kampf* as the result of a Jewish conspiracy: 'If we allow all the causes from which the collapse of Germany has sprung to pass before our mind's eye, the last and most important thing remains is that the racial question and especially the Jewish danger were not seen.'

Furthermore, like many other anti-Semitic conspiracy theorists and racialists, Hitler was convinced that races possessed common, inherited physical and mental characteristics. He therefore regarded miscegenation and blood mixing as the greatest danger to the Aryan, for it would have destroyed 'all the great cultures of the past'. In addition to preventing race mixing, he argued, it was also necessary to rid one's own race of hereditary diseases. In *Mein Kampf* he remarked: 'the state must declare all that is in any way apparently diseased and hereditary burdened – and therefore also hereditary burdensome – unauthorized to procreate, and must also accept the practical consequences associated with this.'

In order to save the Aryan race and secure its future, Hitler ultimately wanted to establish a Greater Germanic Empire populated by a purely Aryan population. The empire would consist of the territory of the Third Reich, the annexed Germanic Northern and Western European countries and Western Poland. The other European countries would become vassal states,

The racial doctrine of the Nazis was certainly not taken seriously by every German, as this cartoon, which probably dates from just before the takeover of power, proves. None of the Nazi kingpins – Hitler, Himmler, Göring, and especially Goebbels (depicted here) – were even remotely close to their racial ideal. (*Private collection*)

and the territory from Eastern Poland and the Soviet Union to the Urals would act as a colonization area for a Germanic peasant warrior class and a buffer against the Asiatic peoples. The Greater Germanic superstate had to be completely self-sufficient and able to compete successfully for world domination. After all, to ensure the survival and dominance of the Aryan race well into the distant future, this empire, populated by pure Aryans, had to become a world power. Ultimately, Hitler argued, racial politics would lead to the ultimate goal: 'A state which, in the age of racial poisoning, devotes itself to the care of the best elements of its race, must one day become master of the earth.'

Hitler could only achieve his megalomaniac goals through traditional power politics – war – and through race politics. That he would act completely ruthlessly, if given the chance, was also announced in *Mein Kampf*: 'However, when people struggle for their existence on this planet, and for them it is therefore about being or not being, then all humanitarian or aesthetic considerations completely disappear; for all these ideas are not cosmic realities, but products of human fantasy…'

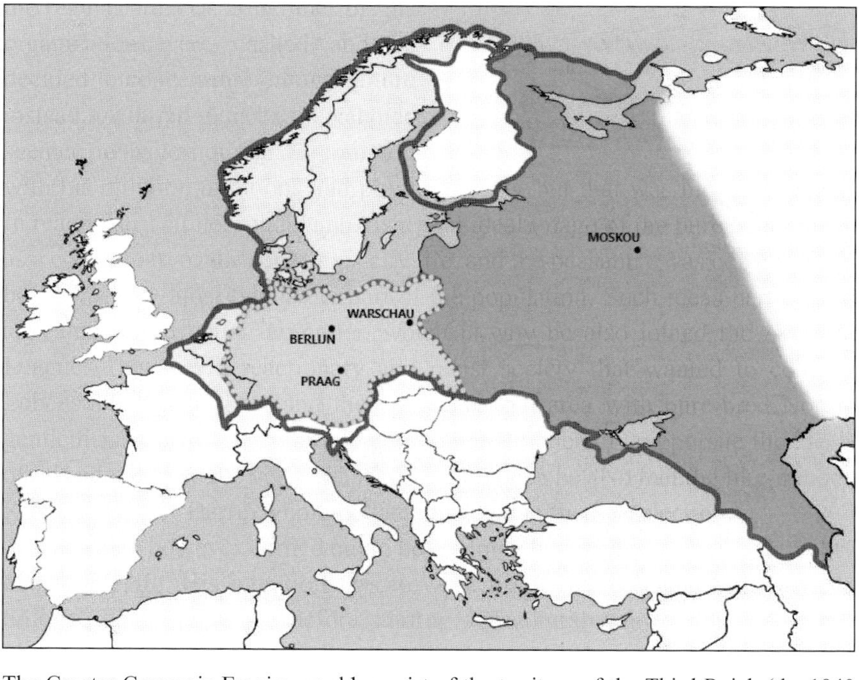

The Greater Germanic Empire would consist of the territory of the Third Reich (the 1940 borders, including annexed territories, are shown here by the dotted line) and the Germanic lands (dark line), with the remaining European countries as dependent vassal states and Eastern Poland and the Western Soviet Union as a colonization area and buffer against the Asian peoples. (*Private collection*)

Legislation

That racial politics was the central element of Nazi ideology was illustrated by the nature and speed of the legislation introduced by the new regime immediately after taking power. Immediately after Hitler came to power, a number of laws were passed that excluded the Jews from social life, and further legislation was designed to prevent the birth of unhealthy children. In the view of the Nazis, this would help to 'purify the German blood'. These racial laws were accepted almost uncritically; proof that such views were already widely held among the German population in the 1930s.

Already on 7 April 1933, exactly two weeks after Hitler's takeover of power, the Al law was introduced (*Gesetz zur Wiederherstellung des Berufsbeamtentums*) which allowed Jews and politically unreliable officials to be fired. Exceptions were made for non-Aryan civil servants who were already employed before August 1914 or who had fought in the army during the First World War (the so-called *Frontkämpferprivileg*), although this privilege would soon expire. The law stipulated that the officials had to present a so-called *Ariernachweis*, a document proving that one had no Jews among one's parents or grandparents.

Nine months later, on 1 January 1934, a new law came into force (*Gesetz zur Verhinderung erbkranken Nachwuchses*) which stipulated that people who suffered from certain hereditary diseases or had other congenital abnormalities could be forced to undergo sterilization. Ultimately, some 400,000 people would be rendered infertile, largely involuntarily. Incidentally, this legislation had already been prepared under the Weimar Republic and forced sterilization was not a typically German measure or invention of the Nazis, being also legally possible in countries such as Canada, Denmark, Japan, the United States, Sweden and Switzerland.

Characteristic of Nazi Germany were the infamous Nuremberg Laws, which came into effect on 15 September 1935. These consisted of three parts, two of which had major consequences for Jewish Germans. The first (*Reichsbürgergesetz*) divided the German population into citizens and subjects. According to the definition, someone was a citizen if he or she 'had German or related blood, and proved by his behaviour that he could and would serve the German people and Reich faithfully'; all others – especially Jews – were considered subjects. Two months later, an ordinance defined who was considered a Jew and deprived the Jews of their civil rights so that they could not claim the protection of the Constitution. The other anti-Jewish law was the 'Law to Protect German Blood and the German Honour' (*Gesetz*

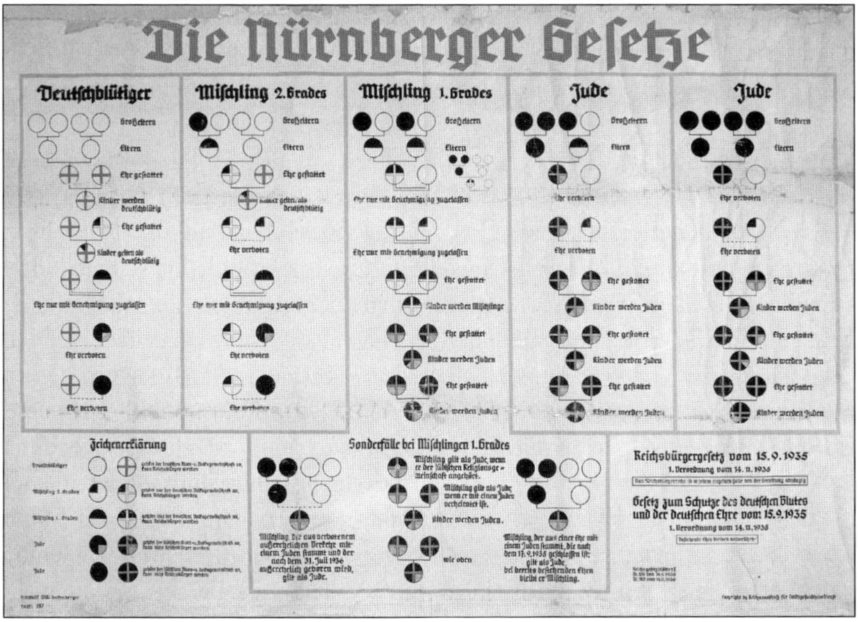

The Nuremberg Laws spelled out precisely who was '*Jude, Mischling, oder Deutschblütiger*' (Jew, half-breed or of German blood). The laws stripped Jews of their civil rights and prohibited sexual relations and marriages between non-Jewish Germans and Jews. (*USHMM*)

zum Schutze des deutschen Blutes und der deutschen Ehre). Beginning with the all-encompassing sentence, 'Pervaded by the fact that the purity of the German blood is the condition for the survival of the German people, and animated by an unyielding will to secure the German nation for all the future ...', the law banned all sexual relations and marriages between non-Jewish Germans and Jews.

On 18 October 1935, the *Gesetz zum Schutz der Erbgesundheit des deutschen Volkes* (Law to Protect the Hereditary Health of the German People) followed, which stipulated that people who wanted to get married had to undergo a medical examination to see if they could produce genetically healthy children. If one of the partners suffered from a hereditary disease, the marriage could not take place unless they were sterilized.

So, within 2.5 years of coming to power, the Nazis had enacted a series of laws aimed at excluding the Jews as much as possible and ensuring that only 'healthy children of German blood' were born in the future. This was called 'racial hygiene' in Nazi terminology.

The Euthanasia Programme

The next step in the radicalization of race politics was the so-called euthanasia programme. Between September 1939 and the end of the war in May 1945, the programme killed several hundred thousand people who, in the opinion of the Nazis, led an 'unworthy life'. Forced euthanasia – in truth nothing more than a euphemism for murder – as a method of making the people stronger by killing the weak, had been suggested before and more often in right-wing extremist circles, including by Hitler. In addition to racial politics, economic arguments were put forward; people who lived in an institution could not work and therefore cost society money due to their necessary care.

The Nazis made propaganda for euthanasia, especially from the second half of the 1930s. Plans and preparations were probably already being drawn up at that time, but Hitler expected resistance from the population and did not want to take such measures until wartime. In practice, therefore, nothing happened until an opportunity presented itself in the course of 1939, which he took advantage of. Parents of a child who had been born with serious physical and mental defects submitted a request to him to have the child killed. After a brief inquiry, Hitler gave his permission and in November 1939 – the order was backdated to 1 September to appear as a wartime measure – he ordered a programme to allow doctors to kill people who were living indecent lives.

Dr Karl Brandt, Hitler's personal physician, and Philipp Bouhler, chief of the *Kanzlei des Führers*, (The Führer's Chancellery) were instructed to 'extend the powers of physicians with decision-making powers in such a way that, in the case of a critical assessment

'A hereditary disease costs the community 60,000 Reichsmarks during its lifetime. Countrymen, that's your money too.' In the 1930s, the Nazis ripened the minds for the 'forced euthanasia' of people deemed to have an 'unworthy existence'. This advertisement appeared in the NSDAP's bureau for race politics monthly magazine, *Neues Volk*. (*Private collection*)

Karl Brandt led the euthanasia programme. This photograph was taken during his trial in Nuremberg. He was hanged in June 1948. (*USHMM*)

of their state of health, the incurably ill, according to human judgment, can be granted merciless death'. From a department of the Reich Chancellery at Tiergartenstrasse 4 in Berlin, a programme was set up that came to be known after the war as *Aktion T4*, after the address of the department. (During the war this designation was not used.)

Child euthanasia had already begun in mid-August. In contrast to the first case, in which the child's parents requested euthanasia, the regime had taken the initiative instead. Doctors, midwives, maternity clinics and hospitals had been required to report children under the age of 3 with mental and/or physical disabilities. The age limit was later raised to 16 years. The doctors involved had to fill in a standard form and send it to the *Reichsausschuß zur wissenschaftlichen Erfassung von erb- und anlagebedingten schweren Leiden* (loosely translated as National Commission for Scientific Registration of Severe Suffering Caused by Hereditary and Congenital Disabilities). The questions on the form were worded in such a way that it seemed the purpose of the registration was to give special care to the children concerned. But the so-called Reichsausschuß was no more than a cover name for a department of the Kanzlei des Führers, Ambt IIb, where a few people, without having seen the children or even the medical records, made a judgment based on the data on the form about life or death. If that final judgment was passed, the child was transferred to a *Kinderfachabteilung* (Special Children's Ward) specially set up for this purpose. In these institutions, the children were deprived of fluids and food, and were usually killed with an anaesthetic. It is believed that between 5,000 and 10,000 children fell victim to this practice.

The euthanasia programme for adults, Aktion T4, was officially launched in October 1939, when all kinds of institutions were required to report patients who had been hospitalized for more than five years, or were considered 'deranged criminals', or were not of the Aryan race or suffered from a specific condition such as schizophrenia, epilepsy, dementia or severe paralysis. The adult patients were assessed in the same way as the children, without looking at a medical file or examining the people themselves. Those sentenced to

In early 1941, victims of Aktion T4 gather at the Bruckberg nursing home in the village of Neuendettelsau, about 20 kilometres southwest of Nuremberg, to be taken away in the waiting buses. Of the 1,205 patients, only 372 survived the war. (*Public domain*)

death were then taken by buses of the *Gemeinnützige Krankentransport GmbH* (Nonprofit Patient Transportation Ltd.), set up by the organization and run by SS men in white coats to give it a medical appearance, to a transit centre in an ordinary hospital. From there it went to one of the six centres specially set up for this purpose, where the victims were killed in gas chambers with carbon monoxide. The family later received a document with a falsified cause of death. The euthanasia programme is estimated to have killed some 200,000 Germans and Austrians and about 100,000 people from other countries. The vast majority of the latter group consisted of Poles, who were taken from local institutions and hospitals and simply murdered by firing squads or with gas.

In the course of 1940, as more and more information about the secret operation in Germany and Austria leaked out, what Hitler had once feared would happen, did. Social unrest arose, petitions were filed and protests were even held, including by doctors who opposed the programme. The church also protested and in August 1941, Hitler ordered the programme to be terminated.

Nevertheless, forced euthanasia continued until the end of the war, albeit less systematically. The exception was *Aktion 14f13*, which Himmler initiated to get rid of concentration camp inmates who were a nuisance to him in some way: sick, unable to work, and later criminals and 'asocials'. Initially doctors assessed the forms – not the people themselves – but later the selection was left to the camp staff. The approximately 20,000 victims of this action also included forced labourers and Russian prisoners of war. A number of leading figures of the Aktion T4, who had gained a great deal of experience in gassing people, would later play an important role in the 'Final Solution to the Jewish Question': the mass murder of the European Jews.

Ethnic Cleansing and Repopulation

To achieve the ultimate goal of the autarkic and pure-bred Germanic state, a large area in the East had to be annexed, before being redeveloped and colonized by people who met the appropriate racial criteria. 'Our mission is not to Germanize the East in the old sense – to impose the German language and laws on the people there', Himmler said, 'but rather to ensure that in the East only live people of pure German, Germanic blood.'[1] To carry out that mission, the Nazis deported much of the original inhabitants of the annexed territories and intended to repopulate them with people who matched their racial requirements.

As later with the mass murder of the Jews, Hitler entrusted Himmler with the implementation of the so-called Eastern Policy. In October 1939, he had been put in charge of an organization specially set up for this purpose, the Reichskommissariat für die Festigung deutschen Volkstums (Reich Commissariat for the Consolidation of German Nationhood; RKF or RKFDV). Although the regime gave the impression that the establishment of the RKF was based on a well-thought-out plan, it was, in fact, a hastily improvised

The Baltenlager in Posen (Poznań), where emigrants from the Baltic countries were housed before being moved into the buildings from which the Polish residents had been forcibly removed, sometimes only hours before. (*Bundesarchiv Bild 137-051843*)

venture designed to evacuate ethnic Germans from the Baltic states.[2] The Soviet occupation of Eastern Poland, part of the Molotov-Ribbentrop Pact, had caused great anxiety in the neighbouring Baltic countries. There, the population remembered only too well the massacres the Russian army had inflicted in Riga and other places at the end of the First World War. The regime in Berlin then decided to bring the ethnic Germans from that area, *Heim ins Reich*, and by the second half of October 1939 the ships with these people were already entering ports in West Prussia. The migrants were housed in homes from which the Polish residents had only recently been violently expelled. The Poles had been given a few hours at most to pack some hand luggage and leave the house clean, after which they were taken to the station with a single suitcase and then deported in open train carriages to the occupied, but not annexed, part of Poland, the *Generalgouvernement*. This hastily planned, improvised action was only the beginning of an unprecedented ethnic cleansing; in the following years, around 1 million Poles were to be forcibly evicted and deported as part of a megalomaniac repopulation plan.

However, expelling and deporting the people who did not fit into the new, pure-bred empire proved easier than finding enough new residents who *did* meet the requirements. As there were far too few people in Germany to populate the new territory, the Nazis began to gather as many Germanic people as possible and so huge population movements were organized. This mainly concerned the Volksdeutsche, which constituted around 10 million people of German descent who were often, but not always, German-speaking, and who had been settled in Eastern and Southeastern Europe for many generations. These people were sometimes voluntarily, sometimes forcibly, removed from their living areas and transferred to large transit camps. There they were extensively medically and racially examined and then, if approved, went to their new place of residence. Furthermore, attempts were made to interest people in other Germanic countries in settling in the annexed territories in the East.

But even these methods did not yield enough Germans to populate the new ideal state and therefore a large part of the population in occupied Central and Eastern Europe was examined for its racial value by racial experts, the so-called SS-Eignungsprüfer. The Nazi 'race experts' believed that among the largely Slavic population there were also people with Aryan blood, and they had to be 'saved' for the Germanic race. The SS-Eignungsprüfer examined millions of people and filled out a 'race card' for each person. This form recorded dozens of different physical features, including eye, hair and skin colour, height, and the shape of the skull, nose and lips. Based on this data, classification into one of the four breed groups followed. The people in

This map from 1942 (titled *umgesiedelte Volksgruppen*; resettled ethnic groups) shows the large-scale population migration in which the RKFDV and the VoMi transferred about 10 million Volksdeutsche to mainly annexed Polish territory. First from the Baltic states occupied by the Soviet Union, later from Eastern and Southeastern Europe and the border area of Ukraine. The map also shows how, in addition to parts of Poland, all of Luxembourg, German-speaking Belgium and the French provinces of Alsace and Lorraine were annexed. (*Private collection*)

groups I and II were considered 'desirable population growth', while those in group III ('average') were eligible to serve as slave labourers and the people in group IV ('undesirable') were to be deported or killed. Nearly 50% of the Poles, Balts and Russians and all Asians, Sinti, Roma and Jews were assigned to the latter group.

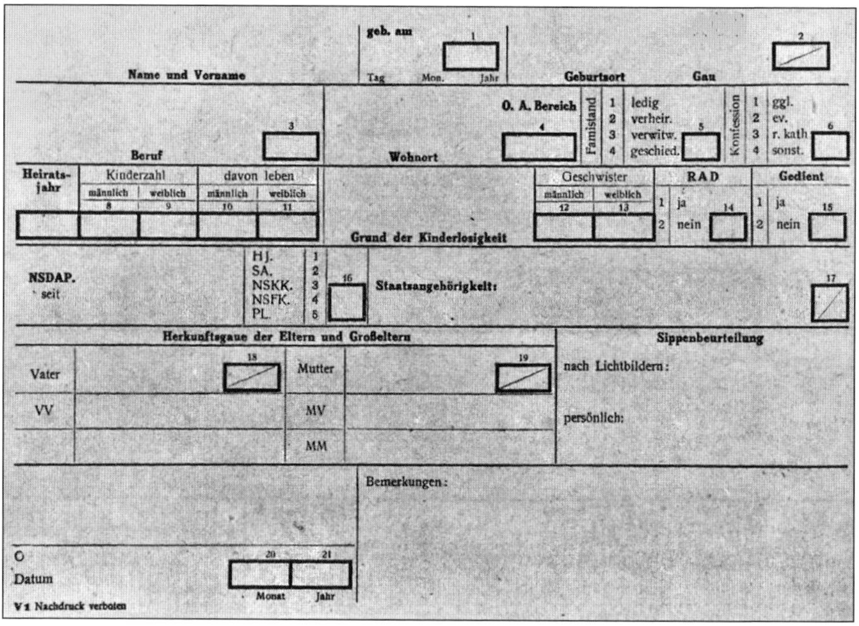

geb. am 1 | Tag Mon. Jahr
Name und Vorname
Geburtsort Gau 2
Beruf 3
Wohnort
O. A. Bereich 4
Famistand: 1 ledig, 2 verheir., 3 verwitw., 4 geschied. 5
Konfession: 1 ggl., 2 ev., 3 r. kath, 4 sonst. 6
Heirats-jahr
Kinderzahl: männlich 8, weiblich 9
davon leben: männlich 10, weiblich 11
Grund der Kinderlosigkeit
Geschwister: männlich 12, weiblich 13
RAD: 1 ja, 2 nein 14
Gedient: 1 ja, 2 nein 15
NSDAP. seit
HJ. 1, SA. 2, NSKK. 3, NSFK. 4, PL. 5 — 16
Staatsangehörigkeit: 17
Herkunftsgaue der Eltern und Großeltern
Vater 18 | Mutter 19
VV | MV
MM
Sippenbeurteilung
nach Lichtbildern:
persönlich:
Bemerkungen:
O
Datum 20 21 | Monat Jahr
V1 Nachdruck verboten

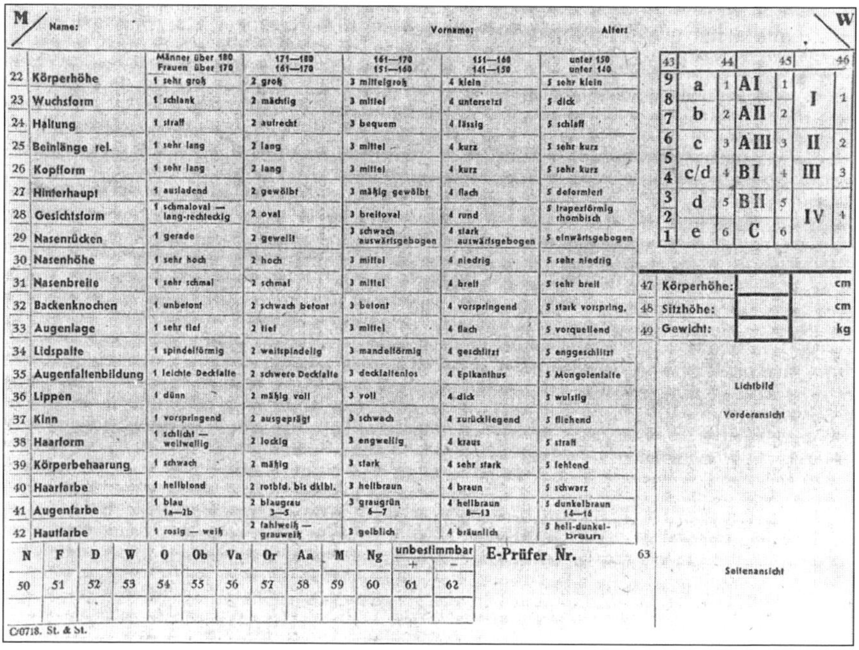

M | Name: | Vorname: | Alter: | W

		Männer über 180 / Frauen über 170	171—180 / 161—170	161—170 / 151—160	151—160 / 141—150	unter 150 / unter 140
22	Körperhöhe	1 sehr groß	2 groß	3 mittelgroß	4 klein	5 sehr klein
23	Wuchsform	1 schlank	2 mächtig	3 mittel	4 untersetzt	5 dick
24	Haltung	1 straff	2 aufrecht	3 bequem	4 lässig	5 schlaff
25	Beinlänge rel.	1 sehr lang	2 lang	3 mittel	4 kurz	5 sehr kurz
26	Kopfform	1 sehr lang	2 lang	3 mittel	4 kurz	5 sehr kurz
27	Hinterhaupt	1 ausladend	2 gewölbt	3 mäßig gewölbt	4 flach	5 deformiert
28	Gesichtsform	1 schmaloval — lang-rechteckig	2 oval	3 breitoval	4 rund	5 trapezförmig rhombisch
29	Nasenrücken	1 gerade	2 gewellt	3 schwach auswärtsgebogen	4 stark auswärtsgebogen	5 einwärtsgebogen
30	Nasenhöhe	1 sehr hoch	2 hoch	3 mittel	4 niedrig	5 sehr niedrig
31	Nasenbreite	1 sehr schmal	2 schmal	3 mittel	4 breit	5 sehr breit
32	Backenknochen	1 unbetont	2 schwach betont	3 betont	4 vorspringend	5 stark vorspring.
33	Augenlage	1 sehr tief	2 tief	3 mittel	4 flach	5 vorquellend
34	Lidspalte	1 spindelförmig	2 weitspindelig	3 mandelförmig	4 geschlitzt	5 enggeschlitzt
35	Augenfaltenbildung	1 leichte Deckfalte	2 schwere Deckfalte	3 deckfaltenlos	4 Epikanthus	5 Mongolenfalte
36	Lippen	1 dünn	2 mäßig voll	3 voll	4 dick	5 wulstig
37	Kinn	1 vorspringend	2 ausgeprägt	3 schwach	4 zurückliegend	5 fliehend
38	Haarform	1 schlicht — wellwellig	2 lockig	3 engwellig	4 kraus	5 straff
39	Körperbehaarung	1 schwach	2 mäßig	3 stark	4 sehr stark	5 fehlend
40	Haarfarbe	1 hellblond	2 rotbld. bis dklbl.	3 hellbraun	4 braun	5 schwarz
41	Augenfarbe	1 blau 1a—2b	2 blaugrau 3—5	3 graugrün 6—7	4 hellbraun 8—13	5 dunkelbraun 14—16
42	Hautfarbe	1 rosig — weiß	2 fahlweiß — grauweiß	3 gelblich	4 bräunlich	5 hell-dunkel-braun

N	F	D	W	O	Ob	Va	Or	Aa	M	Ng	unbestimmbar +	unbestimmbar −
50	51	52	53	54	55	56	57	58	59	60	61	62

E-Prüfer Nr. 63

43		44		45		46
9	a	1	AI	1	I	1
8						
7	b	2	AII	2		
6	c	3	AIII	3	II	2
5						
4	c/d	4	BI	4	III	3
3	d	5	BII	5		
2					IV	4
1	e	6	C	6		

47 Körperhöhe: cm
48 Sitzhöhe: cm
49 Gewicht: kg

Lichtbild
Vorderansicht
Seitenansicht

C/0718. St. & St.

The front and back of the so-called '*Rassenkarte*' on which all conceivable personal data and a large number of 'racial characteristics' were recorded, on the basis of which people were then classified into one of four racial groups. (*Private collection*)

Dealing with the population of the Eastern European countries was mainly based on Himmler's proposals, which he had submitted to Hitler in May 1940 in a short memorandum entitled *Einige Gedanken über die Behandlung der Fremdvölkischen im Osten* (Some Thoughts on the Treatment of non-German People in the East).[3] The piece proposed deporting all Jews to Africa or a colony – the decision to commit mass murder would come later – and to filter out the 'racially valuable' from the population and transfer them to Germany to assimilate. The remaining non-German population would then receive only four years of education. According to Himmler, it was enough for these people to simply learn to count, to write their own name, and to be honest and diligent. He did not consider it necessary to learn to read, but they had to be taught that it is 'a divine commandment' to obey the Germans. This 'education' would eventually create a large proletariat that could be deployed in Germany for special tasks such as building bridges and roads. Hitler judged the Himmler's work as being *'sehr gut und richtig'* ('very good and just'). The memorandum was to form the basis for the population policy, but Hitler did stipulate that the document still had to be treated as top secret and could only be read by a few very high-ranking Nazis.

The plans for the future of the conquered and yet to be conquered areas were further elaborated on Himmler's instructions by the planning department of the RKF under SS-Oberführer Professor Konrad Meyer. In collaboration with a department of the RSHA, a first version of what would later be called the *Generalplan Ost* was drawn up; a detailed, comprehensive plan for the ethnic cleansing, repopulation, settlement and colonization of the East. A small group of scientists affiliated with the SS – specialists in the field of agriculture, racial sciences and economic geography – worked out the plans further and in March 1941 organized an exhibition in Berlin entitled *Planung und Aufbau im Osten* (Planning and Construction in the East). Here, SS-Oberführer Meyer gave a group of senior Nazi officials, including Hess, Himmler and Heydrich, an explanation of the plans and showed them examples of the model villages and farms that were to be built.

In the following months the details were worked out in cooperation with the RSHA and demographic experts and in May 1942, the headquarters of the RKF presented a new version of the plan. Himmler agreed with substantive parts, but instructed Professor Meyer to expand the concept into a complete plan for the whole of Europe, including Alsace-Lorraine, Slovenia, Bohemia and Moravia. It is not known whether this variant was ever completed, but he received approval from Hitler in mid-July 1942 for his plans for Eastern Europe.

The opening of the exhibition 'Planung und Aufbau im Osten'. The head of the planning department of the RKFDV, SS-Oberführer Professor Konrad Meyer, is seen here talking to (from L-R) Reichsminister Hess, Reichsführer-SS Himmler, Reichsleiter Bouhler (co-responsible for the euthanasia programme), Reichsminister Todt and SS-Gruppenführer Heydrich. (*Bundesarchiv Bild 183-B01718*)

Himmler's masseur Felix Kersten, who was present at his headquarters *Hegewald* in Ukraine at the time, reported that on the morning of 16 July 1942 that he could not treat his patient because he was unable to reach the state of relaxation necessary for the massage. 'You can't imagine how happy I am, mister Kersten', Himmler began excitedly.

> The Führer not only listened to me, moreover he did not interrupt me constantly, as is his habit – a habit, by the way, which completely disturbs the train of thought, so that one finally listens to the Führer's views on the subject in question, instead of presenting its own proposal. No, today he went so far as to approve my proposals, ask questions and draw my attention to important details that I had not considered and that required additional investigation on my part. This is the happiest day of my life.[4]

The Generalplan Ost was modified several times, but the various successive versions shared the most important characteristics. The treatment of the population of Eastern Europe was completely based on racial politics, which meant that about 31 million 'racially undesirable' people had to disappear from the area to be colonized. It was foreseen that more than half of these people would die of starvation and deprivation. The rest, an estimated 14 million people, would be used as slave labourers. The implementation of the plans would take at least twenty to thirty years and during this period, the planners reasoned, 'the Jewish Question' would also have been solved.

The Holocaust

Race politics eventually culminated in the Holocaust, with the murder of millions of people whom the Nazis considered harmful or undesirable. The main target of the mass murder was the Jews, and approximately 6 million Jewish men, women and children were killed by bullets, gas or other means. In addition, the Nazi regime murdered several hundred thousand Roma and Sinti (a more precise number is not known), political opponents, people of Slavic origin, homosexuals, prisoners of war and resistance fighters.

The persecution of the Jews in Nazi Germany had begun immediately after Hitler's seizure of power and had been legislated into government policy very shortly afterwards. The Jewish population became victims of social exclusion, libel, harassment and boycotts, arson, vandalism, and extortion and violence. Before the outbreak of war, some 250,000 Jews, about half of the Jewish community, left Nazi Germany, usually after having to give up most of their possessions to the regime.

The German invasion of Poland marked the beginning of a more radical phase of the persecution of the Jews. Special SS-Einsatzgruppen executed

A typical boycott of a Jewish-owned shop. Potential customers would be scared off by an SA man in an heroic pose and the sign saying '*Deutsche! Wehrt Euch! Kauft nicht bei Juden*!' (Germans! Resist! Don't buy from Jews!) The display case has been defaced with the six-pointed star. (*USNA, 541929*)

thousands of Poles, many of them Jews. Subsequently, massive ethnic cleansing took place and the Polish Jews, some 1.7 million people, were gathered in ghettos and imprisoned. Crowded together, many of them succumbed to starvation, lack of medical care and appalling sanitary conditions.

Initially, the Nazi regime wanted to deport the Jews (Madagascar, British Palestine, Eastern Poland and the Soviet Union were mentioned), but at an unknown moment in time during the autumn of 1941, Hitler decided to murder them. Himmler was ordered to organize and carry out the mass murder and on 20 January 1942, a meeting took place at Wannsee Nr. 56/58 in Berlin, where the '*Endlösung der europäischen Judenfrage*' (Final Solution to the Jewish Question in Europe) was discussed under the leadership of the chief of the Sicherheitspolizei and SD, SS-Obergruppenführer Heydrich. Those present included representatives of the Ministries of Justice, the Interior, Foreign Affairs, the Occupied Eastern Territories, the Generalgouvernement,

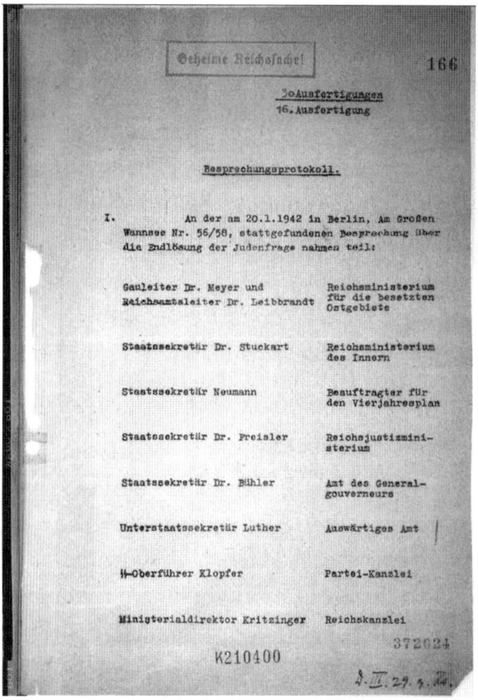

Geheime Reichssache!

166

30 Ausfertigungen
16. Ausfertigung

Besprechungsprotokoll.

I. An der am 20.1.1942 in Berlin, Am Großen Wannsee Nr. 56/58, stattgefundenen Besprechung über die Endlösung der Judenfrage nahmen teil:

Gauleiter Dr. Meyer und Reichsamtsleiter Dr. Leibbrandt	Reichsministerium für die besetzten Ostgebiete
Staatssekretär Dr. Stuckart	Reichsministerium des Innern
Staatssekretär Neumann	Beauftragter für den Vierjahresplan
Staatssekretär Dr. Freisler	Reichsjustizministerium
Staatssekretär Dr. Bühler	Amt des Generalgouverneurs
Unterstaatssekretär Luther	Auswärtiges Amt
SS-Oberführer Klopfer	Partei-Kanzlei
Ministerialdirektor Kritzinger	Reichskanzlei

372024

K210400

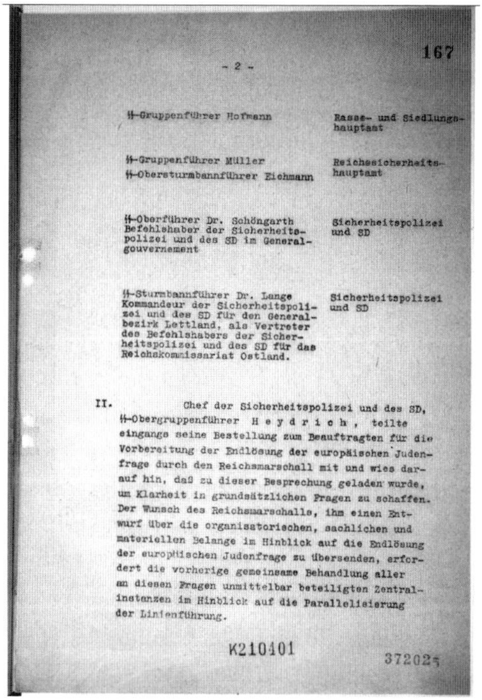

167

- 2 -

SS-Gruppenführer Hofmann	Rasse- und Siedlungshauptamt
SS-Gruppenführer Müller SS-Obersturmbannführer Eichmann	Reichssicherheitshauptamt
SS-Oberführer Dr. Schöngarth Befehlshaber der Sicherheitspolizei und des SD im Generalgouvernement	Sicherheitspolizei und SD
SS-Sturmbannführer Dr. Lange Kommandeur der Sicherheitspolizei und des SD für den Generalbezirk Lettland, als Vertreter des Befehlshabers der Sicherheitspolizei und des SD für das Reichskommissariat Ostland.	Sicherheitspolizei und SD

II. Chef der Sicherheitspolizei und des SD, SS-Obergruppenführer H e y d r i c h , teilte eingangs seine Bestellung zum Beauftragten für die Vorbereitung der Endlösung der europäischen Judenfrage durch den Reichsmarschall mit und wies darauf hin, daß zu dieser Besprechung geladen wurde, um Klarheit in grundsätzlichen Fragen zu schaffen. Der Wunsch des Reichsmarschalls, ihm einen Entwurf über die organisatorischen, sachlichen und materiellen Belange im Hinblick auf die Endlösung der europäischen Judenfrage zu übersenden, erfordert die vorherige gemeinsame Behandlung aller an diesen Fragen unmittelbar beteiligten Zentralinstanzen im Hinblick auf die Parallelisierung der Linienführung.

K210401

372025

Above left and above right: The first two pages of the minutes of what came to be known as the Wannsee Conference, where the 'Endlösung der europäischen Judenfrage' (Final Solution to the Jewish Question) was discussed on 20 January 1942. The attendance list shows that in addition to the SS and the NSDAP, all important ministries were aware of the planned mass murder. (*Public domain*) the Four Year Plan, the Party and Reich Chancelleries, and, of course, the SS: the Rasse- und Siedlungshauptamt, the Reichssicherheitshauptamt and the Sicherheitspolizei and SD.

The minutes of the meeting did not state what the 'Final Solution' actually entailed because instead the obscure language called it the 'Evacuation of the Jews to the East'. But the document did provide a definite answer to the ultimate fate of these people. After first describing how the Jews had to build roads in the East in large columns of labourers, with men and women separated, 'many of which will no doubt fall out through natural attenuation', it was then stated that any survivors had to be treated '*entsprechend*' (in the same way). They formed, according to the minutes, the natural selection, and when released would form the germ of a new Jewish tribe.

While the mass murder of European Jews was being discussed in Berlin, it had already begun in the Soviet Union. The German army had invaded the country in June 1941, closely followed by a number of Einsatzgruppen of the SS, who had orders to shoot all possible 'enemies of the Reich', including not only partisans and civilian and military communist officials, but also the Jewish population. At first this only applied mainly to young men, but later also included the elderly, women and children.

These large-scale massacres took place under the direction and instigation of the SS, but police units, local auxiliaries and even members of the local population also participated. However, it became clear that the mass executions were causing

The murder of Jewish civilians by members of a German SS-Einsatzgruppe near Ivanhorod in Ukraine, 1942. These death squads were responsible for the deaths of over 1 million people. (*Historical Archives Warsaw, public domain*)

severe psychological distress to the killers and were considered both too expensive and time-consuming by their commanders. Consequently, they reverted to the experiences gained during the euthanasia programme. In December 1941, an extermination camp was opened in Chełmno, Poland, the first of a number of camps specifically designed to murder the Jews on an industrial scale. At Chełmno this was done with gas vans – trucks or delivery vans with a closed loading space in which the victims were suffocated with exhaust gas – but other extermination camps were provided with special gas chambers. Those camps included Bełżec, where former Aktion T4 inspector and SS-Sturmbannführer Christian Wirth was the first commander, and the Sobibor and Treblinka camps, both of which were under the command of SS-Sturmbannführer Franz Stangl for a period. He too had played an important role in the euthanasia programme.

The Jews of the Soviet Union and Eastern Europe were the first victims of this mass murder, but from the middle of 1942 the Germans also began to deport Jews from the occupied territories of Europe to the camps in the East, after first locking them up in transit camps. After a days-long journey in crammed cattle wagons, they arrived at the camp, where many were murdered shortly afterwards while others were selected for their ability to work. In most cases, these people also died after a short time as a result of abuse, hard labour, insufficient nutrition, poor hygiene and no or inadequate medical care. This was called 'destruction by labour'. About two-thirds of the 6 million murdered Jews died in the concentration and extermination camps and about one-third were executed by firing squad or in some other way.

A mass grave in Bergen-Belsen concentration camp after the liberation of the camp in April 1945. Among the bodies is the SS doctor Fritz Klein (centre), a Volksdeutsche from Romania who was active in various concentration and extermination camps and was now forced to help bury the bodies. Later that year he was sentenced to death and hanged. (*H. Oakes, public domain*)

IV

THE NEW NOBILITY

Lebensborn: Goals and Means

'Every mother of good blood is sacred to us.'
Heinrich Himmler

Establishment

Lebensborn was founded on 12 December 1935 on Himmler's orders and registered as an association shortly afterwards. There is no doubt that Hitler was aware of and supported the initiative. The fact that the organization was created precisely at this time was probably due to several reasons. Himmler had long been obsessed with the low German birth rates and during this period, as head of the Bavarian police, he was regularly confronted with the problems of unmarried pregnant women and abortion. In addition, the Hilfswerk Mutter und Kind had been founded a year earlier, part of the NSV of the NSDAP, which aimed to support the pregnant Aryan mother and her children. Because racial ideology was the central part of Himmler's worldview, he also wanted to concern himself with the concern for 'right' mothers and children. With Lebensborn he

Himmler at his desk, presumably during a radio speech. Obsessed with racial purity and birth rates, he founded Lebensborn in 1935. (*Private collection*)

wanted to guarantee that the SS, as the standard-bearer of the National Socialist birth, population and race policy, would retain as much influence as possible on this matter, which was essential to him. The establishment of Lebensborn was also an extension of the SS betrothal and marriage order, which stipulated that both the SS man and his bride had to meet racial requirements.

The form of an association was specially chosen because Lebensborn could then own property, but the organization was also part of the SS as main department IV of the Sippenamt, which came under the Rasse- und Siedlungshauptamt (RuSHA). The RuSHA had evolved from the Rasseamt der SS, one of the first three main departments of the SS empire, which had been set up in early 1932 to examine candidates for the SS and their (future) wives for racial purity. In the first years of its existence, Lebensborn was governed by three SS officers appointed by Himmler. One of them, SS-Sturmbannführer Guntram Pflaum, was in charge of the day-to-day operations and also represented Lebensborn externally.

According to its official objectives, Lebensborn was established for 'supporting racially and hereditary biologically valuable, child-rich families', and 'providing shelter and care for pregnant women of racially and hereditary

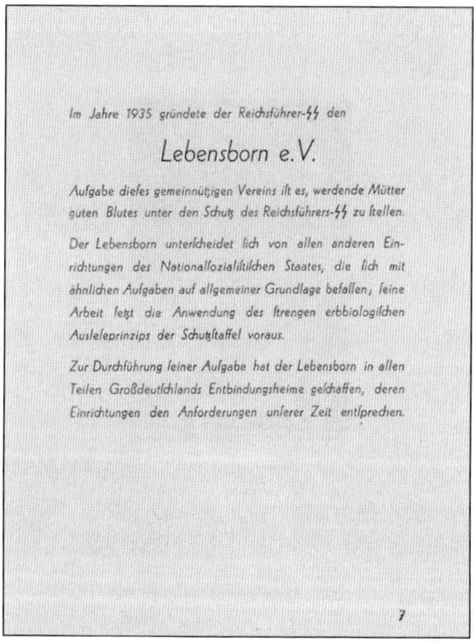
Im Jahre 1935 gründete der Reichsführer-ᛋᛋ den

Lebensborn e.V.

Aufgabe dieſes gemeinnützigen Vereins iſt es, werdende Mütter guten Blutes unter den Schutz des Reichsführers-ᛋᛋ zu ſtellen.

Der Lebensborn unterſcheidet ſich von allen anderen Einrichtungen des Nationalſozialiſtiſchen Staates, die ſich mit ähnlichen Aufgaben auf allgemeiner Grundlage befaſſen; ſeine Arbeit ſetzt die Anwendung des ſtrengen erbbiologiſchen Ausleſeprinzips der Schutzſtaffel voraus.

Zur Durchführung ſeiner Aufgabe hat der Lebensborn in allen Teilen Großdeutſchlands Entbindungsheime geſchaffen, deren Einrichtungen den Anforderungen unſerer Zeit entſprechen.

7

Above left and above right: Two pages from the brochure published by Lebensborn around 1940, with the motto chosen by Himmler – all mothers [including unmarried ones] with good blood will be sacred to the organization – and the main premise: 'Lebensborn differs from all other institutions of the national socialist state engaged in similar tasks on a general basis; in its work, the application of the strict hereditary biological selection criteria of the Schutzstaffel is paramount.' (*Private collection*) value, who, after careful examination by the Rasse- und Siedlungshauptamt-SS of her family and that of the begetter, it can be assumed that equally valuable children will be born'.[1] Lebensborn would also take care of the children and their mothers after giving birth.

But while all Nazi organizations aimed to increase the birthrate of children with 'good blood', Lebensborn was particularly concerned with the racial elite. According to Himmler's worldview, the Nordic race was to be saved from impending doom by gathering all Germans in a future Greater Germanic Empire. To realize this, territory had to be conquered and a racial elite created. This 'new nobility' – Himmler used the words literally – was to form the leading class of the coming Greater Germanic Empire. Populating the new superstate and creating the future leaders required raising the number of births and improving the racial quality. Lebensborn had to contribute to this, in particular by preventing abortions among unmarried, Aryan women.

Expectations were high. Himmler planned to open about thirty Lebensborn clinics in Germany and expressed the hope that thanks to Lebensborn, at least 100,000 abortions would be prevented every year, which he calculated would create an army of about 400,000 in a period of thirty years. According to Ebner, Lebensborn's medical leader from the late 1930s, great financial benefits could also be expected. 'On the premise that each new child adds 100,000 Reichsmarks to the German economy through his later labour', he reasoned, 'about 832 million Reichsmarks will be contributed to the future of the German people through Lebensborn's activities'.[2] Presumably those leading the organization also realized that these estimates were not very realistic and mainly served to gain support for their cause.

Maternity Clinics, Children's Homes and Child Abduction

Between 1936 and 1944, Lebensborn opened a total of about thirty clinics, homes and boarding houses: thirteen in Germany and annexed Austria, eleven in Norway and the rest in Poland and some Western European countries. The organization's first branch was Heim Hochland near Munich, and six more followed by the end of 1938. After that, growth stagnated, mainly due to poor governance and financial problems. In 1940 a new director was appointed, the SS officer Max Sollmann. He carried out a reorganization and managed to improve the financial situation, after which the expansion of Lebensborn was continued. Between 1942 and 1944, the organization opened five branches in Germany and annexed Austria and five others in occupied Northern and

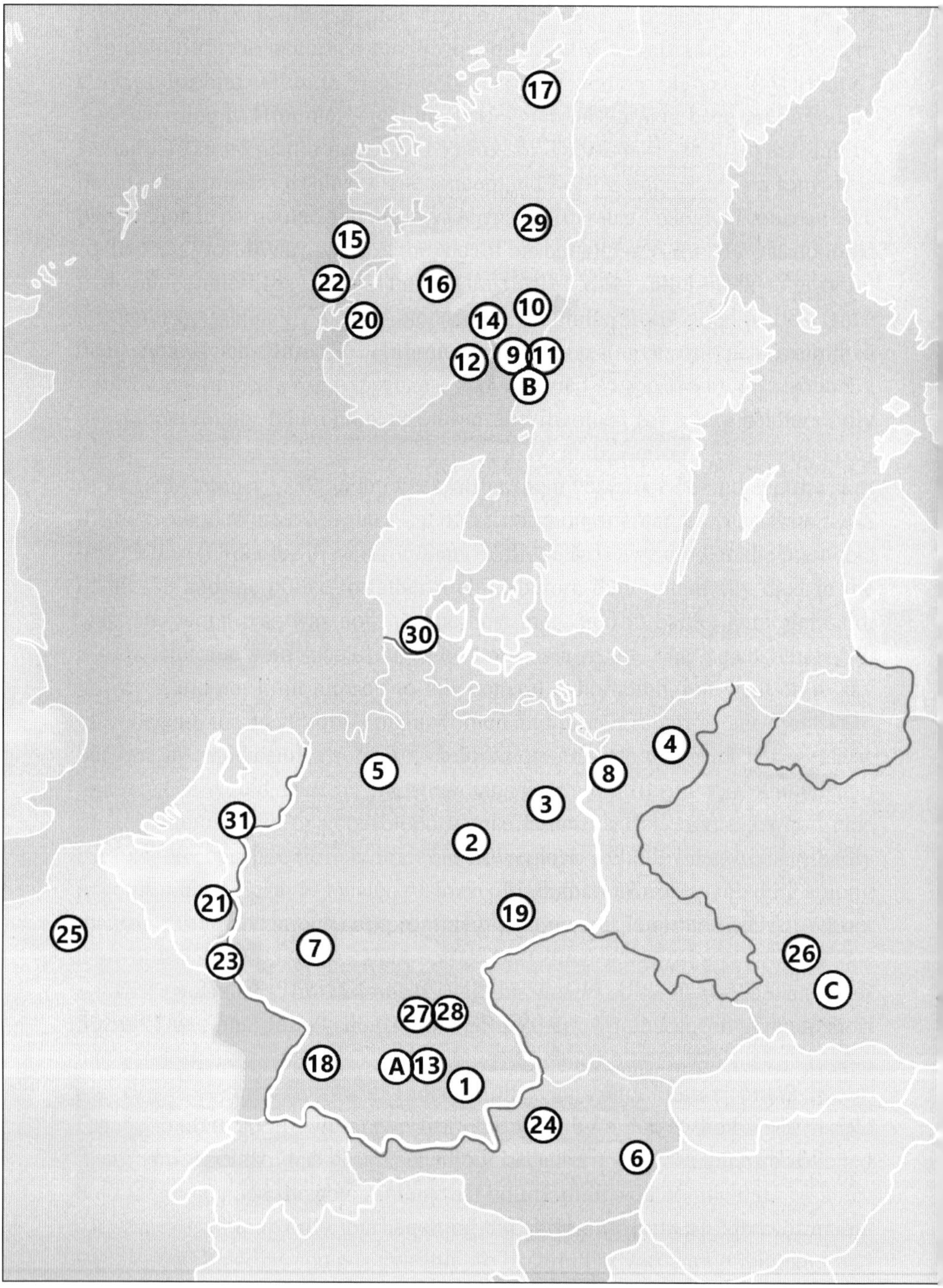
17
29
15
22
16
10
14
20
12
9
11
B
30
4
5
8
3
31
2
21
19
25
7
23
26
C
27
28
18
A
13
1
24
6

The Lebensborn Branches (numbered in order of opening):

A. Munich, Zentrale Lebensborn, Germany.
B. Oslo, Zentralstelle Lebensborn, Norway.
C. Krakow, Aussenstelle Lebensborn, Poland.

1. Heim Hochland, Steinhöring, Germany, August 1936, maternity clinic & children's home.
2. Heim Harz, Wernigerode, Germany, June 1937, maternity clinic & children's home.
3. Heim Kurmark, Klosterheide, Germany, September 1937, maternity clinic & children's home.
4. Heim Pommern, Bad Polzin, Poland, May 1938, maternity clinic & children's home.
5. Heim Friesland, Hohehorst, Germany, May 1938, maternity clinic & children's home.
6. Heim Wienerwald, Feichtenbach, Austria, November 1938, maternity clinic & children's home.
7. Heim Taunus, Wiesbaden, Germany, November 1939, children's home; later also maternity clinic.
8. Kriegsmütter- und Wohnheim Johannistal, Szczecin, Poland, June 1940, guest house.
9. Stadtheim Kristinelund, Oslo, Norway, March 1941, guest house.
10. Heim Hurdalsverk, Hurdalsverk, Norway, August 1941, maternity clinic & children's home.
11. Stadtheim Olav, Oslo, Norway, February 1942, guest house.
12. Kinderheim Godthaab, Oslo, Norway, February 1942, children's home.
13. Mütterwohnstätten, Munich, Germany, March 1942, boarding houses.
14. Heim Klekken, Hønefoss, Norway, May 1942, maternity clinic & children's home.
15. Stadtheim Bergen, Hop, Norway, June 1942, boarding house.
16. Vorheim Geilo, Geilo, Norway, December 1942, maternity clinic & children's home.
17. Stadtheim Drontheim, Trondheim, Norway, circa October 1942, boarding house.
18. Heim Schwarzwald, Nordrach, Germany, November 1942, maternity clinic & children's home.
19. Kinderheim Sonnenwiese, Kohren-Sahlis, Germany, November 1942, children's home.
20. Kinderheim Stalheim, Voss, Norway, February 1943, children's home.
21. Heim Ardennen, Ayeneux, Belgium, March 1943, maternity clinic & children's home.
22. Kinderheim Moldegård, Os (Bjørnafjorden), Norway, April 1943, children's home.
23. Heim Moselland, Luxembourg, July 1943, children's home.
24. Kinderheim Alpenland, Laakirchen, Austria, September 1943, children's home.
25. Heim Westwald, Lamorlaye, France, February 1944, maternity clinic & children's home.
26. Heimstätte, Smoszewo, Poland, April 1944, guest house.
27. Kinderheim Franken I, Schalkhausen, Germany, June 1944, children's home.
28. Kinderheim Franken II, Schalkhausen, Germany, June 1944, children's home.
29. Heim Høsbjør, Brumunddal, Norway, April 1945, maternity clinic & children's home.
30. Heim Tønder (?), Tønder, Denmark, April 1945, maternity clinic & children's home.
31. Heim Gelderland, Nijmegen, the Netherlands, never opened, maternity clinic & children's home.

Western Europe. In addition, from the beginning of 1941, support was provided to the establishment and expansion of the Norwegian Lebensborn.

Initially, almost all Lebensborn locations had a dual function and served not only as a maternity clinic but also as a children's home, but that changed in a later phase. The flow in maternity hospitals was slower than expected because many children sometimes stayed there for two years or more after birth. As a result, clinics became overcrowded, infectious diseases sprang up and infant mortality rose. Therefore from 1942, with a few exceptions, only children's homes were opened in Germany and Austria. However, because the demand for places in both the maternity hospitals and the children's homes almost constantly exceeded supply, Lebensborn also made extensive use of public and private institutions. There, too, the women and children remained under Lebensborn's control and all costs were paid by the organization.

The activities in occupied territories started in 1941. These foreign branches of Lebensborn concerned the children of German soldiers and mothers with the desired racial characteristics of a different nationality. The care for these children was implicitly approved by Hitler in 1941 in the context of the racial policy, initially only for the Netherlands and Norway, but later also for other areas. Norway led the way in opening branches, mainly because of the initiative and commitment of the local SS leader and the Reichskommissar, and a complete branch of Lebensborn was eventually set up in that country. The Norwegian Lebensborn operated according to almost the same rules as in Germany and received personnel and financial support from Munich, but otherwise the local leadership had a great deal of freedom of action.

The branches in the other countries fell directly under the Zentrale in Munich. This concerned two maternity hospitals with children's homes in Belgium and France and a children's home in annexed Luxembourg. Work was also done on branches in Denmark, but presumably only one was completed just in time, a few weeks before the end of the war. In the Netherlands, Lebensborn had already completed a large maternity hospital with a children's home in the spring of 1943, but this establishment was never put into use. In annexed territory in Poland, Lebensborn founded two boarding houses for young working women who had given birth with the organization.

A number of children's homes in Lebensborn not only accommodated children who had been born in their own maternity hospitals or in an ordinary hospital under the supervision of the organization. There were also foreign children who were 'Germanized' and were given a new identity. These were not children of German soldiers and foreign mothers who had voluntarily reported to Lebensborn, but children who had been abducted from abroad because they met the desired racial characteristics.

This kidnapping of children started shortly after the invasion of Poland on the initiative of local German authorities, but from February 1942 Lebensborn was officially involved by the order of Himmler. The organization took over custody, placed some of the youngest foreign children in its homes and even set up one children's home especially for the Germanization of the somewhat older children. They mainly came from Poland, but also from Czechoslovakia and Slovenia. The children were taken from orphanages, kidnapped from school or even pulled from their parents' arms. A number of children whose parents had been murdered or imprisoned in camps because of their involvement in the resistance also met this fate. According to Himmler's views, which were marked by racial delusions, the knife cut both ways in this way. Not only did

15-year-old Marie Doležalová was one of the Czech children taken to Lebensborn after her father was shot and her mother deported to Ravensbrück concentration camp. The Nazis had mistakenly believed that their hometown, the village of Lidice, had been involved in the assassination attempt of Reinhard Heydrich. She was one of the few children to survive the war thanks to her 'racial characteristics' and is seen bearing witness here at the Nuremberg trials. (*USHMM*)

he think he was strengthening the German people, while at the same time weakening the countries concerned, he also believed he was taking away the 'most valuable' children and thus depriving those territories of future leaders.

Munich: the Physical and Spiritual Centre

Lebensborn was founded in Berlin in 1935, but moved to Munich two years later, where the headquarters were also located. This was not just a geographical move, because shortly afterwards Himmler also removed Lebensborn from the organization of the RuSHA and promoted it to an independent department, *Amt L* (Lebensborn), of his personal staff. The form of government was also radically changed. A board of directors was set up with himself as chairman and some of his confidants as members. The fact that the Reichsführer-SS was chairman and the organization formed part of his personal staff gave Lebensborn a great deal of prestige and authority.

There is no doubt about the reasons for the move and the personnel and organizational changes. Lebensborn was one of Himmler's favourite projects, and he personally wanted to keep full control over it. This would be easier in his hometown of Munich than in Berlin, where competing NSDAP organizations

An early period postcard depicting Heim Hochland in Steinhöring with a sun and greeting adapted to the zeitgeist. (*Private collection*)

such as the NSV were based. There were also increasing ideological differences of opinion with Richard Walther Darré, the leader of the RuSHA, of which Lebensborn was a part until the autumn of 1937. Himmler's ideas about the development of a Germanic elite of peasant warriors were increasingly inconsistent with Darré's in this field.[3] Furthermore, Gregor Ebner, Himmler's friend and former family doctor whom he made the organization's medical leader, was also from the area. It is no coincidence that the first maternity hospital annex children's home, Heim Hochland, had been opened a few months earlier in the village of Steinhöring, in the countryside just east of Munich.

From the beginning of 1938, Lebensborn's centre of gravity was, in all respects, Munich. The head office was located in the city and it is where the association was officially registered. In addition, the organization had various offices, residential houses, homes, depots and even a satellite camp of Dachau concentration camp. Munich was also not just physically but mentally a suitable location for the centre of Lebensborn.[4] The Bavarian capital was one of those German cities where concepts such as racial hygiene and eugenics were already commonplace in the nineteenth century and anti-Semitism was very common. Furthermore, the *Gesellschaft für Rassenhygiene* was active from 1907, which, with the Austrian-German doctor and publicist Max von Gruber as chairman, made fanatical propaganda for a population policy aimed at selection on the basis of racial characteristics. He collaborated with Houston Stewart Chamberlain, who combined his belief in the superiority of the Teutons with fanatical anti-Semitism, and Julius Lehmann, a Munich author, publisher, and politician who specialized in populist racism, with Hans Günthers' *Rassenkunde des deutschen Volkes* as one of his bestsellers.

The city was also a hotbed of early right-wing extremist and völkische movements, including the *Deutsche Vaterlandspartei* (DVLP) and an even more extreme political sect called the Thule-Gesellschaft, which in many ways was the immediate predecessor of the

The logo of the Thule-Gesellschaft featured the swastika. This society was also a forerunner of the NSDAP in other respects. (*Private collection*)

NSDAP, not only in terms of ideology, but also in relation to the main characters and symbolism: its members included Rudolf Hess, Dietrich Eckart and Alfred Rosenberg; they used the '*Heil*' greeting; the most important symbol was the swastika; and the organization's motto was *'Gedenke, dass Du ein Deutscher bist! Halt dein Blut rein!'* (Remember, you are a German! Keep your blood pure!).

Not long after the seizure of power, Munich, as the birthplace of the National Socialist movement and the setting of Hitler's failed Putsch in 1923, was given the 'honorary title' of '*Haupstadt der Bewegung'* (Capital of [the National Socialist] Movement). Himmler, therefore, was in his element.

The Lebensborn headquarters was the main branch of the organization and was referred to as the *Reichszentrale*, *Lebensborn-Zentrale* or simply *Zentrale*. The head office was initially located in the villa of the writer Thomas Mann, at Poschinger Strasse No.1. Mann was an acknowledged opponent of Nazi rule and after his house was seized in January 1934, it was made available to Lebensborn by the Bavarian government in November 1937. Following renovation, the main office, which then employed about twenty-five people, moved in in January 1938.

From Munich, the Zentrale managed the maternity hospitals and children's homes in Germany and the annexed Austria and the occupied territories, with the exception of Norway. Although the Norwegian Lebensborn organization, like the German branch, was under the authority of Himmler's personal staff and there was close cooperation on personnel and other matters, it operated largely independently of the headquarters in Munich. There was also a department at the Zentrale that was in contact with representatives of the organization in

From January 1938, Lebensborn's headquarters, the Zentrale, was located in the writer Thomas Mann's villa, at Poschinger Strasse No.1 (today Thomas-Mann-Allee No. 10) in Munich. (*Private collection*)

When Mann's villa became too small, the headquarters moved to Herzog-Max-Strasse, also in Munich, in January 1940. The synagogue located there (the building with the tower) was demolished in 1938 on Hitler's orders, and Lebensborn moved into the associated building in the right foreground, where the administrative centre of the Jewish community in Munich had previously been located. (*Private collection*)

Litzmannstadt (the German name for the Polish city of Łodz), Posen (Poznań) and Krakow (Kraków).

When Mann's villa became too small due to the expansion of activities and an increase in personnel to around 100 employees, the Zentrale moved into a number of buildings in Herzog-Max-Strasse from January 1940. Previously housed in the confiscated property of an opponent of the government, Lebensborn's headquarters now moved into buildings belonging to victims of the Nazi regime, being as it was the religious and administrative centre of Munich's Jewish community. The synagogue had been demolished on Hitler's personal orders in June 1938 (making it the first in the Third Reich to meet this fate) but the associated office building was still there for Lebensborn to move into. Such practices were the rule rather than the exception. Almost all Lebensborn's buildings in Munich had been confiscated by the Gestapo having previously belonged to Jewish institutions or individuals, or other enemies and victims of Nazi rule.

Over the years, as the organization continued to grow – by the spring of 1942 around 220 people worked at the Zentrale – a number of departments were moved to other addresses in the city. In June 1941, part of the administration was established in the so-called Bürgermeister villa in Munich-Bogenhausen. Unlike almost all other buildings of the organization, this villa was not only bought but also paid for. In addition to a few departments of the Zentrale, there were also a few apartments, where managing director Sollman, head of the legal service Tesch, and a few other employees lived. Medical director Ebner also lived here for some time with his wife and two young daughters.

At the beginning of 1944, a number of Zentrale departments responsible for handling essential documents – probably forged birth certificates and similar papers, which were used to hide the identity of unmarried mothers and (stolen) children – were transferred to Heim Hochland in the village of Steinhöring. By moving to the countryside, Himmler wanted to prevent these important departments from being hit by Allied bombs, as would indeed happen. In June 1944 a series of heavy Allied air raids on Munich took place, during which US Air Force bombers destroyed much of the Zentrale and other buildings of the organization in the inner city. The Bürgermeister villa was also heavily damaged and became uninhabitable. Subsequently, the other departments and headquarters staff also moved to Steinhöring, where they were housed in eight barracks on the Heim Hochland grounds. Only the *Rechtswesen* (legal) department went to Heim Alpenland with Maria Merkel. The size of the organization is illustrated by the size of those barracks, each 3m high and with an area of $530m^2$. At that time, around 500 people were employed at the Zentrale. Incidentally, Sollmann and Tesch were not housed in barracks but in their own (wooden) houses constructed for them by the forced labourers.

Until early 1942, this building in Antonienstrasse housed a Jewish children's home. After the children and their carers were deported – of whom only a small number would survive the war – Lebensborn established a Mutterwohnstätte there. The boarding house had a nursery for women who had given birth at the organization and now worked at the Zentrale. (*Private collection*)

Besides the Zentrale, the Bürgermeister villa and the other buildings that housed some administrative departments, Lebensborn in Munich also owned several buildings that were used as depots for looted goods, and a number of houses that housed the so-called *Mütterwohnstätten*. These were a kind of boarding house with a nursery, each with room for fifteen women and their children, set up especially for young mothers who had given birth at Lebensborn and now worked at the Zentrale. Two of these Mütterwohnstätten were located at Antonienstrasse No. 7 and Kaulbachstrasse No. 65, where a Jewish children's home (*Kinderheim der Israelitischen Jugendhilfe e.V.*) and a retirement home (*Israelitisches Pensionat*) had been located respectively. The roughly 100 residents of the retirement home were expelled in February 1942, while the children and their carers were arrested and taken away from the children's home between November 1941 and April 1942. Only a few of them would survive the war. The Jewish association that owned the home was forced to hand it over to Lebensborn, but the set sale price was never paid. The Mütterwohnstätten were already evacuated in August 1943 due to the increasing number of air raids on the city, and the children were then separated from their mothers and taken to Heim Moselland in annexed Luxembourg.

A Jewish clinic with a sisters' house on Hermann Schmid Strasse in Munich was evacuated in May 1942 on Himmler's orders, and the patients and staff were deported to Theresienstadt concentration camp a month later. Of the approximately sixty people deported, only four survived the war. The hospital was then forcibly sold to Lebensborn, but even the unilaterally set, rock-bottom price was never paid. The inventory was temporarily stored at Heim Hochland to be later transferred to the planned *Heimstätte* in Poland.

Himmler planned to renovate the hospital and start a private nursing school for Lebensborn in order to combat the staff shortages and make the organization less dependent on the '*braune Schwestern*' – nurses called 'braun' (brown) both because of the colour of their uniform and their Nazi ideas – of the NSV. However, that plan was cancelled when the renovation was already at an advanced stage, and two departments of the Zentrale were subsequently accommodated and an examination room for the medical director Ebner was set up. There he examined and assessed pregnant women and their husbands who had applied for admission to Lebensborn. In the building, which was destroyed by Allied bombing in 1944, were additional apartments for staff and one of the depots where looted goods were stored. The depots were used for the storage and transit of goods and foodstuffs, in many cases robbed or seized, intended for the supply and furnishing of the clinics and homes.

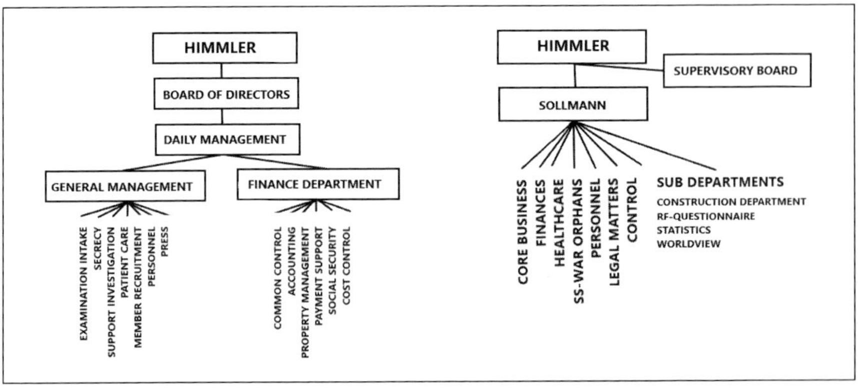

Schematic representation of Lebensborn's organization in the first and second phases of his existence. Initially, Lebensborn came under the Sippenamt of the RuSHA and Himmler was the chairman of a board of directors. The day-to-day management was led by Guntram Pflaum. Under this administration were two main departments, each with six or seven sub-departments. Two years after its foundation, the association moved from Berlin to Munich. Himmler removed Lebensborn from RuSHA, promoted the organization to an independent department (Amt L) of his personal staff, and appointed Gregor Ebner as its medical director. In 1940 Sollmann was appointed as Pflaum's successor and a thorough reorganization followed. There were seven main departments (and some separate sub-departments) directly under Sollmann. He received his orders from Himmler, who was assisted by an advisory board. However, that council was never convened.

The KZ-Aussenlager and the Prisoners

As part of the SS, Lebensborn used forced labourers and concentration camp prisoners, which was a very cheap solution for the ever-continuing shortage of personnel. The SS operated a total of over 15,000 larger and smaller camps and rented out prisoners to private companies for around 4-6 Reichsmarks per day, but Lebensborn, as an SS organization, paid no more than 25 Reichsmarks per prisoner per month. The prisoners were deployed at various locations in Germany for the renovation and furnishing of new clinics and homes, but in Munich, and later in Steinhöring, Lebensborn also had its own labour command.

This command, designated *KZ-Aussenlager 'Lebensborn'* was established in June 1942 in the former *Lipschütz'sche Versorgungsanstalt*, formerly a Jewish retirement home at Mathildenstrasse 8-9. After the residents had been forced to leave, and were deported not much later, the building was to be taken over by the SS for a fixed, far too low price. As usual, the money was never paid.

The KZ-Aussenlager 'Lebensborn' was a satellite camp of Germany's first large concentration camp at Dachau, around 16 kilometres from Munich.

The organization had its own labour command of concentration camp prisoners, the KZ-Aussenlager 'Lebensborn', consisting of several dozen men who were held in this building – a former Jewish retirement home – on Mathildenstrasse. (*Public domain*)

The building in which the prisoners were housed was hermetically sealed and guarded by the SS. The labour command consisted at first of twenty, later around forty, political prisoners, who mainly carried out construction work and maintenance on Lebensborn's many buildings in the city, but were also used for work on the houses of the leading staff, including Sollmann's. The prisoners were mainly Poles, Austrians, Czechs and Germans and were guarded by a six-strong SS unit under a non-commissioned officer, who supervised the work and received his orders directly from Sollmann. Abuses were the order of the day and especially under the last commander of the guard unit, SS-Unterscharführer Sauter, who after being given command in the autumn of 1943, treated the prisoners very badly. Due to the brutal treatment, insufficient food and heavy workload, some of the prisoners regularly became so weak that they could no longer cope with the work. This, of course, was no problem for Lebensborn; Sollmann merely sent the exhausted men back to Dachau and had them replaced by new workers.

After the bombing of Munich in the summer of 1944, the prisoners were first deployed in the city to clear debris and to dismantle unexploded bombs. They then moved with the Zentrale to Heim Hochland. From 20 September, the command was first called the *KZ-Aussenkommando Steinhöring*, but shortly later changed into *KZ-Aussenlager RFSS Persönlicher Stab Amt 'L'* (Satellite Concentration Camp Personal Staff Reichsführer-SS Department Lebensborn). In Steinhöring, the prisoners were mainly used to build office and residential barracks on and near the clinic grounds, but were also forced to unload train wagons with supplies for the home. Until the last weeks of the war, when hunger and starvation prevailed almost everywhere, train wagons full of looted goods, foodstuffs and delicacies such as sugar, coffee, chocolate and oranges, all destined for the inhabitants of Heim Hochland, regularly arrived there.

The administration was also kept on to the end. On 3 April 1945, according to the Dachau registration, twenty-seven prisoners were still assigned to the KZ-Aussenlager RFSS Persönlicher Stab Amt 'L'. On 28 April, just before the liberation of Dachau by the US Army, Sollmann sent the last prisoners back to the concentration camp. In addition to these male prisoners, who usually worked outside, a few clinics also employed female prisoners indoors. This mainly concerned Jehovah's Witnesses (*Bibelförscher*: Bible Researcher), who regarded their imprisonment as a test of faith and therefore presented no danger of flight.[5] In January 1943, Himmler even gave a special order '... Bibelförscher to be employed as staff in our Lebensborn homes, not as caretakers, but as cooks, housemaids, washerwomen and for such tasks.' For example, in Heim Hochland in 1944, around twenty female Jehovah's Witnesses, including some Dutch women, from the Moringen and Ravensbrück concentration camps, were put to work.

Johanna Preisel and Frieda Nixdorf in the garden of Heim Hochland, winter 1944. They were among about twenty female Jehovah's Witnesses from the Moringen and Ravensbrück concentration camps who were put to work there. (*Public domain*)

Overjoyed prisoners wave to American troops liberating Dachau concentration camp on 29 April 1945. The day before, Lebensborn director Sollmann had returned the last prisoners of Lebensborn's labour commando, *KZ-Aussenlager RFSS Persönlicher Stab Amt 'L'*. (*USHMM*)

Financing

Lebensborn thus obtained an important part of its movable and immovable property at relatively low cost through the SS methods of coercion, violence and robbery, and also had cheap labour at its disposal. In the early years in particular, however, when Himmler first came to power and the SS was still limited, the organization had great difficulty in making its budget work. The nursing and care of women and children, the financial support of unmarried mothers, wages and other fixed costs, and the constant expansion of the organization cost many millions of Reichsmarks a year. In 1939 Lebensborn was therefore in a very bad financial situation, a problem not helped by the lack of business acumen of its first director, Guntram Pflaum.

Income was also an issue. Revenues were irregular and came from very different sources. In order of importance, these were donations, contributions and payments for accommodation in the clinics and homes.[6] Lebensborn also sometimes received donations. The largest, which was also by far the most important for Himmler from a moral point of view, was given to the organization by Hitler. In October 1937 he had received the luxurious Kurhaus Luisenbad hotel from the city of Bad Polzin as a gift, and a few months later donated it to Lebensborn, which opened a clinic there in 1938.

Above: The luxurious Kurhaus Luisenbad in Bad Polzin (now Połczyn-Zdrój, Poland) that Hitler was offered by the city council and donated to Lebensborn a few months later. (*Private collection*)

Left: Kurhaus Luisenbad as seen in a Lebensborn brochure. (*Private collection*)

Money also came in by seizing the assets of Jews and enemies of the regime, and of companies that were partly or wholly owned by the SS. The latter category included, for example, Anton Loibl GmbH, which was set up specifically to help finance Ahnenerbe and Lebensborn. Hitler's former driver, Anton Loibl, had invented a reflector for bicycle pedals, and Himmler saw an opportunity to make money in this. Although there was already a previous patent application from someone else, he gave Loibl the patent and set up a company to market the reflector. He then took advantage of his position as chief of police by making the pedal reflector mandatory on all new bicycles. Thanks to the license for which bicycle manufacturers had to pay from then on, Lebensborn alone received 100,000 to 150,000 Reichsmarks annually from 1939 onwards, just from the bicycle reflectors.[7]

Initially, the NSV was the main source of income and this NSDAP organization subsidized Lebensborn in the first period of its existence with hundreds of thousands of Reichsmarks per year. Although Lebensborn was much smaller than the NSV, which was also involved in population politics, Himmler's brainchild was initially the only Nazi organization allowed to operate maternity hospitals. Presumably the NSV wanted to exert influence on Lebensborn through the financing until, in 1939, most likely at the instigation of NSDAP Reichsleiter Bormann, the money tap was turned off. As a result, Sollmann, who was appointed the new director of Lebensborn in the spring of 1940, found himself in charge of an almost bankrupt organization. However, he soon found another source of income. First, Sollmann twice persuaded the Ministry of Finance to donate 1 million to Lebensborn, and in 1942 he received a commitment that the organization would receive an annual fixed contribution of 3 million Reichsmarks, which covered about two-thirds of all expenses.

Another part of the costs – in the years 1937-39 about 20% of the total, later less – was covered by the dues paid by the association's members. In principle, every German could become a member, but this non-commitment did not apply to senior SS men after Himmler had made membership in Lebensborn compulsory for them in September 1936. The lower ranks were expected to volunteer. The results must have disappointed him. Although the SS at its greatest size was nearly 500,000 strong, Lebensborn never had more than some 17,000 members.

The cost of membership for the SS men depended on rank, age and number of children. The higher the rank and age, the more had to be paid; the more children, the lower the compulsory contribution. For Himmler this was not just a matter of money. According to him, it was not simply a personal choice to have many children, but a duty to the German people. Anyone who failed to fulfil this obligation would, in any case, support the population policy by making a

A pin with the symbol of Lebensborn, the elhaz rune, the letters SS and HH (Heinrich Himmler), surrounded by the organization's motto *'Heilig soll uns sein jede Mutter guten Blutes'*. Presumably such pins were intended for the members of the association. (*Private collection*)

substantial financial contribution that could amount to almost 8% of their gross salary.

Finally, income was still obtained from the health insurance of the mothers admitted to Lebensborn and a compulsory contribution from the fathers. The latter contribution was only paid without issue in a small minority of cases.

Secrecy Versus Recruitment

Lebensborn was not a secret organization. On the contrary, it had a press department, published information brochures and was the subject of articles in SS publications and commercial magazines. It made no secret of the fact that a strict varietal selection was applied. Lebensborn also placed advertisements to recruit staff and to inform pregnant women of the existence of the clinics. There was even work undertaken on an information film, although it was never completed. The existence and function of Lebensborn was soon known outside Germany as well. For instance, in November 1940 the organization was mentioned in the Dutch-East Indies newspaper *De Sumatra Post*: 'Himmler encourages his men to have illegitimate children: unmarried mothers of Schutzstaffel descendants are nursed free of charge in royal hospitals'. (The newspaper was wrong a line later in claiming that the largest clinic was called 'Lebensborn'.)

However, even if the existence of Lebensborn was not a secret, many of the things that happened within the organization were. This mainly concerned the identity of the unmarried pregnant women. There is no doubt that the ability to give birth anonymously was the main reason for an unmarried expectant mother to turn to the organization. In order to attract as many pregnant women as possible, it was therefore in Lebensborn's interest to guarantee anonymity. But secrecy was not an obligation; it was a choice

klaarblijkelijk zelf bedacht heeft.

De aanstaande echtgenooten van S.S.-mannen moeten een grondig onderzoek ondergaan over haar politieke denkwijze en haar geschiktheid voor het moederschap. Himmler moedigt zijn mannen aan onwettige kinderen te krijgen: ongehuwde moeders van Schutzstaffel nakomelingschap worden gratis verpleegd in vorstelijke ziekenhuizen. Het grootste hiervan, gelegen in de Beiersche Alpen, is door Heinrich zeer toepasselijk Lebensborn, „Levensbron", gedoopt.

Lebensborn was by no means a secret organization. The identity of unmarried mothers (and fathers) was protected, but its activities and accommodations were advertised inside and outside the SS, and the organization was also known outside Germany at an early stage. For example, its name is seen here in the Netherlands East-Indies newspaper *De Sumatra Post*, from 13 November 1940. (*Public domain*)

of the expectant mother. Most unmarried women opted for secrecy, while married women almost never did.

Lebensborn had all the facilities to guarantee anonymity, starting with the location of the buildings, which were almost always on park-like private grounds in a rural area, usually guarded and surrounded by a wall or fence. After a woman had applied through the Zentrale in Munich and had passed the strict selection process, she was – if she appreciated secrecy – placed in a Lebensborn clinic far from where she lived to minimize the chance of being seen by someone she knew. Once in the clinic, the rule was that the women were only allowed to address each other with 'Frau' (Mrs), followed by their first name. This was prescribed not only to conceal identity, but also to make no distinction between married (Frau) and unmarried women (Fräulein) (Miss). Furthermore, it was explicitly stated in the house rules of mother clinic Heim Hochland – although they certainly also applied in other locations – that 'the women and staff are strictly forbidden to ask for the name of the father of their child, or to spread any existing rumours about this. Violation of this rule will result in immediate removal.'

The organization also carefully monitored the identity of the mother and father from an administrative point of view. Because it was mandatory in Nazi Germany from the beginning of 1938 to inform the police about the home address, Lebensborn had several fake addresses that the pregnant women could provide. In many cases this concerned residential addresses of Lebensborn staff in Munich and the surrounding area. From the second half of 1939, the use of false addresses was no longer necessary, as by this time Himmler had ordered special offices (*Meldestellen*) for the organization to be set up, which kept the addresses secret.

More than a year earlier, Lebensborn had already received permission from the Ministry of the Interior to establish its own civil registry office (*Standesamt*) in each clinic. This meant that birth registrations could also be kept secret. These legal exceptions would serve the organization well in the 'Germanization' of foreign children because they could provide them with a new identity and new papers without outside interference. If desired, Lebensborn could also take on the custody of the children born in the maternity hospitals, thus excluding interference from the government's youth services and allowing the identity of the parents to remain secret. This happened to about half of the children born at Lebensborn.

Welchen Schutz findet die alleinſtehende werdende Mutter?

Um die alleinſtehende werdende Mutter guten Blutes vor der immer noch drohenden Gefahr der Verfemung zu ſchützen, wurde der Lebensborn mit Sondereinrichtungen ausgeſtattet, die die Geheimhaltung von Schwangerſchaft und Niederkunft unter beſtimmten Vorausſetzungen gewährleiſten; auch der Vater des erwarteten Kindes kann der Außenwelt gegenüber völlig in die Geheimhaltung einbezogen werden, wenn er ſeine ſelbſtverſtändlichen Pflichten erfüllt.

1.) Jedes Heim verfügt über ein eigenes Meldeamt.

Genaue Anweiſungen über die Durchführung der polizeilichen Abmeldung werden von Fall zu Fall geſondert erteilt.

2.) Jedes Heim verfügt über ein eigenes Standesamt.

Durch die behördlichen Einrichtungen des Lebensborn (Meldeämter und Standesämter) können alle nötigen Beurkundungen innerhalb des Lebensborn-Bereiches durchgeführt werden.

Under the headline 'What protection does the single expectant mother receive?', a brochure explains that Lebensborn had its own Meldestellen (or Meldeämter), which meant that a person's whereabouts no longer had to be reported to the local police station. It also had its own Standesämter (civil registry bureaus), so that a birth could be kept secret from the outside world. (*Private collection*)

V

BABY MACHINES?

The Role of Women in the Third Reich and at Lebensborn

'Women's emancipation is just a word invented by the Jewish intellect.'

Adolf Hitler

Subordinate

In the National Socialist world view, women were subordinate to men in all respects. At the first general meeting of the NSDAP in January 1921, women were already formally excluded from all leading positions. Although it is true that during the Third Reich women could hold higher posts within specific organizations that were active in the fields of youth, women and family, such as the *NS-Frauenschaft* and the *Bund Deutscher Mädel* (BDM), according to the ideal image they would assume the role of housewife or have to fulfil a 'typically female' profession as a nurse.

Lebensborn was illustrative in this regard. A large number of women worked there, for the most part in such typical female professions, but few of them held high positions within Nazi Germany. That was made possible by the nature of the organization – it involved children – but at the same time there were limits. For example, Inge Viermetz, who played an important role at Lebensborn, represented the organization on foreign missions and led various departments, although she was only a department manager in practice. On paper she was classified as a subordinate because a woman was officially not allowed to hold such a high position.

Whatever role or function a woman had, it should in any case be subordinate to that of the man: 'Women's emancipation is just a word invented by the Jewish intellect', Hitler declared on the 1934 *Reichsparteidag*. According to him, female behaviour was determined more by feeling and instinct than by common sense and sober deliberation, and 'the education of the woman …

A gymnastics performance by the Bund Deutscher Mädel (League of German Girls), where girls between the ages of 14 and 18 received ideological training, learned household chores and were prepared for motherhood (according to some, the abbreviation BDM stood for *'bald Deutsche Muttter'*; 'soon German mothers'). Membership became compulsory in 1936 and in 1944 the BDM had 4.5 million members. (*Bundesarchiv Bild 183-2000-0110-500*)

must be absolutely directed to the education of the girl to be a mother-to-be'. She also had to take a subordinate position from a legal point of view. In *Mein Kampf* he remarked: 'The German girl is a subject of the state and only becomes a citizen of the state through her marriage'.

If, according to the National Socialist ideal, the woman was therefore an obedient housewife and mother who took care of her husband and (as many) children as possible, the reality often looked different. Due to the increasing shortage of men, the trend in the Third Reich was actually reversed: more and more women exercised traditional men's professions in the service of the government, the business community or even the armed forces. In Munich, for example, a quarter of all workers in the arms industry were women in 1939, and that share would only increase in subsequent years. In addition, previously imposed restrictions on studying were quickly lifted and women were later encouraged to follow certain studies and higher education. So while the Nazis intended to stop or even turn back time, their actions ultimately resulted in the

Although the Nazis regarded women primarily as mothers and housewives, the need for personnel in the war changed their role in society and even the SS began recruiting women. This advertisement is for the *Weibliches Nachrichtenkorps* (Female Signal Corps), which was renamed the SS-Helferinnenkorps in 1943. (*Private collection*)

opposite development. A so-called *SS-Helferinnenkorps* (Help Corps) was even set up in the SS. During the war, several thousand carefully selected volunteers served there, mainly as secretaries and in the liaison service.

But the main function of women remained to give birth to as many healthy and racially valuable children as possible, because according to Nazi ideology, that offspring determined the future of the nation and race. For example, at the party convention in 1936, Hitler declared that he would measure the success of the efforts of the NSDAP above all by the German child and youth. 'If it grows, then I know that my people will not perish and that our efforts have not been in vain.'

The idea that women should primarily be housewives and mothers of many children was the norm in Germany in the first decades of the twentieth century. But a new element introduced to motherhood by the National Socialists was the notion of 'genetic and racial hygiene'. What that meant is illustrated by the 'Ten Commandments for Mate Selection', published in 1934 in the *N.S. Frauen-Warte*, the only Nazi Party-approved women's magazine. The first six commandments were:

1. Remember you are German.
2. If you have no hereditary diseases, you will not remain unmarried.
3. Keep your body clean!
4. You shall keep your mind and soul clean.
5. As a German, only choose a partner of the same or Nordic blood.
6. When choosing your partner, ask about his ancestors.

To secure the future of the race and to ensure there were enough soldiers for the foreseeable future, women were constantly encouraged to bear as many children as possible. At school and within party organizations, girls and young women

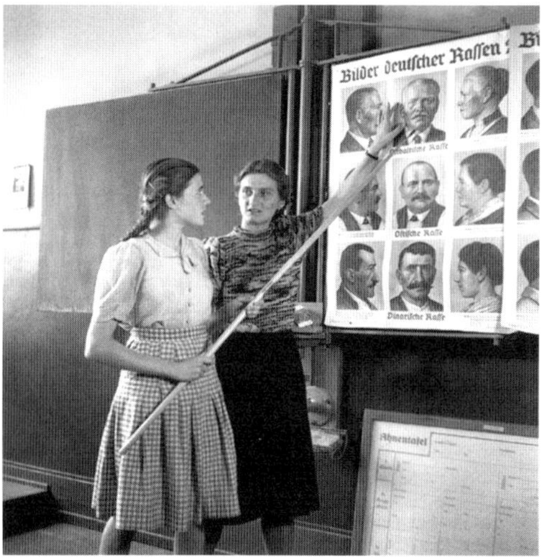

Above and left: It was considered of paramount importance to choose the right partner. This is why young women received information about heredity and racial hygiene (left), and lessons in racial science. Such subjects belonged to the permanent curriculum in German education. (*Public domain*)

were indoctrinated from an early age. In addition, the birth of a child was often equated with the achievements of a man on the battlefield: both sexes had to make sacrifices for the people and the fatherland. That was the message. Such propaganda was not without results, however, as when the Nazis launched the campaign 'Give the Führer a child', a considerable number of German women responded to this exhortation.

Im Namen
des
Deutschen Volkes
verleihe ich
Gisela
geb.
Königsberg (Pr)
die dritte Stufe
des
Ehrenkreuzes
der Deutschen Mutter
Berlin, den 1. Oktober 1939
Der Führer

The Ehrenkreuz der Deutschen Mutter was awarded as 'a sign of gratitude from the German people to the child-rich mother', provided that the children were healthy and 'of German blood' and the mother met all ideological and racial requirements. There were three variants, bronze, silver and gold, respectively for four or five, six or seven, or eight and more children. The award was less reverently referred to as the 'Rabbit Order'. (*Public domain*)

Mothers with many children, provided they were healthy and met the racial requirements, were awarded the *Ehrenkreuz der Deutschen Mutter* (Cross of Honour of the German Mother), which was introduced in December 1938 as a 'visible sign of gratitude from the German people to the child-rich mother'. The condition was, of course, that the mother was of 'Germanic blood' and was hereditary healthy and had a morally impeccable lifestyle – the latter, of course, according to National Socialist norms and values.

Those norms and values were very different for men and women, and also for Lebensborn. For example, it was no problem at all for the organization if a married man fathered one or more children with his mistress. However, a woman who had children from different men was judged to be racially inferior. And a young mother who was diagnosed with a venereal disease during her stay in a Lebensborn clinic had to leave immediately after giving birth. Also, a married woman who was pregnant with a child out of wedlock was not included, because that would support her husband's deceit. However, a man responsible for two pregnant women giving birth at the same time in a Lebensborn clinic was criticized only because he should have planned it better.[1]

In the Third Reich, therefore, women were first and foremost seen and judged as potential mothers, with a sharp distinction being made according to their racial value. As many children as possible had to be born, but they had to be of good blood. On the one hand, there were high penalties for abortion – the death penalty was introduced for such an act in 1943 – but on the other hand, sexual relations between Germans and people who were 'racially inferior' were prohibited. Furthermore, women (and men) who suffered from certain hereditary diseases or had congenital abnormalities could be forced to undergo sterilization. It was the totalitarian state at its best: free will and personal preferences no longer counted, not even in the choice of partner.

Himmler's 'Vision'

In the SS, the choice of a wife who met all racial and medical requirements was essential. As the SS was to form the racial elite of the future Greater Germanic Empire, its members were obliged, according to the aforementioned Verlobungs- und Heiratsbefehl der SS, to marry a healthy, hereditary stable and at least racially equal woman. If possible, it was more important for her to be racially purer than the man himself, so that procreation meant not only preservation, but even 'improvement' of the race.

In order to make the right choice, the SS man – as was explained in *Das Schwarze Korps*, the official weekly magazine of the SS – had to gain knowledge of the racial aspects beforehand, so that he could choose a suitable bride. However, this advice apparently did not result in a massive conversion of Himmler's subordinates to the Nordic ideal of beauty. In a speech in 1936, the Reichsführer-SS argued that marriages were still far too often made with girls of lesser racial value, because they 'always mature earlier' and are 'more sexually attractive and more compliant' than the less attractive, but racially more valuable, girls. Seven years later, the situation had apparently still not improved when the head of the marriage office of the RuSHA, SS-Brigadeführer and Generalmajor der Polizei Otto Heider, argued for the establishment of a written marriage mediation because 'racially valuable women, who are particularly attracted to domestic

According to Himmler, marriage in its current form was a diabolical invention of the Catholic Church and because it was impossible for a man to live with one woman all his life, he was forced into infidelity. He himself had an extramarital affair with his secretary. (*Bundesarchiv 183-572707)*

and caring valuable occupations … only very rarely find a marriage partner'.[2] By directly linking these women to SS men, the quality of the offspring would be guaranteed, the SS-Brigadeführer believed.

The racial quality of the bride was not the only aspect of married life the top brass of the SS interfered with. The need to father as many children as possible was also repeatedly emphasized. Apart from the notorious October 1939 order for his subordinates to father a child before they might die in the war, and the 'Order for the Last Sons' of a similar nature three years later, the same subject came up again and again in Himmler's speeches, and each time the desired number of offspring increased. Two children were no longer enough and neither was four; every woman was supposed to have as many children as possible and personal opinions counted for nothing. In fact, in 1942 Himmler declared that it 'is unnatural to want to limit the number of births for personal gain'.[3]

The way Himmler and the SS ideologues viewed women was simultaneously backward and modern. Backward because of the view of the subordinate and one-sided biological function of the woman as a 'baby machine' of the desired offspring, while at the same time 'modern' because the woman did not have to be married to have children and the unmarried mother also had to be treated with respect. Yet this view clashed with the prevailing conservative view of marriage and motherhood, and although every Nazi organization aimed for a high number of children, the promotion of unmarried motherhood met with widespread resistance, including from most party members.

For Himmler, whose views on this subject were no doubt influenced by his grandfather also being an illegitimate child, it was ultimately all about getting as many offspring from good blood as possible. For that reason, according to his masseur Kersten, he argued that 'marriage in its present form was a devilish invention of the Catholic Church'. After all, according to Himmler, 'a man could not possibly live with one woman all his life, he was now indirectly forced into infidelity'.[4] (This statement also applied to his own situation. Ten years after his marriage, Himmler began an extramarital relationship with his secretary that would last until his death. They would have two children together.) The existing marriage laws, according to the Reichsführer-SS, evoked 'marital difficulties, mutual aversion to partners and' – worst of all – 'childlessness', leaving millions of children unborn. After the war, he continued, Hitler would change the legislation to allow certain SS leaders the right to a second wife and a high, well-paid state job to enable the chosen one to support two families. All three spouses would, of course, have to be rigorously selected, for the goal was double the number of children 'of the purest and most valuable blood'. However, if such a polygamous marriage remained childless for five years, the

RuSHA would intervene. An investigation into the infertility was initiated and, if necessary, an operation was performed on the woman at state expense (it was never the man at fault). If that did not result in a baby after two years, the marriage was automatically dissolved. Himmler took the view that the German people would no longer be able to afford childless marriages after the war.

However, it did not stop there. According to Kersten, Himmler then declared that everything would change after the war:

> Every pure-bred female being, insofar as it was still childless after the age of 30, would in fact be declared outlaws. The Rasseamt [RuSHA], then called the National Health Service, could issue a call to make itself available to the Lebensborn on such and such a day and at such and such an hour to allow them to be inseminated. A refusal would automatically entail banishment from the community.[5]

Whether Kersten gave a truthful representation of Himmler's fantasies here cannot be verified. It is certain, however, that in the spring of 1942 the Reichsführer-SS had given Lebensborn director Sollmann the 'highly secret order' to draw up plans for the construction of a large Zentrale for Lebensborn, 'with a view to the currently approximately 400,000 women already present, who cannot get men because of the war and its casualties ... The building must be beautiful and presentable, reflecting the noble thought and honour of the unmarried woman.'[6] It is not known exactly what Himmler wanted with this construction, which would never be realized. The plan may have been indirectly related to the note that Reichsgesundheitsführer

Leonardo Conti was an early NSDAP member and co-founder of the *Nationalsocialistisches Deutschen Ärtzebund* (National Socialistic Doctors Union) and was appointed Reichsgesundheitsführer (Reich Health Leader) in 1939. He took part in the experiments that preceded the 'forced euthanasia' at Aktion T4. At the beginning of 1942 he proposed to Himmler that artificial fertilization be used to increase the birth rate more speedily. (*Bundesarchiv Bild 183-1989-0309-501*)

(Reich Health Leader) Conti had submitted to him and Reichsleiter Bormann around the same time. After the deadlock of the attack on the Soviet Union in the winter of 1941-42, the Nazi leadership realized that the war would not be decided quickly. There was a long battle ahead that would cost many lives and that was reason to look again at how birth rates could be increased quickly. Conti proposed, among other things, the use of artificial insemination, but Himmler resolutely rejected the proposal, expecting great social resistance and finding it completely unnatural. Even more important was his belief that artificial insemination would negatively affect heredity, which contradicted everything Himmler advocated.

Selection for Lebensborn

The expectant mother who wanted to give birth in a Lebensborn clinic had to meet strict requirements and go through a large number of steps. The procedure started with a written application for inclusion, addressed to Lebensborn's headquarters, the Zentrale in Munich. The head office then sent the woman two lists, labelled 'KM' (*Kindesmutter*; child's mother) and 'KV' (*Kindesvater*; child's father), containing a large number of very detailed and personal questions about the health of the parents-to-be and their families. In the latter aspect, Lebensborn was mainly concerned with ruling out hereditary diseases that could be passed on to offspring. In addition, the woman had to hand in a handwritten life history, with a photograph in which her entire figure was clearly visible. The future father also had to submit a similar photograph.

Another condition for admission was that both prospective parents had an Ariernachweis (Proof of Aryan Descent), with which they could prove they were of pure Aryan blood. To this end, they had to submit a completed *Ahnentafel* (Family Tree Overview) dating back to the year 1800, in

The *Ahnenpas* contained an Ahnentafel (family tree overview) with which the holder had to prove they had no Jewish ancestors from at least 1800. (*Private collection*)

which no Jewish ancestors were allowed to appear. The completed personal details of those ancestors had to be proven with official papers (birth certificates and marriage certificates) from the civil registry, and these documents had to be sent with the application.

Since the father-to-be also had to provide this information, his identity was known to the Zentrale in Lebensborn but was otherwise kept carefully secret. If the couple were not married, the mother had to take an oath on paper that the man she had designated was the father. Members of the SS, their wives and future wives who had already been granted permission to marry, did not have to submit the said papers because they had already been assessed and 'approved' when applying for marriage.

Once this first administrative selection was passed, an examination by a doctor into the health and possible hereditary diseases within the applicant's family followed. This was carried out according to a questionnaire drawn up by Lebensborn, which was sent to the doctor in question, and which he had to complete and return to the Zentrale in a sealed envelope (without giving the persons under examination access to it). On the basis of the data provided and the various studies, a racial assessment was made, which, together with the hereditary health, formed the essence of the selection.

The aim was to include only perfectly healthy women, from a family without hereditary diseases, who were of 'pure Aryan descent', who fulfilled the desired outward ideal and who were therefore expected to give birth to a child with the same racial characteristics. The various

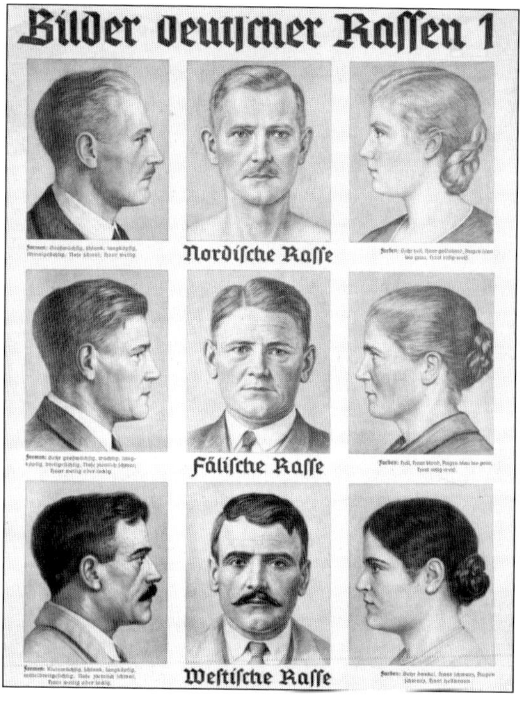

Bilder deutscher Rassen 1 (Pictures of German Races). With the help of posters like this, the German people were taught about racial science. From top to bottom are images of the so-called nordische, fälische and westische races. (*Private collection*)

external characteristics, including height, figure, posture, hair and eye colour, face and nose shape, and skin colour determined the classification in a particular race: designated *nordisch, fälisch, westisch, dinarisch, ostisch* and *ostbaltisch* (Nordic, Falian, Western, Dinaric, Eastern and Eastern Baltic). Initially only an SS doctor was allowed to pass judgment on the racial classification, but after the outbreak of the war, when the SS had a shortage of doctors, ordinary doctors were also allowed to do so. Ultimately, Ebner, the medical director, made the decision on whether to accept the applicants. In the last years of the war, the racial assessment was carried out mostly by the Heimleiters (SS doctors), who used the book *Rassenkunde des deutschen Volkes* by Hans Günther as a guideline.

About 75% of applications for admission to a Lebensborn maternity clinic were assessed positively.[7] This meant that the majority of the women who applied for inclusion were well informed about the racial selection beforehand. This is not surprising as the organization made no secret of this. On the contrary, on the very first page of the promotional brochure that Lebensborn published around 1941, titled *Aufgabe und Ziele des Lebensborn*, (Tasks and Purposes of Lebensborn) this was made very clear: 'Lebensborn differs from all other institutions of the National Socialist state that deal with similar tasks on a general basis, because its work puts first the application of the strict hereditary biological selection principles of the Schutzstaffel'. To put an end to all ambiguity, a page further, under the subheading 'Who is being admitted?', it was stated again: 'For admission it is required proof of health, hereditary health and Aryan descent of the grandparents and the father and mother of the expected child'.

During the existence of Lebensborn, selection criteria were sometimes stricter and sometimes more flexible. Until late 1941 and early 1942, when Nazi Germany was at the height of its power and the war seemed to be turning in its favour, the criteria became stricter; after that, the admission requirements became more flexible. For example, pregnant women who did not meet all the external criteria could sometimes still be admitted if they were convinced Nazis or had the right connections. Women from the conquered areas in the East who were pregnant by an SS man were also occasionally admitted to a Lebensborn clinic. In many, if not all cases, personal permission from Himmler was required. 'Unfortunately', he wrote to a senior SS officer, he had to 'compromise between the necessary quantity and the best possible quality'.[8]

Just because a mother-to-be passed the selection and was admitted to a Lebensborn clinic did not mean that the assessment was complete. She had only fulfilled the requirements of health, heredity and appearance. A final judgment was made only after her character had also been assessed. To this end, the young woman was, without her knowledge, observed during her stay at the Lebensborn clinic. After all, not only did she have to give birth to a healthy child, she also had to behave like a good mother.

The final assessment, including a long questionnaire in which all criteria were included and provided with an evaluation, was drawn up by the Heimleiter and head nurse after the young mother was discharged. This included her attitude within the community, her behaviour in a crisis situation (childbirth), and her political views. Some information about the father was also included. The report concluded with answers to the questions: 'Does the child's mother conform to the elite character of the SS in terms of a) race; b) world view; c) character?' This highly secret personal file, which was kept at the Zentrale, was called the *RF-Fragebogen* (Reichsführer Questionnaire) because it was presented to Himmler personally. Himmler did not simply read through them, but carefully studied the assessments and regularly commented on the conclusions of his subordinates, who quickly changed their judgment in response to criticism. The Reichsführer-SS also developed the system by which the women were classified in a certain category and later made 'improvements' at least twice. Initially, the women were given the brief rating of 'good, mediocre, or poor', but he later 'refined' his system and divided them into groups:

> I = fully meets the elite criteria of the SS.
> II = good cross-section.
> III = does not meet the elite criteria.

Later, in January 1942, after believing he had caught the Lebensborn personnel in a serious error during an assessment and classification, Himmler drew up a schedule with four categories:

Geheim! Heim:

RF-Fragebogen
(Nur für RF ϟϟ bestimmt!)

The heading for the R.F. Fragebogen (Reichsführer Questionnaire), the form specifically intended for Himmler, on the basis of which it was assessed whether the women who gave birth to Lebensborn met the criteria of the SS.

I = the mother and father are acceptable in character, worldview, race, heredity, and health.
II = acceptable in character and worldview, but deficient in health, race, or heredity.
III = defects in character or worldview, or greater defects in health, race, or heredity.
IV = unwanted mother or father, defects in character and worldview, or racially rejectable, or definitely rejectable because of health or hereditary characteristics and therefore undesirable as a begetter/producer of children.[9]

The consequences of a bad assessment were far-reaching, because it inevitably resulted in Lebensborn ceasing to support mother and child. The young mother was completely left to her own devices with her baby: she had to leave the home, received no financial support and was not given shelter or a job.

Lebensborn was only for people who met the selection criteria for the SS, especially those babies born in the organization's clinics. Only children who met the desired external characteristics and were healthy were allowed to stay in a Lebensborn ward. If they were born with abnormalities or showed a clear developmental delay at a young age due to a physical or mental deficiency, measures were taken immediately. First, Lebensborn refused custody, with far-reaching financial consequences for the parent(s). They were also examined again for possible hereditary diseases and could be told that they were not allowed to have any more children. The consequences for the child were often even more drastic. For a baby who was born in Heim Hochland in Steinhöring in 1943 with black hair, dark eyes and a (light) coloured skin, the consequences were not too bad: mother and child had to leave the Lebensborn clinic as soon as possible. The same measures applied to children with mild disabilities – no guardianship and stay in the home – and the parents could also be urgently advised to have them sterilized.

Babies born in a Lebensborn clinic with more severe mental or physical disabilities were doomed. They were taken to a special facility misleadingly known as Kinderfachabteilung. There, the children were first deprived of fluids and food, and then usually killed with an anaesthetic. It is estimated that a total of 5,000 to 10,000 children were killed in these institutions, including several dozen who were born in Lebensborn clinics. Here, as far as is known, the highest number of victims came from Heim Sonnenwiese, where at least nine children were killed in a Kinderfachabteilung. The official cause of death, as reported to the registry office and to the parents, was almost always pneumonia.

The Stay in the Maternity Clinics

The stay in the Lebensborn institutions was precisely organized and followed clear rules, which had to be strictly adhered to. Anyone who did not comply with the rules could be immediately evicted from the home. All aspects of the stay were laid down in detail, from the daily schedule, the meals, the activities and duties of the mothers, their domestic and ideological education to the required manners. Given the large group of people who lived together in such an establishment – from dozens up to perhaps 200 women and children – a tight organization was necessary, but it also served an ideological purpose. This was described in a brochure prepared by Lebensborn as follows:

> The mother-to-be, who wants to be admitted to a Lebensborn home, must know that a home community awaits her. Community in the National Socialist sense, however, means real comradeship. The expectant mother should also know that a Lebensborn-Heim is not a sanatorium. Every mother should participate in light household chores as the supervising physician deems necessary for the improvement of her physical and mental well-being. Every mother is expected to perform her assigned light duties cheerfully and conscientiously. It is essential to comply with the house rules established by the Reichsführer-SS. Mothers-to-be who think they cannot fit in with the comradely spirit of the home, because they expect a carefree period of cheerful activities, will be disappointed in the Lebensborn-Heimen.

To stimulate the emergence of the aforementioned sense of community and camaraderie, Himmler had, as mentioned, drawn up a number of house rules. These were mainly aimed at minimizing the differences between rich versus poor and married versus unmarried. For example, expectant mothers were expected to bring only underwear, a few dresses, shoes and shoe polish, toiletries and – if insured – a certificate of insurance, plus clothes for the journey home for the expected child. Initially, upon arrival, the women were provided with the same standard clothing they were required to wear in the clinic, although it seems this dress code became less strict over time.

The way individuals were addressed (as previously discussed) was of great importance. It was Frau for everyone, followed by their first name. Not only did this protect their identity, but more importantly it abolished the distinction between the married (Frau) and the unmarried (Fräulein). After all, unlike

Himmler and his ideological followers, the Germans in general, and married women in particular, still looked down on unmarried mothers. Naturally, this did not help the desired sense of community.

Meals were taken collectively and at set times, and everyone received the same. The meals were eaten simultaneously in three groups, with the expectant and young mothers, the children, and the staff each having their own table or room, of course with fixed seats. Although there were occasional complaints about food, the Lebensborn sites were well supplied until the end of the war, with foodstuffs and delicacies available that most Germans had not seen for years. Himmler was personally concerned with the diet of the inhabitants and regularly interfered with the smallest details.

In addition to training in practical domestic and caring skills, the women also received 'lessons' in politics and ideology, of course on a strict National Socialist basis. SS-Oberführer Ebner, the medical leader of Lebensborn, was responsible for the ideological training. The aim of the lessons was to educate the mothers to be good National Socialists and to have them leave the clinic with the right world view. The content of the teaching programmes differed

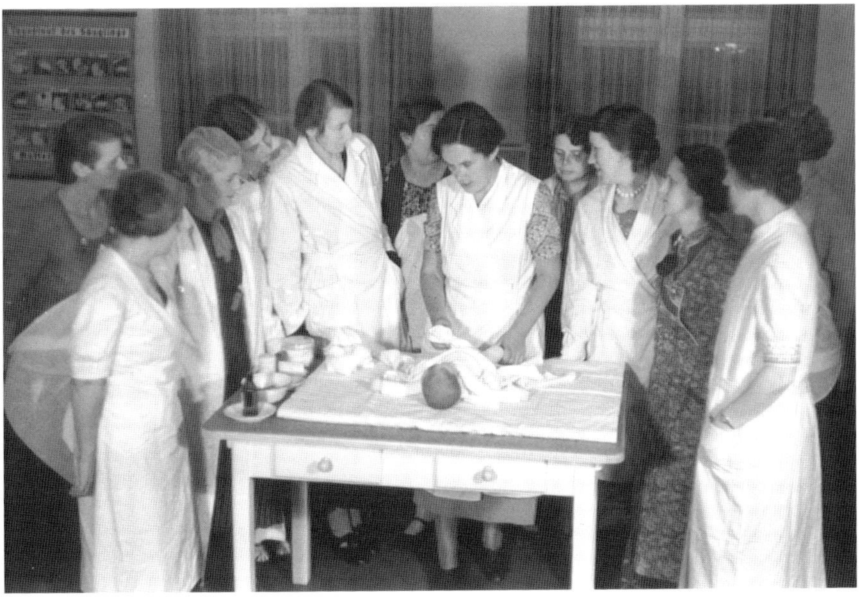

The regular programme components of the daily routine naturally included lessons in the field of childcare. This photograph was probably taken at a so-called Mütterschule (mother school), where young women were taught childcare, household chores and the correct world view. SS brides and women admitted to Lebensborn were required to attend a six-week course. (*Public domain*)

per home and mainly depended on the management. Regardless, the regular lessons included listening to the speeches of Hitler, Goebbels, Rosenberg and other senior Nazis; reading (aloud) from *Mein Kampf*; lectures and slide shows on topics such as 'the enemies of the German people' (Judaism, Freemasonry, Bolshevism), racial science and law, runic science and the sippe (clan). In addition, subjects such as 'the woman as a propagandist of National Socialism' or more practical matters such as air protection and first aid could also be included in the programme, and singing folk songs together was part of the standard repertoire. The Heimleiter was responsible for the programme and took care of part of the lessons, which had to be held three times a week, but officials from outside the homes were also involved. The leader of the RuSHA, SS-Gruppenführer Pancke – who had succeeded Darré – nevertheless found the teaching programmes too non-committal. He wanted to have a training programme developed 'after the war' that was geared towards Lebensborn's interests. Incidentally, the leadership was of the opinion that the worldview influence had the additional advantage that it not only benefited discipline, but also had the effect of 'virtually disappearing the chatter that is customary among women'.[10]

The pregnant women and young mothers admitted to Lebensborn were in a very privileged position. Housed in luxurious buildings in a rural setting and

Throughout the war, more and more women reported to Lebensborn because its clinics were located in the countryside, far away from the increasingly bombed cities. The remains of Heilbronn are seen here in 1945. (*Public domain*)

with every modern comfort, they were well cared for and fed, and were far removed from the horrors of war, which soon affected many German cities. In addition, a number of young women had escaped the censure and exclusion that befell an unmarried pregnant woman or young single mother. They felt protected by the powerful organization that often provided them with work and shelter after giving birth. This is proven by a large number of letters from grateful women to Himmler that have been preserved and the testimonies given by former Lebensborn mothers after the war.

On the other hand, there were many complaints about Lebensborn. This was partly due to the way Lebensborn had treated some of the young women. They had passed the scrutiny and rigorous selection to which the organization had subjected them, and so they now felt part of the elite who would lead the coming Greater Germanic Empire. Or at least that is what they were told. The feeling of belonging to the chosen ones, however, was not always consistent with the strict rules they had to comply with in the Lebensborn houses, which prescribed their daily activities in detail. In addition, it seemed more women who had an education and job that were much better than those of the average German woman reported to Lebensborn,[11] which probably also made them more assertive and self-confident. There were complaints about the food, the compulsory long suckling of the babies and the prolonged expression of breast milk. There were also frequent complaints about the behaviour and care provided by the medical and nursing staff. Several women felt they were being treated merely as producers of the future elite and protested the impersonal treatment, with some certainly not mincing their words. For example, a young mother complained about the impersonal treatment, saying that they were not 'baby machines', and another woman refused a doctor's order, saying that she 'was not in Dachau after all'. Disagreements, especially with such language, was not common among the SS, and the later comment therefore cost the woman in question dearly when Ebner removed her from Heim Hochland.[12] The women did, however, have the right to file complaints and had to do so in writing to the Zentrale or to Himmler personally. In an official regulation of an unidentified maternity hospital, it was stated that 'the Reichsführer-SS [would] personally read every letter'.[13] Given Himmler's close involvement in the organization, this was probably not an empty promise.

This did not alter the fact that many became disappointed in the projected community life and comradely interaction. If it became known that a woman was unmarried, not only did the married women often look down on them in the Lebensborn clinics, but many NSV nurses also adopted a condescending and disapproving attitude. Over time, the number of married women in the maternity hospitals also increased, because the comfortable and well-equipped Lebensborn locations were a safe distance from the increasingly bombed German cities. This group regularly included women of high-ranking SS and party officials. These ladies naturally received preferential treatment and enjoyed many privileges, such as a single room, exemption from household duties or permission to receive men – something that was normally forbidden. And these privileges extended not only to the wives of the Nazi elite, but also to their pregnant mistresses.

Hygiene and regularity were paramount in the care of the infants, especially the physical side of the care. The babies were changed six times a day and breastfed five times a day, all on a strict schedule. Outside these periods, they had no contact with their mothers and stayed together in a separate infant ward to which only medical staff had access. The underlying idea was that the young children initially only needed good physical care, because mental development would not start until around the second birthday and education had to start only then. The mothers were told to treat the children at a distance, not to spoil them and to teach them rules as early as possible.

As unmarried mothers were often unable to take their children with them when they were discharged from the maternity hospital because of the desired secrecy or their work, they were allowed to stay in the institution for a maximum

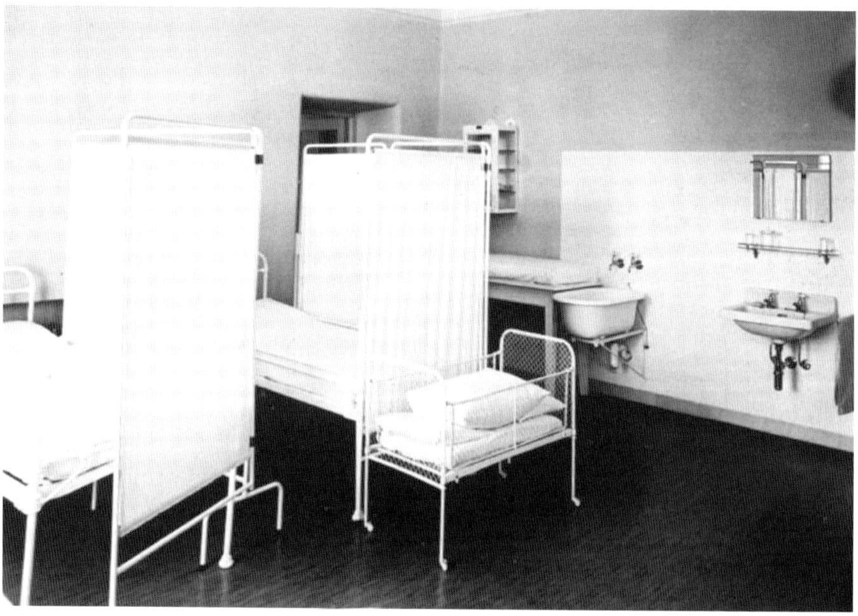

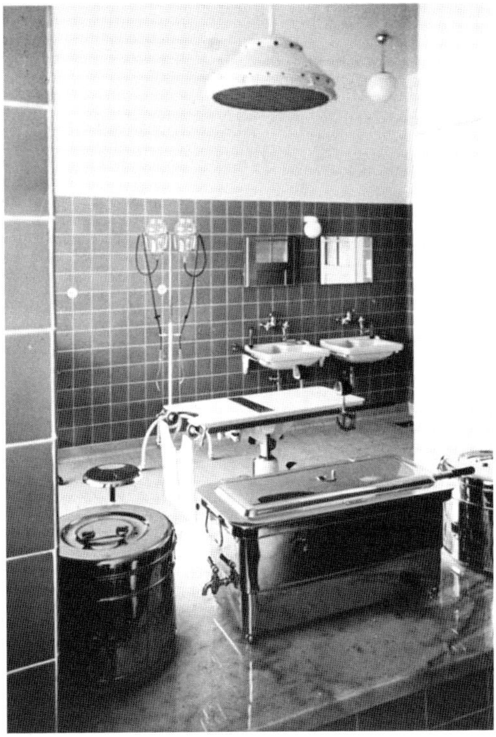

Opposite, right and below: The examination room, delivery room and infant ward in one of the maternity hospitals, most likely Heim Hochland (*Bundesarchiv B-145-Bild F051638-0065, F051638-0065-0063 and F051638-0065-0061*)

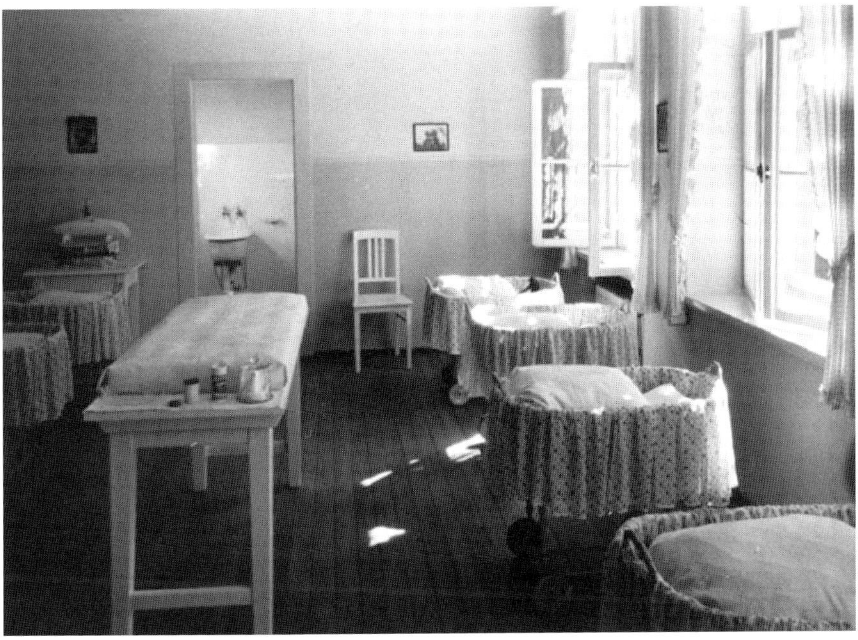

of two years. If the mother was still unable to take the child with her after that period, the organization would seek out a foster family with her permission. On the one hand because there was an increasing lack of space in the clinics, on the other hand because it was felt that the racially valuable children should not be brought up in a home.

For the same reason, such children were not to be placed with a random family, with Himmler in particular wanting them placed with childless SS couples. Initially, those potential foster parents had no choice in the matter as they were simply forced to accept, but there were limits to the power of the Reichsführer-SS. In the summer of 1938, the RuSHA reported to Himmler that of the ten SS members who had been required to take in foster children in the previous three months, nine had refused and had left the SS.[14] Not much later it was decided to make foster parenting voluntary and the organization tried to find interested people within the SS. However, this had insufficient results, which is why many children ended up living with their grandparents or other relatives. There, incidentally, they remained under the supervision of Lebensborn and regular reports had to be made on the well-being of the children.

There were therefore no objections to placing a child in a suitable foster family, but this only applied to the adoption of children born in Lebensborn clinics. Lebensborn went to great lengths to persuade the mothers who wanted their children to be adopted, and Himmler's personal consent was required in all cases. For ideological reasons, they wanted the mother to keep her child with her, because 'the racially high-quality mother does not, in principle, renounce her child'.[15] Furthermore, he did not approve of childless marriages being 'artificially' maintained through adoption as a result of infertility of one of the partners. According to Himmler, a divorce would be much better, because then the other could have healthy children with a new partner. Entirely in line with National Socialist population policy, it was therefore not about personal happiness, but only about bringing as many racially high-quality children into the world as possible.

Namensgebung: the Nazi Baptism

One of the most remarkable expressions of Himmler's efforts to provide his new knighthood with special rituals was the ceremony of the so-called *Namensgebung*. This ritual was in fact intended to replace Christian baptism, in which a swastika flag and an image of Hitler took the place of the altar, and the holy water was replaced by an SS dagger. At this ceremony, the child was officially named and symbolically placed under the protection of the SS. It was the mother's choice whether or not to have her child participate in the Namensgebung and from the scant known figures it seems that around half did.

The Namensgebung was intended as a festive gathering. In the presence of a number of guests, often including senior SS and party officials, a number of children were usually 'baptized' one after the other. The ceremony took place in a spacious hall, with a table at the front decorated with a bust or picture of Hitler, swastika flags and flower arrangements. The mothers sat in the front row with their children; behind them were the SS men who would become godfathers. In the rows behind them were the other guests and the women who stayed in the clinic. After a musical introduction, an SS-Führer pronounced a motto appropriate to the meeting, after which the Heimleiter spoke and explained the meaning and purpose of the Namensgebung. This mainly referred

Right, below left and below right: Around half the women who had a child in a Lebensborn clinic had it 'baptized' in a so-called Namensgebung ceremony. These photographs were taken during such an event in Heim Taunus in Wiesbaden. (*Bundesarchiv Bild 146-1969-062A-56, 146-1969-062A-58 and 146-1981-0501*)

to the (existing or not) customs of the ancestors, praised the young mothers and emphasized the great importance of the birth of a new child. 'Every woman who bears a child to the nation wins with this birth a battle for the life of her people', was one of Hitler's oft-quoted sayings.

After the speech, the mothers with the children came forward one by one and the actual naming took place while the *Deutschlandlied* (national anthem) was played. The Heimleiter asked the mother the question 'German mother, do you commit yourself to raising your child in the spirit of the National Socialist worldview?' (or the variant: 'Are you prepared to raise your child in the faith of Adolf Hitler?') The mother had to confirm her yes with a handshake. The Heimleiter then turned to the SS godfather standing next to the mother and said: 'Are you, SS comrade, prepared to personally protect this mother and her child when they are in distress and danger?' The Heimleiter then asked him: 'Are you prepared to always monitor the education of this child in the spirit of the sipping thought of our Schutzstaffel?' Another handshake and confirmation were to follow. After this, the Heimleiter moved an SS dagger over the child, touched his head with the weapon, and said: 'I hereby take you into the protection of our sippe community and give you the name […] Honour this name.' Finally, the mother was handed the certificate with the child's name. The meeting ended with the joint singing of the *Treuelied* of the SS, followed by coffee.[16]

Himmler automatically became godfather to all children born on his birthday, although naturally only if the child met all racial and genetic requirements. He kept himself closely informed of their development and sent them small gifts and healthy food. As with his subordinate SS godfathers, he never seems to have interfered with the education of the godchildren. The entire Namensgebung ceremony was ultimately a mere ostentation, with no concrete consequences for those involved, and presumably only impressed the true believers.

VI

HIMMLER'S HENCHMEN

The People Behind Lebensborn

> '*... our moral views of right and wrong are directed only to the interests of our people. Good is that which benefits the people, and bad is that which harms our people.*'
>
> Gregor Ebner

Old Comrades

Lebensborn was Himmler's favourite project. He devoted a disproportionate amount of time and energy to the organization, interfered with the smallest details and until the end of the war had himself informed on the ups and downs of the Lebensborn mothers and, especially, their children. He placed the leadership of the organization in the hands of people he knew and trusted.

The main three, Guntram Pflaum, Max Sollmann and Gregor Ebner, respectively the first and second director and the medical director of Lebensborn, were, like himself, among the first supporters of the Nazi movement, earning their spurs early on with far-right paramilitary groups. Like Himmler, Pflaum and Sollmann had taken part in the Hitler Putsch and all three had been members of the Freikorps Oberland. There is therefore little doubt they knew each other well. This was certainly true of Ebner, a former member of the *Freikorps Epp*, who from the late 1920s was not only Himmler's general practitioner, but also his friend.

Given their shared past in paramilitary units, these three men were not afraid of violence, and in a sense also symbolized the different blood groups within the SS. Pflaum, the organization's first director, was a model for the extreme right's 'man of action'. He was an ambitious, aggressive Nazi and race fanatic, who had no problems in using brute force against defenceless victims. Ebner, the medical leader of Lebensborn, represented the large body of German physicians and academics who were not only staunch adherents of racialism, but who were also prepared to select people by race, accepting all possible consequences. Sollmann, Pflaum's successor, was, like his predecessor and Ebner, a convinced Nazi, but not a racial fanatic. He represented the SS technocrats, the men who carried out their orders as closely as possible without moral consequences.

SS-Sturmbannführer Guntram Pflaum

Guntram Pflaum (1903-1945(?)), the first director of Lebensborn, had been a member of the NSDAP since 1932 and had joined the SS that same year. Shortly afterwards he was assigned to Himmler's personal staff at the SS-Sippenamt, a department of the Rasseamt (from 1935 RuSHA), which was responsible for the racial examination of SS members. In early 1936, SS-Sturmbannführer Pflaum was subsequently appointed the daily leader of Lebensborn.

Although he belonged to the fanatics in the ideological field, it soon became apparent that the highly ambitious Pflaum was not very suited for this position. He was unable to lead an organization like Lebensborn and pursued only his personal goals. When Himmler took Lebensborn out of the Sippenamt in early 1938 and placed it under his personal staff, he promoted the SS doctor Gregor Ebner, the medical leader of the organization, to co-director in order to limit Pflaum's power. At about the same time, in April 1938, the now promoted Pflaum was on an assignment for which he was better suited. A few weeks after the Anschluss of Austria, he arrived at the Wienerwald sanatorium in Feichtenbach with a Gestapo unit to seize the institution in Lebensborn's name. One of the founders and owners, the renowned Jewish pulmonologist Hugo Kraus, received the delegation led by SS-Obersturmbannführer Pflaum. Kraus died in hospital three days later, presumably as a result of a knife or bayonet stab inflicted on him by one of the SS men.

SS-Obersturmbannführer Guntram Pflaum, an ambitious, aggressive Nazi, was the first director of Lebensborn. He was replaced in early 1940 and continued to carry out special duties for Himmler until the end of the war, finally receiving the nickname Reichsfliegendiktator (Reich Fly Dictator). This is the only known photograph of Pflaum. (*Private collection*)

Within the leadership of Lebensborn, conflicts swiftly escalated when Pflaum opened a new branch of Lebensborn in Bromberg (Bydgoszcz, in the annexed part of Poland), intended to support the Volksdeutsche living there who had fallen victim to Polish violence during the German invasion. Such an initiative was not one of Lebensborn's objectives and Ebner was strongly against it, but he apparently could not stop Pflaum. Gradually, a power struggle ensued that eventually got so out of hand the employees were divided into two camps – one behind Ebner, the other behind Pflaum – who spied on each other. Pflaum's position did not improve when, in 1939, it turned out that the financial administration was in chaos and Lebensborn was deeply in debt. The power struggle was soon decided in favour of Ebner. In February 1940, at a meeting with Himmler, his right-hand man Karl Wolff, Pflaum and Ebner, in the *Vier Jahreszeiten* hotel in Munich, the latter requested that he be discharged from the SS because of the unworkable situation. Himmler decided otherwise: Pflaum had to go.[1] To save him face, it was announced he had repeatedly asked to be reassigned to a military branch of the SS and was also appointed to the supervisory board of Lebensborn. They would never come together anyway.

SS-Obersturmbannführer Pflaum did not disappear from view and briefly ran the Bromberg branch until it was divested. He then became active again in the field of race and population politics. In the autumn of 1941, Himmler sent him to Russia to track down Germanic children as leader of the *SS-Sonderkommando Pflaum*. In the Belarusian town of Babruysk, Pflaum, now promoted to SS-Standartenführer, founded a children's home where he brought together children who met the desired racial characteristics in order to transfer them to Germany at a later stage. It seems that it was an experiment in which German and selected Belarusian children were raised together so as to 'Germanize' the latter more quickly. Between the summer of 1942 and the autumn of 1943, when the home was closed, it is believed that several hundred children were abducted – some from orphanages and some from their parents.[2] Lebensborn was not involved in this operation: Pflaum carried out this task on behalf of Himmler in his position as RKF.

From August 1943, Pflaum served as Rasse- und Siedlungsführer with the HSSPF Ostland, and there are indications that he may also have been in charge of Heim Kurmark for some time that year. Finally, in January 1944, he was appointed special representative of the Reichsführer-SS in the field of pest control, based in the Auschwitz-Birkenau concentration camp. His task mainly consisted of combating the malaria mosquito, which caused many cases of illness among the SS guards. Pflaum had a work command of about forty SS men and eighty concentration camp prisoners and was nicknamed '*Reichsfliegendiktator*' (Reich Fly Dictator).[3]

SS-Oberführer Gregor Ebner

Gregor Ebner (1892-1974) was the winner of the power struggle with Pflaum and from 1937 until the end of the war the medical leader of Lebensborn. Born in Ichenhausen in Bavaria, during the First World War he had served as an assistant field physician and after completing his medical training in the early 1920s, started a practice as a general practitioner in Kirchseeon near Munich in 1923. Ebner was a supporter of extreme right-wing ideas from a young age and had joined the Freikorps Epp after the First World War. In 1930 he joined the NSDAP and met Himmler that same year, according to him at a meeting of the student association *Apollo*. Not only did he become Himmler's family doctor, but they also became friends. Mutual visits were made, they dined together with their wives, and their children also regularly played together.

Not long after his acquaintance with Himmler, Ebner joined the SS and was given an official position as doctor of SS-Oberabschnitt Süd. About five years later, in May 1936, he was appointed as a physician at Heim Hochland, the organization's first maternity hospital. At Lebensborn his star then rose rapidly. In 1937 he was appointed Chief Physician of the entire organization, a year later he was included in the executive board, and in April 1939 he was promoted to SS-Oberführer (senior colonel). He would remain the highest in rank at Lebensborn until 1945. Ebner was not only responsible for the health of the mothers and children, but he also carried out racial tests and selections, for example on twenty-five alleged orphans who had been transferred from Romania to Germany in 1941. He rejected five children because of racial and hereditary characteristics; three of them were judged by him to be mentally underdeveloped and had to be sterilized. Of the remaining children, Ebner gave five the highest rating, deeming them acceptable for Lebensborn.[4]

SS-Oberführer Gregor Ebner, doctor and race fanatic, was Himmler's friend and Lebensborn's medical leader from 1937 until the end of the war. This photograph was taken after the war while he was awaiting trial in a US military court. (*Public domain*)

He also held a number of positions in other Nazi organizations and had good contacts at the highest level within the party and the SS. Besides Himmler, his circle of acquaintances included SS-Gruppenführer Hermann Fegelein, Eva Braun's brother-in-law, and the Higher SS and Police Leader Ernst-Heinrich Schmauser. Ebner was a National Socialist from the very beginning, and a convinced and fanatical supporter of the racial doctrine. In addition to his medical and administrative tasks, he was responsible for the ideological training of both the women admitted to Lebensborn and the staff. In that capacity, and as a speaker on behalf of the *Rassenpolitische Amt der NSDAP* (a party department that was mainly concerned with propaganda and 'information'), he gave lectures on topics such as 'the large family as the foundation of the state', 'the danger of miscegenation' and 'the sterilization and castration of the inferior'.[5] In January 1939 he addressed SS top brass about Lebensborn: 'When we as SS men protect the unmarried mother of good blood against the slander of the environment … we do so only on the basis of the idea not to waste a single drop of good blood … If both the father and the mother are of good blood, then we can certainly expect a hereditary healthy, valuable child, and because of this child the mother must be helped.' Incidentally, Himmler closely monitored Ebner's ideological activities and had also reviewed and corrected this speech beforehand.[6]

SS-Oberführer Ebner was also the chairman of the disciplinary court of the *Nationalsozialistische Deutsche Ärtzebund*, (National Socialistic German Physician's Association), an organization that propagated, among other things, the racial doctrine, a task he once again carried out with fanaticism. Until the very end he adhered to the National Socialist and racist worldview and believed in final victory. In the last months of the war, he reported a Luftwaffe doctor assigned to Lebensborn to the Gestapo for undermining morale and anti-state propaganda. The man was in a Gestapo cell from November 1944 to April 1945 and only survived the war thanks to the German defeat.

SS-Standartenführer Max Sollmann

Max Sollmann (1904-1978), who succeeded Pflaum as Lebensborn's director in March 1940 and would remain in that position until the end of the war, was of the same generation as his predecessor. He was born on 6 June 1904 in Bayreuth (Bavaria), went to school in Munich and was employed by various companies from 1920, where he mainly performed administrative and financial work. Like Pflaum and Ebner, Sollmann was a supporter of right-

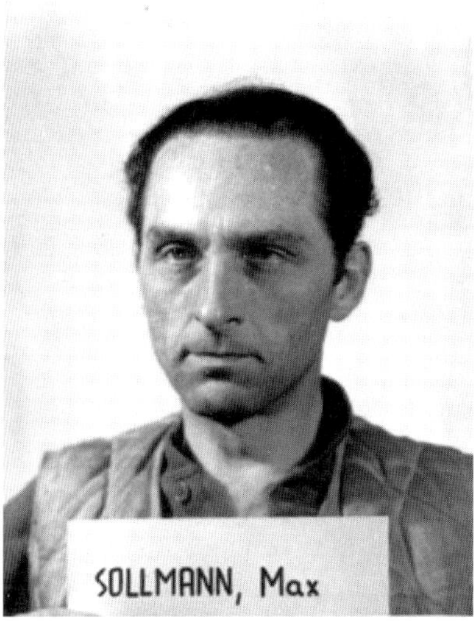

SS-Obersturmbannführer Max Sollmann, photographed in prison after the war, was the general manager and leader of Lebensborn from 1940 to 1945. He was a convinced Nazi from an early age and a staunch follower of Himmler, but not a race fanatic. This photograph was taken in US captivity. (*Public domain*)

wing extremist groups from an early age. He joined the Freikorps Epp and the Freikorps Oberland at the age of 16 and in 1921 took part in the fighting in the suppression of a Polish uprising in Upper Silesia. He joined the NSDAP that same year and in November 1923 took part in the failed Hitler Putsch. When Hitler was serving his prison sentence a few months later, Sollmann, representing the *Jung-Bayern-Bund Munich* – yet another right-wing paramilitary organization – paid him a personal visit to congratulate him on his birthday.

In 1929 he left for Colombia, where he worked in business for several years before returning to Germany in January 1934. The situation in the country had changed dramatically after Hitler had taken power and Sollmann's fellow party members now had control of the state. He had by no means missed this, because in April 1933 he had already sent a letter to Hitler in which he congratulated him and reminded him of their meeting in 1924. In the same letter he stated that he was 'delighted to be able to place his person and knowledge at the disposal of the movement', whether in the German Reich or abroad.[7]

It is not known whether Sollmann received a response to his letter or whether it benefited him in some other way, but it is certain that he was rewarded for his activities in earlier years. Despite his relatively young age, he belonged to the so-called *Alter Kämpfer* (Old Warriors), a name for members of the NSDAP who already belonged to the party before the takeover of power. These veterans of the movement received preferential treatment in Nazi Germany and, if necessary, were offered suitable employment. Sollmann also benefited from the new relationships. After his return to Germany, he was awarded both the gold party insignia and the 'sign of honour of 9 November 1923'. He received the latter award – colloquially known as the *Blutorden* (Blood Order) – for his participation in Hitler's failed coup. In addition to this tribute, his career in the new Germany got off to a flying start. After Sollmann enlisted in the SS in June 1937, he was immediately promoted to SS-Untersturmführer (second lieutenant) with retroactive effect, and received the same salary as he had previously earned in a private company, which was considerably higher than the salary corresponding to his rank.

According to Sollmann, he enlisted in the SS at the suggestion of a friend, SS-Sturmbannführer Bruno Galke, the head of the economic support department of the personal staff of the Reichsführer-SS and the business manager of the *Ahnenerbe-Stiftung*. He was included in Galke's staff and, on behalf of Himmler, carried out a few special assignments as manager of several SS companies, including the Allach porcelain factory. On 1 January 1940, he was subsequently transferred to the recently established Reichskommissariat für die Festigung deutschen Volkstums (RKFDV), but less than six weeks later Himmler called on him again and Sollmann was instructed to thoroughly examine Lebensborn's structure and finances. Not only was the power struggle between Pflaum and Ebner raging, the organization had also fallen into a deep financial and organizational crisis due to Pflaum's arbitrary and risky actions.

Sollmann vetted Lebensborn within weeks and then submitted a report of his findings, on the basis of which Himmler made a sweeping decision. After Pflaum was relieved of his duties, he appointed Sollmann as the new director of Lebensborn in March 1940. It is not certain whether Himmler had already envisaged him as Pflaum's successor beforehand, but it is certain that Sollmann, who had meanwhile been promoted to SS-Obersturmbannführer, was appointed to the post because of his business and financial experience, and because Himmler trusted him completely. The two men had a common past and Sollmann was an unconditional follower of the Reichsführer-SS. Himmler's will was law to him, as he once stated explicitly, and he did everything in his power to make Lebensborn comply with his demands. Immediately after his appointment, he therefore began a thorough reorganization with the aim of 'giving Himmler a financially healthy and optimally functioning instrument'.[8]

The appreciation was mutual. Not only did Himmler write in his preamble to Sollmann's written assignments *'Lieber Sollmann'* (Dear Sollmann), Sollmann was also judged to be 'ostisch-dinarisch' according to the racial criteria of the SS, and although he thus fell far short of the Nordic ideal pursued by Lebensborn, he was still responsible for the 'future nobility' of the Greater Germanic Empire. The other staff, and at least the nurses, had to meet the racial requirements. Another indication of the close relationship between the two men was the lenient punishment Himmler inflicted on him after he was found drunk during an official visit to Reichskommissar Terboven in Norway in late February or early March 1941. Although Sollmann had damaged the

Himmler with his retinue at the Ekeberg German military cemetery, near Oslo, during his visit to Norway to discuss Lebensborn, late February/early March 1941. The officer to the left behind Himmler, with the thick fur collar, is SS-Obersturmbannführer Sollmann (*Public domain, Bundesarchiv Bild 101III-Moebius-03022*)

reputation of the SS in public and in front of senior officers and the Norwegian guests – a very serious misstep – Himmler only imposed a one-year alcohol ban on him, even though he usually punished transgressions of his subordinates mercilessly.[9]

Apart from this incident, Himmler had put the right man in the right position with Sollmann. After his appointment he went to work and within two months had set up a completely new structure. He also managed to solve the organization's biggest financial problems within a short period of time and then led the consolidation and expansion of Lebensborn. Sollmann was the undisputed leader of Lebensborn and would remain so to the end, despite the fact that his highest rank would be SS-Standartenführer (colonel), one rank below Ebner. He was immediately subordinate to the Reichsführer-SS and received his instructions directly from Himmler or through his adjutant. Thanks to the short line to Himmler, Sollmann was a powerful man in Nazi Germany, even outside Lebensborn's immediate field of activity. He corresponded with stationery with the heading '*Der Reichsführer-SS, Persönlicher Stab, Amt L*' and had a large budget, blank identity cards and travel papers for the entire Reich territory and the occupied territories. In the spring of 1942 he was assigned SS-Hauptsturmführer Wolfgang Überschaar as an adjutant, a member of the Waffen-SS who had been so badly wounded in Russia that he was no longer suitable for front service.

Sollmann was a convinced National Socialist but not a racial fanatic like Himmler, Pflaum and Ebner. He was a technocrat who carried out the orders of the Reichsführer-SS punctually and conscientiously, whatever they meant. Yet just because he was not a fanatical racialist did not mean he did not accept the consequences, quite the contrary. He personally ordered that children born to Lebensborn with a serious abnormality be transferred to an institution for *Sonderbehandlung* (special treatment), the common euphemism for murder.[10] He also took an active part in and was responsible for the 'Germanization' of kidnapped, foreign children. It is also certain that he knew in detail the horrors and massacres committed by his organization in the East.

Inge Viermetz

Inge Viermetz (1908-1997) was probably Sollmann's most important collaborator from 1940 to 1943.[11] She was born in Aschaffenburg in Bavaria, attended primary and secondary education there and from 1923 worked as a shorthand typist for various companies. She married in 1932 and moved to Austria, but soon left her husband and returned to Germany in 1935. There she worked in various administrative positions until she lost her appointment in early 1938. In the autumn that same year, through the mediation of the employment office, she got a job as a shorthand typist at the Zentrale van Lebensborn in Munich, where administrative staff were desperately needed.

Little is known about her world view, but in 1937 Viermetz had become a member of the NSV, the *Nationalsozialistische*

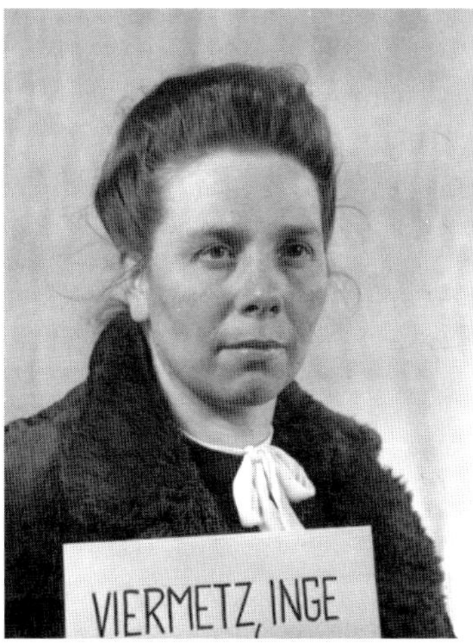

Inge Viermetz was one of Sollmann's most important employees from the end of 1938 to the end of 1943. By the standards of Nazi Germany, in which women formally had very little say, she held several senior positions and represented Lebensborn at home and abroad on important missions. Viermetz was also arrested after the war and is photographed here in captivity before her trial. (*Public domain*)

Frauenschaft (National Socialist Women's League) and the *Reichskolonialbund* (Reich Colonial Association). Whether this was out of conviction or out of opportunism, in the hope of finding a job more easily under the new regime, is not known. In any case, it is certain that she ended up at Lebensborn by chance, where she turned out to be particularly well suited. She was automatically assigned to *SS-Gefolge* because of her work; women who worked for the SS in civilian positions, but were not members of the SS. They worked in administrative and economic departments such as secretaries, typists and telephone operators, in medical services as doctors and nurses, or as overseers in concentration camps.

Viermetz started as a shorthand typist in the recordings sub-department but was already unofficially promoted to head of this department in the autumn of 1939, when the war had broken out and many men had been called up. Not much later she was also put in charge of the sub-department that looked for jobs for women who had given birth at Lebensborn. Her job, which included business trips to various German cities, was completed so well that Sollmann, who took over the management during this period, noticed. In the reorganization that followed his appointment, Viermetz was promoted to deputy chief of the main department A (admissions, guardianship, foster and adoption mediation, statistics and registration). She first led it together with her male colleague SS-Hauptsturmführer Ernst Ragaller, but when that cooperation did not work out, Sollmann transferred Ragaller leaving Viermetz to manage the department alone. As a woman was not allowed to hold such a high position in the Third Reich, she was officially registered as the deputy chief, but in practice she headed the main department. There she performed important work for Lebensborn and was repeatedly sent to the Berlin Ministry of Justice to negotiate exemption from the state control of adoptions of children born to Lebensborn.

Inge Viermetz must have had a particularly strong character. In the male-dominated Third Reich, where the SS also symbolized some of the most unpleasant masculine traits, women played a subordinate role in every way. Viermetz was one of the few exceptions who succeeded in obtaining – and maintaining – a position in which she interacted on an equal footing with high-ranking members of the SS, party and government officials. Sollmann had great confidence in her abilities. This became apparent, for example, when he sent her to Berlin in March 1942, together with Lebensborn's legal adviser, SS-Hauptsturmführer Dr Günther Tesch, for consultation with the leadership of the NSV. Lebensborn had long been in fierce competition with this powerful NSDAP organization and now a new conflict had arisen over a group of alleged orphans from the Warthegau who were eligible for 'Germanization'. Viermetz and Tesch successfully refuted the claims of Hilgenfeldt, the leader of the NSV, and she subsequently played a leading role in the process by which the children were transferred to Germany.

It is not clear whether Viermetz was a convinced adherent of Nazi racial ideology, but it is certain that she operated according to those standards. When she was sent to Posen (Poznań) in the spring of 1942 to arrange the transfer of children from the Warthegau to Lebensborn homes, she proposed not only to select them on racial characteristics, but also to examine them from a characterological and psychological point of view after admission to Lebensborn, to see if they met the selection criteria of the SS.[12] Only if that turned out to be the case would Lebensborn have to take over custody and place the children in foster homes selected by the organization after six to eight months. At the end of their vocational training, the Reichsführer-SS would then have to decide on their final destination, according to Viermetz's proposal. Viermetz was also aware of the fate of children born to Lebensborn with a congenital defect, as in the case of Jürgen Weise in Heim Pommern (see p.146).

In May 1942 she had to give up her leading position in main department A to Ebner, presumably because there was still criticism that such an important department was led by a woman. Viermetz was deeply disappointed and asked to be fired. She argued that she should take care of her husband's business – she had since remarried – who was absent due to military service. But Sollmann was very keen to keep her for Lebensborn and refused the dismissal. Instead, he relieved her of her duties at the Zentrale and, from the summer of 1942, increasingly sent Viermetz on special missions at home and abroad.

For a short time she was Lebensborn's representative in Litzmannstadt (Łodz), which was one of the most important centres of German repopulation policy. The city housed the second largest Jewish ghetto, where more than 200,000 people were imprisoned at times. Litzmannstadt was also home to the headquarters of the *Einwandererzentralstelle* (EWZ) immigration service for ethnic Germans, and housed the *Polen-Jugendverwahrlager der Sicherheitspolizei* (Poland Security Police Youth Detention Centre). This was a special concentration camp where non-Jewish children – officially between the ages of 6 and 16, but often younger – were imprisoned. The children were mainly of imprisoned, deported or murdered parents and performed forced labour, although they were also examined by the SS for their racial characteristics. Viermetz was one of the people who decided whether a child was 'valuable' enough to be Germanized under the care of Lebensborn. She was also engaged in similar tasks in Romania and Slovenia.

In the 'Polen-Jugendverwahrlager der Sicherheitspolizei' (Poland Security Police Youth Detention Centre) in Litzmannstadt (Łodz), the SS held non-Jewish children of imprisoned, deported or murdered parents. The children were officially between 6 and 16 years old, but in practice were often younger. Seen here is a group of girls at roll call. (*Instytut Pamieci Narodowej*)

From the second half of 1942, Viermetz carried out various assignments in Western Europe, where Lebensborn wanted to expand its activities and planned to open new maternity hospitals. Discussions in The Hague ultimately yielded no results, but in Belgium and France, where she bore the title *'Lebensborn-Beauftragten für Belgien und Nordfrankreich'*, she was more successful. She prepared for the opening of a clinic in both countries, and in the spring of 1943 also administered the new Belgian establishment, Heim Ardennen, in Wégimont Castle near Liège for several months.

Despite Viermetz's abilities and great merits for the organization, she was summarily dismissed at the end of 1943. Following her mission in Belgium, she was accused of having had scarce and luxurious foodstuffs sent from Lebensborn depots to Germany for her own use and had also made expensive private purchases at a Brussels department store without paying for them. She was further accused of misusing blank identity cards and travel documents, which she had available to hide the identity of pregnant women if necessary.[13] Finally, there was a long list of accusations of other matters, giving the impression that they wanted to take the opportunity to get rid of her, regardless. Sollmann has stated on several occasions that she was very energetic and capable, but had a particularly difficult character. Even so, he had rejected her request for resignation a year and a half earlier. Why she consequently had to suddenly disappear from Lebensborn has never been clarified.

In the spring of 1943, the Lebensborn clinic Heim Ardennen was opened in Wégimont Castle near Liège. As Lebensborn-Beauftragten für Belgien und Nordfrankreich, Viermetz was responsible for all preparations and also conducted the administration during the first few months. (*Private collection*)

Other Staff Officers

In addition to the quartet described above, there was another small group of people working directly under the management at Lebensborn who fulfilled a number of important functions. In addition to Inge Viermetz, this included a second woman named Maria Knipp-Merkel, as well as the SS officers Günther Tesch (Sollmann's official deputy), Erich Schulz and Hans-Hilmar Staudte – all three graduate lawyers – and Ernst Ragaller, who, like Tesch, acted as Sollmann's deputy.

Maria Knipp-Merkel (date of birth and death unknown) was an important Lebensborn employee about whom very little is known apart from her activities in the organization. Before joining Lebensborn at an unknown time, she appears to have been a secretary at the newspaper *Münchener Neuesten Nachrichten*. At Lebensborn she performed various tasks and, among other things, led the main personnel department for a while. In the autumn of 1942, Knipp-Merkel was sent to Krakow, where she headed the new Lebensborn branch at the HSSPF with orders to set up maternity hospitals for Volksdeutsche in the Generalgouvernement.[14] From September 1943, Knipp-Merkel was Heimleiter of Heim Alpenland, which was specially intended for the Germanization of foreign, mainly Polish children, and from there she also headed the R IV department of the Zentrale, where she was responsible for the mediation of the so-called 'Volksdeutsche Orphans'.

Günther Tesch (1907-1989) was Lebensborn's most important legal adviser and leader of the legal department. He was included in the statutes in April 1942 as the official replacement for Sollmann and was therefore authorized to sign documents. SS-Sturmbannführer Tesch dealt with tax matters, land ownership and guardianship, among other things. In June 1942, after long negotiations with the Ministry of the Interior, Tesch managed to make sure the government no longer supervised the foster children in Lebensborn's care. Later, the ministry also agreed to his proposal to legally consider the abducted foreign children as foundlings. This allowed Lebensborn to officially determine the date of birth, place and name of the children themselves, and thus give the foreign children a new, falsified identity. Tesch was also a judge at an SS court.

Hans-Hilmar Staudte (1911-1979) was the second man and deputy head of the legal department. SS-Obersturmbannführer Staudte was also a judge at the NSDAP Gau court in Munich. During his testimony at the Nuremberg trial on 10 March 1947, Staudte stated that Lebensborn had regularly received letters from women asking if the organization could help them find a partner who would father a child with them.[15]

Erich Schulz (1901-1979) was the leader of the 'Standesamt L München', founded in 1943, which registered children of German soldiers and foreign mothers who wanted secrecy. Before that, he was one of Sollmann's two deputies from 1941-1943 alongside Tesch. SS-Sturmbannführer Schulz was also responsible for creating false birth certificates and changing the names of foreign children.

SS-Sturmbannführer Günther Tesch was the organization's main legal man and Sollmann's official replacement. He managed to remove the foster children under the care of Lebensborn and the foreign children at the organization from government supervision. He, too, was brought to trial after the war. (*Public domain*)

Ernst Ragaller (1895-1951) joined Lebensborn in 1940 and at the end of 1941 led the main department A for a number of months with Inge Viermetz, then the main department war orphans and later again the main department A. From May 1943, SS-Sturmbannführer Ragaller was also Sollmann's official deputy. In the summer of 1944 he was transferred to occupied Norway and headed the Lebensborn department at the Reichskommissariat from Oslo.

SS-Hauptsturmführer Willy Ziesmer (date of birth and death unknown) worked at Lebensborn from 1935 and held various important positions. He had a part in the establishment of the department in Bromberg for the Volksdeutsche, led the main department SS-War Orphans at the Zentrale in Munich for a time, and was sent by Sollmann in December 1944 to Denmark to set up new branches there.

The Staff in the Maternity Clinics and Children's Homes

Throughout its existence, Lebensborn suffered from a great and growing shortage of medical personnel. From the beginning it was difficult to get enough doctors and nurses, and of course that became more and more difficult as the war progressed. It was only because of Himmler's power and prestige that Lebensborn received any medical personnel at all in the latter phase of the war. The shortage was further combated by making a virtue of necessity: an important part of Lebensborn's staff consisted of women who had given birth themselves at the organization.

Each Lebensborn maternity hospital was run by a so-called Heimleiter, usually an SS doctor with the rank of SS-Hauptsturmführer (captain). However, due to a shortage of doctors, this was not always the case and – even more curious – practically none of the Heimleiters who were doctors specialized in gynaecology or paediatrics, Ebner, Lebensborn's chief physician and medical director, being a prime example. At Lebensborn, the National Socialist world view of the doctors was more important than their medical qualifications.

To assist the Heimleiters in word and deed, a number of specialists were available to provide regular and incidental medical support and advice. Despite this, complaints were made several times about the actions of various Heimleiters. The help of midwives, better qualified doctors and hospitals had to be regularly called in urgently, and a number of Heimleiter doctors were even removed from their positions. Their dismissal was not always the result of professional shortcomings, however, but also of ideological differences of opinion and disturbed personal relationships. The Lebensborn leadership

Group photograph of the staff of a Lebensborn branch, in this case the Norwegian maternity hospital Hurdalsverk. Back row (centre) is the SS doctor and Heimleiter, with presumably the secretary on his right, surrounded by '*blaue*' and '*braune*' nurses. The woman with the long white coat (front row, centre left) is most likely the midwife. In addition to the medical staff, who were all German, local residents were also employed for less important functions. (*Schwert und Wiege*)

had high expectations of the Heimleiter, which were not primarily medical: he was above all 'to be a paternal friend and adviser to our mothers, who are reminded only in emergencies that he is a doctor', Ebner wrote.[16] They must also be an ardent Nazi, of course, who could convey his worldview to the young women.

Immediately below the Heimleiter were the Oberschwester (head nurse) and the Verwalter (administrator), the secretary, and a midwife at the maternity hospital. The rest of the staff consisted of several nurses, as well as cleaning, kitchen and maintenance staff. The wages of the leading staff and nurses were higher than was usual for such positions outside Lebensborn. Most of the nurses – and always the Oberschwester – came from the NSV. These nurses were not only medically qualified but also National Socialist trained, and were called *braune Schwestern* because of their ideology and of the colour

This insignia must be related to Lebensborn: a so-called elhaz or tree of life rune is depicted, which Himmler chose as a symbol for Lebensborn, surrounded by a laurel wreath and the SS symbol of the two lightning bolts. It may have been intended for higher (female) personnel of the organization. (*Private collection*)

of their tunic. The turnover among these nurses at Lebensborn was strikingly high, which was probably due to the gulf between their own views and the daily confrontation with unmarried mothers – unmarried motherhood was grounds for dismissal in the conservative NSV. Because the NSV could not provide enough nurses, 'normal' nurses were also hired. They wore a blue tunic and were therefore also called *'blauen Schwestern'*. The personnel, like the mothers-to-be, had to meet the requirements of the SS in terms of race and have the correct worldview.

To combat the shortages and high turnover rates, at the end of 1941 Himmler ordered that Lebensborn would start its own nursing training. According to Ebner, this also had the advantage no longer being dependent on the NSV and that the self-trained nurses would have 'the right inner attitude towards Lebensborn'. Preparations were made for more than a year and a half, and the

NSV leader Hilgenfeldt is welcomed during a working visit by a reception committee of *braune Schwestern,* nurses who were not only medically trained but also National Socialists. (*Private collection*)

nursing school was to be established first in Munich and later in Steinhöring. A number of student applications had already been received when, in the autumn of 1943, Himmler decided to cancel the project, much to Ebner's disappointment. He probably did this in exchange for concessions from NSV leader Erich Hilgenfeldt – who was strongly against competing nurse training – on another part of the population policy.

A relatively large proportion of the staff, estimated to be at least 25-30%, had given birth in a Lebensborn clinic and had subsequently been employed by the organization. This included doctors and nurses as well as secretaries and other staff. This practice benefited both sides. The young women were not only well paid, could live with their children under one roof and had access to childcare, they were also not exposed to the prejudices about unmarried mothers and secrecy was guaranteed. In return, Lebensborn received loyal personnel who – just as importantly – had already proved they met the racial criteria of the SS. Moreover, these women did not need to be made aware of the importance and necessity of secrecy.

In Munich, Lebensborn had a number of special boarding houses – Mütterwohnstätten – where young mothers who worked at the Zentrale could live; during the day their children could go to the accompanying crèche. Jobs outside the organization were also arranged, as much as possible in the vicinity of the Lebensborn maternity home where the child was housed.

Incidentally, in was standard procedure for women who became pregnant in the service of Lebensborn to be transferred to another clinic to give birth. The correct image had to be maintained and at all costs the already existing prejudices about the organization as a breeding institution or luxury brothel must not be confirmed. As a result, the Gestapo was called in whenever another story to this effect surfaced, and they conducted several investigations in search of the source of the rumours.

VII

ARYAN BABIES

Lebensborn's Institutions in the German Reich

'The number of cradles must exceed the number of coffins.'
Heinrich Himmler

Germany and Austria

Between 1936 and 1944, Lebensborn opened a total of twelve branches in Germany and annexed Austria. They were initially housed in buildings that Lebensborn bought or had been gifted from the government for a fraction of the value, but later most of the accommodations were acquired by force. The clinics of the organization opened from 1936 to the end of 1938, and all but one had a dual function, serving not only as a maternity hospital but also as a children's home, where the children born in the clinic could stay for several years. At the start of the war, in September 1939, Lebensborn had seven

Wo liegen die Lebensborn-Heime?

Werdende Mütter können in folgenden Heimen Aufnahme finden:

Heim „FRIESLAND"
Heim „HARZ"
Heim „HOCHLAND"
Heim „KURMARK"
Heim „OSTMARK"
Heim „POMMERN"
Heim „TAUNUS"

Die Namen der Heime bezeichnen allgemein ihre landschaftliche Lage.

Die genaue Anschrift der Heime wird mitgeteilt, wenn dem Aufnahmeantrag wahrscheinlich entsprochen wird. Um Verzögerungen zu vermeiden, muß der Antrag auf Heimaufnahme an die Reichszentrale des Lebensborn e. V. München 2, Herzog-Maxstraße 3–7 gerichtet werden.

An die Heime gerichtete Aufnahmeanträge werden der Reichszentrale zur Bearbeitung weitergeleitet.

A page from a brochure for Lebensborn intended for women interested in admission to one of the organization's clinics. With seven institutions listed, the brochure must date from 1939 or 1940. The clinic mentioned here as Ostmark would be renamed Wienerwald shortly afterwards. (*Private collection*) institutions with room for approximately 250 women and approximately 450 children.

Between 1939 and 1941, no new maternity hospitals or children's homes were opened in Germany and Austria. After the rapid growth of the early years and the financial and organizational chaos – a consequence of the actions of the first director Pflaum – the new staff was mainly concerned with consolidating the situation. In addition, Pflaum's successor, Sollmann, was busy with the new set-up of the organization, while the Zentrale in Munich also provided support for the establishment of the Norwegian Lebensborn. Plans were made for expansion and the opening of new homes and clinics in Germany, and possible new locations were visited at Trier and Braunschweig, but nothing came of this.

From 1942 Lebensborn entered a new phase. Institutions were opened in the occupied territories, while in the territory of the Third Reich emphasis was placed on children's homes. Five branches were opened there between 1942 and 1944, only one of which had the dual function of maternity hospital and children's home; the remaining four were only intended to house children, primarily because the demand for places in children's homes continued to grow. More children remained in the clinics after birth and the length of stay was longer than expected. In addition, places were also taken up by the young children of mothers who continued to work at Lebensborn after giving birth. A third reason was the influx of foreign children; babies from Norwegian Lebensborn clinics, but also older children, particularly from Poland, Czechoslovakia and Slovenia, who were taken to Germany to be 'Germanized'. The children's home Alpenland, where the foreign children were subjected to a strict regime, was even opened especially for this purpose.

In the last phase of the war, as the Allied armies approached from all sides, one Lebensborn location after another had to be evacuated, starting with the foreign settlements. Finally, in May 1945, three institutions were still more or less in operation, including Heim Hochland, where US troops would later find around 160 babies and infants.

This type of armband, of which some slightly different ones are known, was probably worn by Lebensborn personnel when they went on official business outside the Lebensborn establishments. (*Private collection*)

In total, approximately 8,000 births were registered at the German and Austrian branches between 1936 and 1945. Because the capacity of their own maternity hospitals was not large enough, a large proportion of deliveries took place elsewhere, in public hospitals and private institutions, but under the responsibility and control of Lebensborn.

Maternity Clinics with Children's Homes

Heim Hochland was Lebensborn's first branch. It was a maternity hospital with a children's home, located in Steinhöring, a village with a few thousand inhabitants about 30 kilometres east of Munich. Hochland consisted of a main building with a number of outbuildings on a 5.5-hectare site. After an extensive and costly renovation, the first Lebensborn branch opened there on 15 August 1936. That Bavaria had great sympathy for the organization is proven by the purchase price. Although the estimated value was about 1 million Reichsmarks, Lebensborn only paid 55,000 in total.

Heim Hochland remained the parent and model site of the organization throughout Lebensborn's existence, not only because it was the first clinic, but also because of its location in close proximity to Munich, where the headquarters and management of Lebensborn resided. Hochland was highly regarded and was officially recognized as a children's hospital so that specialized nurses could receive their training there. Initially, the maternity hospital had a capacity of thirty mother's and forty-five children's beds, but soon after the opening they started with an expansion and in 1940 Hochland had fifty-one places for (future) mothers and 106 places for children. Between September 1936

The main building of Heim Hochland in Steinhöring, Lebensborn's first maternity hospital. This photograph was taken around spring 1936, when renovations for the opening were in full swing. (*Public domain*)

The *'die Stillende Mutter'* (the breastfeeding mother) statue was erected by Lebensborn in the park of Heim Hochland in around 1940. It is still there. (*Private collection*)

and May 1945, a total of 1,438 births and thirty-four deaths were recorded.

SS-Oberführer Gregor Ebner, Lebensborn's medical chief, was also the Heimleiter of Hochland from 1936 until the end of the war. Under Ebner, a racial fanatic who maintained an authoritarian rule over patients and staff, was a workforce of around fifty people, not counting the prisoners. Like the expectant mothers, Ebner also subjected the staff to a strict selection, because everyone in Hochland had to meet the required racial characteristics and also have the right world view. If it later turned out that their attitude was no good or if someone broke the rules, immediate dismissal followed. This happened, for example, to a young mother who refused an assignment with the remark they 'were not in Dachau after all' and a nurse who had slapped a child.

The daily schedule, tasks and obligations of staff and residents were laid down in detail and there was no deviation from the schedule. As in the other locations, the mothers-to-be had to do light household work and were expected to be happy to do so:

> For the real Lebensborn mother, the concept of "Heim" is equivalent to the concept of "home". She does not experience the Lebensbornheim as an institution or facility which she uses in times of need and where she uses nursing and care, but otherwise does not feel responsible. […] The Lebensborn mother is the founder of this beautiful institution, she is grateful and takes pride in expressing this gratitude through her entire demeanour.[1]

The women were obliged to attend classes of the *Reichsmütterdienst* on housekeeping and childcare and were ideologically trained through lectures, communal reading and singing, or listening to radio broadcasts; everything, of course, to teach them the correct world view or to confirm it. According

When the weather was fine, the babies' cots were placed outside, as seen here in front of the southern facade of Hochland. (*Public domain*)

to the same ideas, people in Hochland also celebrated *Julfest* (the National Socialist's so-called Germanic version of Christmas) and there were festive gatherings for the Namensgebung and the *SS-Eheweien* (the SS wedding). Other highlights included visits by important Nazis, including Reichsführer-SS Heinrich Himmler, Reichsgesundheitsführer Leonardo Conti and the Bavarian Gauleiter Adolf Wagner.

Heim Hochland had mainly double and quadruple rooms and a few single rooms for very important guests, all of which were very comfortably furnished. The institution also had a number of common areas, kitchens and washing rooms, offices, an examination room, a delivery room, infant wards and a nursery. The care was of a high standard; everything was spotlessly clean and supplies and food were not lacking until the last weeks of the war. Because of this, and because the clinic was located in the relative safety of the countryside, Hochland became an increasingly popular destination for pregnant women of high-ranking SS men during the course of the war.

For the same reason – namely the increasing air danger in Munich – administrative parts of the organization began to be transferred to Steinhöring in the second half of the war. In September 1943 and March 1944, eight large barracks were set up near Hochland by Lebensborn's own labour command, the prisoners of KZ-Aussenlager 'Lebensborn'. First, a number of departments of the Zentrale were housed there, and in the summer of 1944, after a bombing raid on Munich, the rest of the staff still working in the city followed.

In addition to the male forced labourers, female prisoners were also employed in Heim Hochland. This concerned about twenty Jehovah's Witnesses

Heim Hochland, circa 1943. The clinic started in the building on the left, which was given the narrow, high extension just before opening. Later followed the two-part extension on the right and the single-story building on the far right. Slightly to the right of centre, faintly visible, is the statue of the breastfeeding mother. From the end of 1943, eight more large barracks were built near Hochland, housing the greater part of the Zentrale, plus two houses for Sollmann and Tesch. (*Steinhöring*)

who were deployed to Lebensborn from the beginning of 1943 on Himmler's instructions. The female prisoners who had to do all sorts of domestic work in Steinhöring came from the concentration camps of Moringen and Ravensbrück. Although they worked long and hard days in Hochland, living conditions and their treatment there were much better than in the camps. Most of the women were German, but there were also a few Austrian and Dutch, and one Polish woman.[2]

In the last phase of the war, when most of Lebensborn's other settlements were gradually evacuated due to the advance of Allied troops, more and more children, pregnant women and staff from other homes were transferred to Hochland. Together with Heim Friesland, this was the last settlement reached by the Allied units and thus Lebensborn ended in the same place where it started.

Heim Harz was the first of two clinics with children's homes that Lebensborn opened in 1937 and was located in the town of Wernigerode. The first building of Heim Harz, which consisted of several buildings separated by a street, was donated to Lebensborn by the NSV in January 1937. The first recordings followed in June, but it was not until 1 September of that year that it was officially opened with fourteen mother's beds and five children's beds. By purchasing a number of nearby buildings, the capacity was gradually expanded to thirty places for pregnant women and forty-eight for children.

Between 1937 and 1945, 1,103 births were registered at Harz, the majority of which took place under the control of Lebensborn in a regular maternity hospital or hospital in one of the nearby cities (Hannover, Braunschweig or Magdeburg). Also, a private nurse, living in Wernigerode, regularly received payments from Lebensborn, which were more than once registered under the reference 'Kind Himmler'.

Heim Harz was located in Wernigerode, about 50 kilometres southeast of the city of Braunschweig and not far from Quedlinburg, where you will find the tomb of King Heinrich I. It was opened in 1937 and gradually expanded thereafter. (*Private collection*)

This armband, with the rune but without the 'SS-Lebensborn' text, was worn by personnel of Heim Harz. (*Private collection*)

One of the head nurses, Oberschwester Luise W. (full surname unknown), was definitely a fanatical Nazi, a fact that nearly cost the life of Eberhard Brandenburg, a Luftwaffe doctor who had been transferred to the clinic in May 1944. He was reported to the Gestapo by Ebner in 1945 for undermining morale and anti-state propaganda, after the Oberschwester had reported these statements to the Lebensborn Zentrale. Brandenburg was arrested in November 1944 and held in a Gestapo cell until the end of the war. He owed his life to Germany's surrender.

Heim Kurmark, a maternity hospital with a children's home, was located in the former sanatorium Klosterheide in the town of the same name, about 40 kilometres northeast of Berlin. Kurmark opened in September 1937 and had a capacity for twenty-eight mothers and thirty children. In later years, the number of places for mothers was reduced and that for children increased to twenty-three and eighty-six beds respectively. The home was evacuated at the end of 1944 when the Red Army approached. More than 1,000 children were probably born here.

Heim Pommern was the first of two maternity hospitals with children's homes that opened in 1938. This institution was housed in the former Kurhaus

Heim Kurmark in Klosterheide, about 40 kilometres northeast of Berlin, was housed in a former sanatorium. In the second half of its existence, this maternity clinic and children's home accommodated twenty-three women and eighty-six children. (*Public domain*)

Luisenbad. The luxurious complex was donated to Hitler in October 1937 by the city of Bad Polzin (now Połczyn-Zdrój, Poland), who gave it to Lebensborn not much later. This must have been an extraordinary event for Himmler, as not only would this allow Lebensborn to expand its capacity quickly and at low cost, but even more importantly had Hitler's explicit support. It was opened on 1 May 1938 after a thorough renovation and expansion and had a capacity of

Heim Pommern, in the city of Bad Polzin, was located in the former Kurhaus Luisenbad. The city council had offered it to Hitler in 1937, who shortly afterwards donated it to Lebensborn. (*Private collection*)

A community room in Heim Pommern. The building was spaciously furnished and equipped with central heating. (*Lebensborn brochure*)

sixty mother's beds and seventy-five children's beds. It is not known how many children were born here in total, but in September 1943 there were already 970 births registered here. In a later phase of the war, Polish and Czech children were also placed here to become 'Germanized'.

Some surviving letters illustrate the fate of a little boy named Jürgen Weise, who was born at Pommern on 5 June 1941. Some six months after his birth, a report noted that while the child had developed well physically, he appeared to be mentally underdeveloped. 'It is inevitable that the child will be referred to a psychiatric institution', the conclusion read. Two months later, Inge Viermetz wrote to SS-Oberführer Ebner that 'SS-Standartenführer Sollmann has decided that the child will be transferred to the *Landesanstalt* in Görden'. What this meant was perfectly clear to everyone, but it was reaffirmed in writing a few weeks later, when Ebner wrote a short note to the leader of Heim Pommern: 'Dear Comrade Düker, in case the *Landesheilanstalt* has not sent Görden a message, I share with you herewith for your information that the child Jürgen Weise died in the institution there on February 23'.[3]

The home was closed in late February 1945 as the Red Army approached rapidly. The children were taken first to Wiesbaden (Taunus) and then to Heim Franken.

Heim Friesland was established in the village of Hohehorst near Bremen.[4] In September 1937, the SS bought the large manor house Löhnhorst with outbuildings and a 17.5-hectre park from the German state. Although the value of the whole was still set at over 743,000 Reichsmarks on 1 January 1935, it passed into the hands of the SS for 60,000 Reichsmarks not much later. After a major renovation, an extremely luxurious maternity hospital with a capacity for thirty-four mothers and forty-five children was opened on 1 May 1938, with the first baby being born a week before the official opening. The baby's mother was Margot Holm, who also became the clinic's first Oberschwester. In total, 217 children are said to have been born in Heim Friesland.

The Bavarian SS-Untersturmführer Otto Bachschneider was the home's first administrator. He lived with his wife and two children in the left gate house of the extensive complex. It is unknown whether Bachschneider was a faithful follower of Himmler and fanatically obeyed his orders about begetting as many children as possible, or whether he was guided mainly by his hormones. However, it is certain that, despite his marital status, he offered himself to a blonde, childless nurse as a potential partner. The young woman was not interested and applied for a transfer, but he had more success with another staff member, whom he approached a few weeks later. The woman would later go on to have two children by him. Bachschneider was sent to Poland by Lebensborn in 1940, where he was involved in the establishment of the Kriegsmütterheim Stettin. He was later transferred to the Höhere SS- und Polizeiführer Russland-Mitte, where, according to a friend of his wife, he 'performed very unpleasant work' before losing his life there in an unknown manner at the end of 1942 or early 1943.

Above and below: Heim Friesland, also very luxuriously decorated, was located in the former country house of Löhnhorst, in Hohehorst, near Bremen. It was opened in May 1938 but closed in early 1941 because of the bombing of Bremen. Due to the increasing lack of space, Friesland was put into use again in the second half of 1944. (*Private collection*)

Due to the lack of a Heimleiter, the course of events was determined by the Verwalter (administrator) and the Oberschwester, who were about the same level in the hierarchy. The head nurse was responsible for everything that happened within the walls of the clinic and was in charge of about twelve nurses in total. In Bachschneider's period in charge, the aforementioned Margot Holm, whose child was the first baby born in Heim Friesland, held the position of Oberschwester for a while. This was curious to say the least, since Holm had no medical or nursing training whatsoever, and therefore most likely owed her position to the status of her child's father. It is certain that he was one of the highest SS men and some colleagues were sure that it was Reinhard Heydrich. Even more puzzling was her forced departure; in the course of 1939 Holm had to leave the clinic after being accused of having a lesbian relationship with another member of staff.

Shortly afterwards the capacity of the clinic was expanded to forty places for women and sixty-four for children, but at the beginning of 1941 Heim Friesland was closed. The premature closure of one of the largest and most luxurious Lebensborn clinics was a direct result of the increasing number of RAF bombing raids on nearby Bremen. In the worst case, the clinic could be affected, but even without such an incident, the situation would have gradually become unsustainable. Due to the nightly air raids, which had started in June 1940, all residents and staff of the clinic had to rush to the air raid shelters and

The Löhnhorst country house in the early twenty-first century. On the outside, apart from the front gallery, little has changed since 1945. (*Public domain*)

wait there for the attack to end. The fear of the bombs and the exhaustion from the many sleepless nights ate at the resident's physical and mental condition and disrupted the desired order and regularity. On 6 January 1941, the order came to evacuate the clinic and three days later, forty-nine babies and ten mothers who were still breastfeeding were taken by Himmler's private plane to Heim Hochland in Steinhöring. Not much later, a number of employees were transferred to Norway to work in Lebensborn branches there.

In the second half of 1944, however, the demand for places in the Lebensborn clinics was so high that Heim Friesland was opened again. In this last period the home was led by Heimleiter SS-Sturmbannführer Walter Albrecht Lang, who had previously led the Heim Ardennen in Belgium in 1944, with Else Schwartmann as Oberschwester. It now mainly served as a children's home, where children and young mothers from other homes were taken care of. This included a group of thirty-two babies and infants who were brought here in November 1944 from Norwegian Lebensborn homes. In the first months of 1945, three more children were born. On 5 May, the estate was finally occupied by British troops and the war had finally come to an end for the staff and residents of Friesland.

Heim Wienerwald was Lebensborn's first settlement on former Austrian territory. After the German army entered the country in March 1938, the Anschluss was ratified by popular vote just one month later. There were now new opportunities here for Lebensborn and there was a great need for this, because on the one hand the lack of space in the clinics and homes increased and on the other hand it became increasingly difficult to find suitable buildings in Germany. With widespread mobilization and the establishment of numerous military and paramilitary organizations, most of the usable shelters in that country had already been seized.

It was the medical chief of Lebensborn, SS-Oberführer Gregor Ebner, who took the initiative. Less than a month after the Anschluss, he and SS-Standartenführer Pflaum, at that time still the business leader of the organization, approached Himmler with a request for the Gestapo's help in seizing homes and their contents.[5] Ebner had prepared well. Earlier, presumably even before the official Anschluss, the SS-Oberführer had travelled all over the country looking for buildings that would be suitable for opening a new branch. He was in a hurry not only because of the lack of space at Lebensborn, but also because he no doubt realized that many other military and paramilitary organizations had similar plans and that Lebensborn had to be quick to claim a share of the loot.

Ebner was successful. Shortly after the Anschluss, the Gestapo seized three buildings at his direction that were owned by Jewish families or other 'public enemies'. These were a children's home in Neulengbach, a lung sanatorium in Feichtenbach, and Schloss Oberweis in Laakirchen, near Gmunden. The first complex, the children's home, would remain the property of Lebensborn but would never be used by the organization. It seems the necessary renovation would have cost too much money and so the building was instead rented to the Wehrmacht. Schloss Oberweis also turned out to be less suitable on closer inspection and selling the complex was initially considered, but a few years later it was put into use.

The sanatorium Wienerwald in the town of Feichtenbach, about 60 kilometres northwest of Vienna, met most of Lebensborn's requirements. The extensive, very luxurious complex was built in 1904 on the initiative of two Jewish pulmonologists, Hugo Kraus and Arthur Baer. Thanks to the expertise of the doctors – especially Kraus, was world famous – the modern medical devices and techniques, and the well-equipped accommodation, meant the sanatorium soon acquired a particularly good reputation and was able to treat the Austrian upper class to its patients. The sanatorium was repeatedly modernized and expanded and just before the war the complex consisted of a large main building with a collection of outbuildings on a 34-hectare site.

On 21 April 1938, Lebensborn reported to the sanatorium in the person of SS-Obersturmbannführer Guntram Pflaum, accompanied by a Gestapo unit,

Heim Wienerwald could accommodate up to forty-nine women and eighty-three children. (*Public domain*)

and was received by Kraus. It is not exactly known what happened then, but brute force was used and Kraus was probably stabbed in the chest with a knife or bayonet. He died in hospital three days later. Whether he was mortally wounded by the SS or committed suicide out of desperation has never been clarified. His colleague Baer survived the meeting with Lebensborn's delegation a little longer. He was taken to Vienna by the Gestapo and, after a day-long interrogation, during which he was undoubtedly badly abused, he left the sanatorium. After he was released, Baer fled to his brother in the Protectorate of Bohemia-Moravia where he died penniless in 1941, officially of a heart ailment but possibly by suicide. After Wienerwald had thus fallen into the hands of the Gestapo, it was handed over to Lebensborn in its entirety, including its contents, and any cash and securities that were found on the spot.

The sanatorium was renovated in the summer and autumn, and on 1 November 1938, the organization opened a maternity hospital there. It was initially called Ostmark (Austria's official name since October 1938), but the name was soon changed to Wienerwald for unknown reasons. The clinic housed up to forty-nine women and eighty-three children. Between November 1938 and April 1945, between 1,200 and 1,700 babies were recorded there, the vast majority of which were born in normal hospitals or maternity hospitals. It is said that this was Himmler's favourite clinic, and he is frequently mentioned as godfather in the clinic's birth records.

A postcard from around 1940 showing Lebensborn Heim Wienerwald in Feichtenbach, in annexed Austria. (*Österreichische Nationalbibliothek*)

In April 1942, the Heimleiter wrote to Ebner that 'a mentally underdeveloped infant' had to be transferred to the Wiener Städtische Fürsorge-Anstalt Am Spiegelgrund because they were engaged in '*Ausmerze*' (extermination).[6] Unusual in this communication was the open language; that Lebensborn would kill children with mental or physical disabilities. In the spring of 1943 Sollmann was called twice by the Heimleiter, at that time SS-Hauptsturmführer Schwab, who had a thorny problem with a pregnant Gestapo employee admitted to his clinic. Because the matter also had to be recorded on paper, Schwab wrote him a letter shortly afterwards:

> This is about the mother Agnes Spangenberg. Already at the beginning of her stay here she caused considerable unrest among the mothers by gossip about her activities with the Gestapo in Smolensk. She gave detailed descriptions of mass executions of Jews, in which infants were also allegedly killed by a shot in the neck. I made it very clear to her at the time that such descriptions certainly do not belong in a birth clinic.[7]

The 'talk', however, did not seem to be the biggest problem and Sollmann and Schwab did not go into further detail about the mass murder and the gruesome details. The straw that apparently really broke the camel's back – and the immediate reason for Schwab to contact Sollmann – was that Gestapo employee Spangenberg now also had complaints about the food, made all kinds of demands, and had stated that the care in the East would have been much better. In consultation with Sollmann, the woman was removed from the clinic a few days later.

Heim Schwarzwald in Nordrach, about 30 kilometres southeast of Strasbourg, opened in November 1942. It was the last institution in Lebensborn to combine the functions of maternity hospital and children's home. Schwarzwald was housed in a luxurious building that had belonged to the Adelheid von Rothschild foundation since 1905 and served as a sanatorium for Jewish girls and women with lung diseases. On 29 September 1942, the sanatorium was surrounded by the SS and the patients and staff were rounded up and taken to the Theresienstadt concentration camp. Most of them would later be killed in Auschwitz.

Shortly after the SS took over the sanatorium, Lebensborn opened the Schwarzwald maternity clinic there. The first Heimleiter and doctor was SS-Obersturmführer August Hagemeijer who served there until February 1943. Between the end of 1942 and April 1945, when the home was evacuated, around

An early twentieth-century postcard showing the sanatorium for Jewish girls and women with lung diseases in Nordrach. After it was seized by the SS in 1942, the patients and staff were deported and for the most part would be murdered in Auschwitz. Lebensborn later opened the Schwarzwald maternity hospital there. (*Private collection*)

250 children are said to have been born there. Ironically, the same institution – located about 20 kilometres from the French border – was used by the French authorities after the war to detain children of German mothers and French fathers (former prisoners of war and forced labourers, but also soldiers of the occupying forces) before deciding whether they were eligible to be transferred to France.

Heim Taunus was not far from Wiesbaden and opened its doors on 1 November 1939. It was housed in a complex where the Catholic children's home *Antoniusheim* had been located a few months earlier. In September 1939, under heavy pressure from the Gestapo, it was handed over by the church and leased to the SS for a period of ninety-nine years. Taunus was initially only a children's home with room for fifty-five children, making it the first Lebensborn location without a maternity hospital.

Taunus was closed in November 1941 and only reopened after an extensive renovation in the autumn of 1943, now also as a birth clinic. Between 1943 and the end of the war, about 500 births took place there, some of them to 'ordinary' mothers from Wiesbaden, where the general birth clinic had

Above and below: A postcard of the future Lebensborn home Taunus, which first housed a restaurant and then a Catholic children's home before it was taken over by the SS. Opened on 1 November 1939 and closed two years later due to poor structural conditions, Taunus reopened after a renovation in the autumn of 1943 as a maternity hospital. (*Private collection*)

been destroyed by bombing. In addition, deliveries must have taken place of women who were previously admitted to other Lebensborn locations. From August 1944, Heim Taunus was used as an intermediate station for the children, mothers and staff of the homes that had to be evacuated due to the Allied advance. It was closed in March 1945, just before the arrival of the US Army.

Children's Homes

Heim Sonnenwiese was opened in November 1942. It was located in the town of Kohren-Sahlis, about 50 kilometres south of Leipzig, and was housed in a recently built nursing home. It was completed in July 1941, but less than three months later, under heavy pressure from the SS, the city council sold it to Lebensborn. The official opening took place on 1 November 1942, when the building was converted into a children's home with 170 places. However, the first children had already arrived in the summer, presumably because of the gradual closure of Kinderheim Taunus. An average of 130 children lived in Sonnenwiese, most of them being 3 years old or younger.

Around thirty-five employees worked in Sonnenwiese, of which about twenty were nurses under the 'braune' Oberschwester Erika Wittmann. The first doctor of the home was soon succeeded by Hildegard Feith, a fanatical and early supporter of the Nazis. (This also applied to her husband Alfons Feith, an SS-member since 1933, who participated in a five-week training course at the SS-Totenkopfverbände in Dachau and from 1937 was assigned as a volunteer to the Leibstandarte-SS Adolf Hitler.)

During the period that Hildegard Feith was a doctor in Sonnenwiese, eight or nine children who were born with abnormalities were transferred to

The Kinderheim Sonnenwiese in Kohren-Sahlis, about 50 kilometres south of Leipzig, opened in November 1942. (*Private collection*)

This decorative dish, decorated with an eagle and a swastika, was presented to Oberschwester Erika Wittmann by the employees and residents of Heim Sonnenwiese for her anniversary. The inscription reads: '*Der Leiterin des Lebensborn Heimes "Sonnenwiese" / Erika Wittmann / zu Ihrem Jubiläum / Von den Mitarbeiter und Bewohner des Heim / Dr. N. Sauer H. Soling. W. Jandzincky. F. Ballach. P Kemper. B. Skonlock(?) / R. Bauer. M. Peterson G. Stulz. A. von Reitzensie. F. (?) / April 1943.*' (*USHMM Collection 2001.204.6*)

a special institution to be murdered, including some children born in Norway. In most cases they were taken to the Kinderfachabteilung of the Landesanstalt Grossschweidnitz near Dresden, where the children were first starved and dehydrated, after which they were killed with medicines.

The home also played an important role in the Germanization of foreign children from Slovenia, Poland and especially Norway. About 150 to 200 very young children came from the latter country. It was also used in the last months of the war to house women and children from the former occupied territories. Sonnenwiese was closed in April 1945.

Heim Alpenland was the second Lebensborn house on the territory of annexed Austria.[8] The children's home was opened after a renovation in the autumn of 1943 and furnished with six freight wagons using items delivered by the Gestapo that had been taken from Jewish families. It could accommodate forty to fifty children and was set up especially for the Germanization of foreign children. About twenty-five people worked there, mostly unmarried women who had given birth in a Lebensborn clinic, but also a number of SS men and female prisoners from Ravensbrück concentration camp.

The home was located in Schloss Oberweis, in Laakirchen near Gmunden on the Traunsee. After the Anschluss, the owner was arrested because was considered an 'enemy of the state' and transferred to Dachau concentration camp. Shortly afterwards, the manor was confiscated by the Gestapo and handed over to Lebensborn in April 1938. When business manager Pflaum arrived a month later to inspect the new property, he ordered the wife of the owner, who still lived in the property, to leave within three days. Ebner, in turn, threatened the housekeeper with arrest if she did not leave immediately when he came to vacation there with his family in the summer.

The country house and its outbuildings was situated on a spacious 14-hectare estate close to an important thoroughfare and train station, and was therefore very suitable in terms of location. However, the structural condition was so bad that a very costly and time-consuming renovation would be necessary to make it suitable as a maternity hospital, which was the original intention. The decision was taken to sell it, but when no buyer had been found by the end of 1940, it was leased to the VoMi. This organization set up a transit camp for Volksdeutsche, until Lebensborn took over again in the summer of 1943 and opened the Alpenland children's home in September of that year after a renovation. The caretaker was SS-Oberscharführer Jakob Pfaffenberger, a member of the Waffen-SS who was unfit for active service due to a serious war

An eighteenth-century engraving of Schloss Oberweis in annexed Austria, where Kinderheim Alpenland was established in 1943. (*Private collection*)

injury and who had previously worked in Heim Pommern. The Heimleiters were all female: first Maria Plate, then Hedwig Ridder and from September 1944 to April 1945 Maria Knipp-Merkel, one of Lebensborn's most important collaborators. She had worked at the headquarters in Munich and the Krakow branch and combined her position in Alpenland with that of head of department R IV of the Reichszentrale. This department was responsible for the mediation of the so-called 'Volksdeutsche orphans' and was transferred to Alpenland when Munich had become too dangerous due to Allied air raids. The other parts of the Zentrale had moved to Hochland in Steinhöring.

It was no coincidence that Knipp-Merkel went to Alpenland with this specific department. This children's home was established and used exclusively for the 'Germanization' of foreign children, especially from Poland, who were brought here from the Gaukinderheim Kalisch. In September 1943 the first sixteen children arrived, with the final group arriving in December 1944. In total about 230 foreign children stayed in Alpenland; all between 4 and 15 years old. In addition to Poland, a small number of children came from the Banat (an area on the border of Romania, Serbia and Hungary), the annexed part of Slovenia that had been given the German name Südsteiermark, and two boys from Czechoslovakia. The latter two areas concerned children whose parents had been murdered or sent to concentration camps because of alleged resistance activities.

Alpenland was the only Lebensborn settlement where only foreign children were housed and the treatment differed greatly from that in the other children's homes. The aim of the stay was to Germanize them as quickly and thoroughly as possible and to that end the children lived according to a strict programme, mainly involving German: speaking, writing, reading and singing. The daily walk after lunch consisted of marching while singing National Socialist songs.

Although some testimonies from children say they were treated well, most, the boys in particular, stated that Alpenland had a very strict regime, that they often went hungry and that they could be severely punished for 'misconduct'. Not a word of Polish was allowed to be spoken, every assignment had to be carried out immediately, all contact with the outside world was forbidden and they were absolutely not allowed to leave the home. Those who did not immediately obey, spoke Polish or broke any other rule could be beaten or kicked, locked in a small dark box, or be forced to stand for hours at night on roll call and not be given food – sometimes for three days. The boys were subjected to strict paramilitary training by the Hitler Youth cadre and had to practise with weapons in uniform before they were 10 years old, sometimes even at night.

After the children in Alpenland had, in the opinion of the management, been sufficiently Germanized, they were eligible to be placed with German foster parents. Although they had not been treated kindly at all during their stay at the home, Lebensborn subjected potential foster parents to thorough research to ensure that the children would receive proper care. Their financial situation, state of health and housing (the foster child had to have their own bedroom) were viewed, a long questionnaire had to be completed and statement about their behaviour had to be submitted. Contrary to what one might expect, the political affiliation of the prospective foster parents was not decisive.

If the foster parents met all Lebensborn's requirements, they were invited to come to Laakirchen and choose a child from Alpenland. The desired age was announced in advance and people had let them know whether they wanted a boy or a girl. On arrival, the future foster parents were received by Knipp-Merkel and then taken to a room where there were some children who met the foster parents' wishes. After being left alone with the children for some time, the foster parents were able to make a choice and pass it on to Knipp-Merkel.

The building where Alpenland was located as seen at the beginning of the twenty-first century. Its outside appearance has probably changed little from its time during the Third Reich. (*Public domain*)

After that, the formalities were immediately taken care of, with the child being handed over and leaving with its new foster parents that same day. Lebensborn's own registry office provided the correct papers and, if desired, changed the child's name to that of the new foster parents. However, the children were not adopted and did not disappear from Lebensborn's sight either. The foster parents were required to report quarterly and Lebensborn staff also made home visits. There is a known case of a foster child who turned out to be abused, after which the organization had the child placed in another family.

The vast majority of the approximately 230 children who stayed in Alpenland eventually ended up with German foster parents. When the home had to be evacuated at the beginning of April 1945 due to the military situation, twenty-six boys were still present. They finally experienced the end of the war in a childcare camp, 50 kilometres away.

Heim Franken I and II were the last branches that Lebensborn opened. It concerned two children's homes near Ansbach-Schalkhausen in Bavaria. Due to the increasing danger of air raids, Lebensborn had started looking for suitable locations sometime in the first half of 1944 and two buildings were found at Schalkhausen that suited its purposes. On 1 June of that year, a request for exemption from the construction ban was submitted to the Reichsministerium Speer for two 'temporary children's homes for areas endangered by air raids'. According to the application, not much needed to be done, just painting and some improvements to the sanitary facilities. In addition, Lebensborn reported that it had the necessary items and that 'the renovation work would be carried out by its own workers'. This undoubtedly meant that forced labourers would be used.

The homes were taken into use in June 1944. It was no coincidence that they were in the south of Germany, as far away as possible from the approaching Allied forces from the East and (later) from the West, and within the fictitious Alpenfestung – the sector some believed to be the last position of the German army. Both homes were mainly used for the temporary care of children from settlements that were threatened by the enemy advance and air raids, and who later often went to Heim Hochland in Steinhöring.

Kinderheim Franken I was located on the Bocksberg in Ansbach-Schalkhausen on the western side of the city. The building housed a convalescent home from 1928, until it was sold ten years later and served for some time as a training centre where 'hereditary healthy' young men received paramilitary training. Franken II was settled a few kilometres to the southeast and was housed in the former Heil- und Pflegeanstalt Ansbach. In 1940 and 1941, almost 900 patients were deported and murdered from this institution, a

Above: Kinderheim Franken I was located on the Bocksberg in Ansbach-Schalkhausen and was opened in June 1944 to receive children from other homes who had to be evacuated due to aerial threat or the advancing enemy. (*Public domain*)

Right: *Neues Volk* was the monthly magazine of the *Rassenpolitischen Amtes der NSDAP* and – as the name says – was completely devoted to race politics. The magazine had a circulation of many hundreds of thousands and was mainly filled with articles about the superiority of the Germanic race, the threat of the Jews etc. The magazine also published a calendar and the front cover of this 1938 edition shows the Aryan ideal, although it is curious that only one child is depicted. (*Public domain*)

former care and nursing home, as part of Aktion T4, while about 150 disabled children were killed on the spot. Hundreds of patients also died of starvation and forced sterilization took place on a large scale.

Little is known about the leadership, the number of places and the occupation of Franken I and II. The capacity was probably several dozen children. The home was evacuated and closed in April 1945.

VIII

CHILD ABDUCTION

Lebensborn in Central and Eastern Europe

'I really intend to get Germanic blood in all the world, to rob and steal where I can.'

Heinrich Himmler

Racial Selection

To realize the aim of the pure-bred, autarkic Greater Germanic state, the territory of the German Empire had to be expanded eastwards, mainly at the expense of Poland and the Soviet Union. After that, the newly acquired territory had to be stripped of the population and populated with people who met the highest racial requirements of the Nazis. In practice, this policy meant the mass murder of the Jews, the expulsion of a large part of the remaining Slavic inhabitants and the repopulation of the annexed areas with people selected on the basis of racial aspects.

Two organizations were set up especially for the ethnic cleansing and repopulation of the annexed territories. The first was the *Umwandererzentralstelle* (UWZ), initially called the *'Amt für die Umsiedlung der Polen und Juden*'. This organization was charged with deporting undesirables. At the beginning of the war, before the Holocaust was decided, German policy was aimed at expelling the Jews to the East, together with the other inhabitants of the annexed Polish territory, who were undesirable to the Nazis. The UWZ had to carry out this task and between the end of 1939 and the spring of 1941 it deported almost half a million Poles and Jews from the areas to be 'Germanized'. Because of the way this happened, without proper preparation, means of transport, shelter or care, many thousands of deportees died of deprivation.

The other organization for the repopulation policy was the Einwandererzentralstelle (EWZ). It was responsible for the return, selection, resettlement and integration of ethnic Volks- and Reichsdeutsche. On arrival from their original residential areas, these people were thoroughly examined

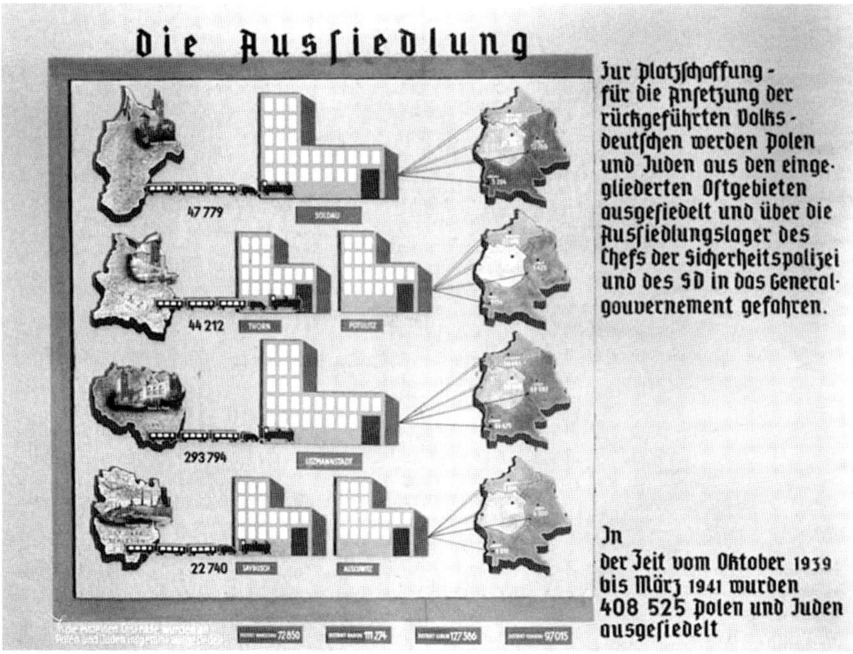

The deportation of 'undesirables' from the annexed Polish territories was no secret. Indeed, diagrams like this showed exactly what was happening. The text reads, 'To make room for the settlement of the returned Volksdeutsche, Poles and Jews are expelled from the annexed areas in the east and taken to the Generalgouvernement via the transit camps of the chief of the Sicherheitspolizei and the SD.' 'In the period from October 1939 to March 1941, 408,525 Poles and Jews were expelled.' (*Private collection*)

by the EWZ, including health, racial characteristics and political views, and then assigned to a certain class. This classification determined where they were sent next: the German Empire, the annexed territory in the East, or back to their original homeland.

It was not just ethnic Germans who were brought in for the repopulation, but also Germans and residents of other occupied, Germanic countries who were encouraged to move to the East. However, because there were not enough settlers, the non-German population of the annexed territory was also subjected to a racial survey. The German racial ideologues generally regarded Poles, Russians and Czechs as inferior because they belonged to the Slavic people, but they also considered the Slavs as a mixed race, in which parts of 'good blood' could also be found. This had to be removed by means of a varietal study and those that were considered valuable as varietal, and therefore suitable for 're-Germanization' (*Wiedereindeutschfähig*), could remain in the territory of the Third Reich or

Above: Driven from their village, a long column of Polish civilians set out on foot under German guard towards an uncertain future. According to the original caption, the photograph was taken in Wartheland, the German name for part of the annexed Polish territory. (*Bundesarchiv R-49-Bild-0131*)

Left: An official of the Einwandererzentralstelle addresses a group of Volksdeutsche, presumably to inform them that they will be assigned a house (of an expelled Pole). The group is in a compartment of a special EWZ train. (*Bundesarchiv Bild 137-068859*)

the newly annexed territories. All the others – the vast majority – were to be expelled, enslaved, or murdered according to guidelines Himmler proposed to Hitler in 1940 and later laid down in the Generalplan Ost.

Children had special attention in Himmler's plans for the future, and not only because of the desired population growth. The Reichsführer-SS was so convinced of the hereditary properties of good blood that he thought he

The 14-year-old Czesława Kwoka was one of the unfortunate children deported and sent to Auschwitz as part of an 'unwanted population'. Upon arrival, Polish prisoner Wilhelm Brasse took these standard identification photographs of her. He survived the war and later stated that he remembered her because she looked so young in the prisoner's clothing. When the SS guard called her number, he said, she did not understand because she did not speak German. She was immediately whipped in the face by the woman. These photographs, taken straight after, show her bloody lip and look of dismay. Czesława was murdered on 12 March 1943 by an injection of phenol in the chest cavity. (*Public domain*)

could prevent the emergence of a leading class in the subjugated countries by transferring the racially valuable children to Germany. As early as November 1938, almost a year before Nazi Germany unleashed war, he declared:

> All the good blood in the world, all the Germanic blood that is not on the side of Germany, may one day spell our downfall. Therefore, every Germanic with the best blood that we bring to Germany and make into a German-conscious Germanic is a fighter for us and one less on the other side. I really intend to get Germanic blood in all the world, to rob and steal where I can.[1]

When Himmler put down his plans for the future of the original population of the conquered territories in the East, he paid extensive attention to the children. For example, in the previously cited *'Denkschrift über die Behandlung der Fremdvölkischen im Osten'22* he called the education and selection of youth a 'fundamental issue'. Non-German children were to have a very minimal education at a four-year primary school; no other education was allowed. Parents who wanted to give their children a better education had to submit an application to the SS. The verdict mainly depended 'on whether the child is racially perfect and meets our criteria' and 'if we recognize such a child as our blood', Himmler continued, then the child would be allowed to go to school in Germany. The parents were given the choice of relinquishing the child – 'then they will probably not father any further children, so that the danger disappears that this "Untermenschenvolk des Ostens" acquires a dangerous, for us equal, leadership class through such people of good blood' – or had to come to Germany and become loyal citizens there. In addition to these special cases, he proposed an annual survey of all 6 to 10-year-old children to select those with 'valuable blood' and transfer them to Germany. The parents would be faced with the same choice as those whose children would go to school in Germany.

Although there was not enough time to put all the plans into practice, a large number of children from Central and Eastern Europe were abducted during the German occupation. The exact numbers have never been traced, but it is certain that many tens of thousands of children were involved, with estimates ranging from 50,000 to several hundred thousand. By far the largest number of them came from Poland, but children from the Soviet Union (particularly Belarus and Ukraine), Yugoslavia (Slovenia) and Czechoslovakia were also deported. Most of the kidnapped children were taken to Germany as forced labourers, where they were employed as farm or factory workers or as maids. The minimum age was initially around 14 years (in occupied and annexed Poland the Germans had introduced a legal obligation to work from that age), but later much younger children were also taken and used as forced labourers. In addition, an unknown number of older non-German boys received military training and ended up in the German army or the SS.

In the summer of 1941, in the vicinity of Minsk, Kostja Pablowitsch Harelek was personally chosen by Himmler to be Germanized. Together with his brother Pawel, he eventually ended up at the national school for Volksdeutsche in Rouffach, in Alsace (at the time territory annexed by Germany and called Rufach), now renamed Konstantin Gerelik. Himmler personally kept himself informed about the boys' fate. (*Public domain*)

Lebensborn participated in the kidnapping of children in Central and Eastern Europe, but played a minor role. The organization was engaged in the shelter and Germanization of a number of the 'racially most high-quality' children, probably about 1,000 girls and boys in total, but it had no involvement with the vast majority of the abducted children. Other German authorities, including the RuSHA, RSHA (as part of the RKFDV) and the NSV, were responsible for this.

Poland: Mass 'Germanization'

In Poland, the Nazis' race and power politics were practiced to the extreme because a large part of the country was designated for German colonization and the racial ideologues regarded the population mainly as inferior. The occupation was characterized by lawlessness, terror and violence on an unprecedented scale, annexation of territory, large-scale looting and slave labour, ethnic cleansing, mass deportations, repopulation, child abduction, elimination of the ruling class and the mass murder of Polish and foreign Jews.

The German army invaded Poland on 1 September 1939, followed by the Red Army on 17 September. At the beginning of October, the last Polish unit was forced to lay down its arms and the German-Russian occupation began, dividing the country into three parts. The eastern half was annexed by the Soviet Union, the middle part became the so-called Generalgouvernement under German administration, and the western provinces were annexed by Germany. The latter area was divided into three new Reichsgaue with the names Danzig-Westpreussen, Wartheland and Oberschlesien.

In these annexed areas, the so-called *Deutsche Volksliste* (DVL) was introduced, the most important instrument of the Germanization policy, with people who appeared on the list being considered German. Depending on the category into which one was placed (I to IV), this could result in rights and privileges, including in regard to food supply and education, but also duties, such as conscription in the German army. Part of the population volunteered, but many others resisted inclusion on the list: most Poles did not want to be registered as German. The criteria for inclusion on the DVL were applied very differently per Gau and depended on the politics of the local Nazi leader.

In addition to Germanizing the population with the help of the DVL, the occupiers in Poland also went in search of Polish children who would qualify for Germanization because of their racial characteristics. Most of the children who would fall victim to these practices came from the Reichsgau Wartheland. This area was governed by Reichsstatthalter and SS-Obergruppenführer Arthur

Greiser, an early member of the Nazi Party and the SS and a racial fanatic, who was determined to Germanize his territory in the shortest possible time and by all means necessary.

In Litzmannstadt (Łodż), the capital of this particular Gau, Polish children were already being investigated in the autumn of 1940 for the possibility of Germanizing them, initially in orphanages as little resistance from the population was expected. To conceal the origin and nationality, also for the (future) foster parents, the children were called 'German orphans from the regained areas in the East' or simply of '*Ostkinder*'. The Germans wanted to pretend that these were orphans of ethnic German parents who had been given a Polish name by the pre-war authorities. In the vast majority of cases this was not true and it concerned Polish children. In the search for 'racially desirable' children, the occupiers thus initially focused on orphanages, but later foster children who had been placed with relatives or children who simply lived with their parents were also abducted. In many cases they were called for a so-called health examination. Often the 'approved' children had to stay immediately after such an investigation and the family was told that they would return 'after the war'. But brutal violence was also not shunned and sometimes the children were taken from school, picked up on the street or literally pulled from the arms of their (foster) parents at home.

Many of the victims were children of parents who refused to undergo a racial test or to be registered on the DVL, children from German-Polish marriages or unmarried mothers, and children of forced labourers, (concentration camp) prisoners, or Poles who had been murdered by the occupying forces. From the end of 1941,

Polish boys being examined for their racial value at an unknown location. The logo on the white coat leaves no doubt about the agency that is carrying out the selection. (*Public domain*)

when the so-called Special Criminal Law for Poland had come into effect and the Polish population had also been legally degraded to a nation with virtually no rights, this German law was often used to 'legalize' the kidnapping of children. Resistance by the guardians or parents was futile and often ended in imprisonment.

After the kidnapping and Germanization of Polish children on the initiative of local German authorities had been going on for more than a year, an official policy document was published in February 1942, designated Decree 67/I. It was commissioned by Himmler by the Chief of Staff of the RKFDV, SS-Obergruppenfüher Ulrich Greifelt, and was entitled 'The Germanization of Children from Polish Families and Former Polish Orphanages'. The document described in detail why and how Polish children had to be Germanized and a number of German authorities were assigned a task in these practices. As justification, it was again – and wrongly – proclaimed that many children with Nordic parents had been systematically placed in Polish orphanages and with Polish foster parents and had been given Polish names. That practice now had to be overturned: 'The children whose racial characteristics indicate Nordic descent must be reclaimed for the Deutschtum; it is therefore necessary that

A Polish girl seen being forcibly taken away from her family. This photograph was taken in the Zamość region, where the Germans carried out large-scale ethnic cleansing (*'Aktion Zamosc'*) between November 1942 and March 1943. At the same time, approximately 30,000 children were abducted and then classified according to their race value. (*Public domain*)

a racial and physical selection is carried out among the orphans in Polish orphanages or with Polish foster parents. The children who are considered a valuable asset to Germanism must be Germanized.'[3]

Although the decree only referred to orphans, the relevant German authorities had previously agreed not to limit themselves to this. This group would also be followed by the children who had one or more parents eligible for Germanization, and finally also the children of parents who did not: in other words, all children. From May 1943, children were even taken from Auschwitz, several hundred in all, all with blond hair and blue eyes.

According to the procedure laid down in the decree, the children first had to be subjected to a racial examination at the RuSHA office in Litzmannstadt by the SS-Eignungsprüfer – in practice this also happened at other locations. The assessment was based on twenty-one physical characteristics such as the shape of the skull, face and nose, and the colour of the eyes, hair and skin. This data was recorded on the so-called R-Karte (Race Card) which would accompany the child on his or her further journey through the institutions. A series of photographs were also taken. Based on this information, the race value was determined and the child was assigned to one of four groups: from 'racially valuable' to 'racially undesirable'.

For the children who met the highest racial requirements, a very extensive health examination followed, including X-rays and a tuberculosis test, after which – if found to be healthy – they were transferred to a special children's home where they would stay for six to twelve weeks for observation and to learn

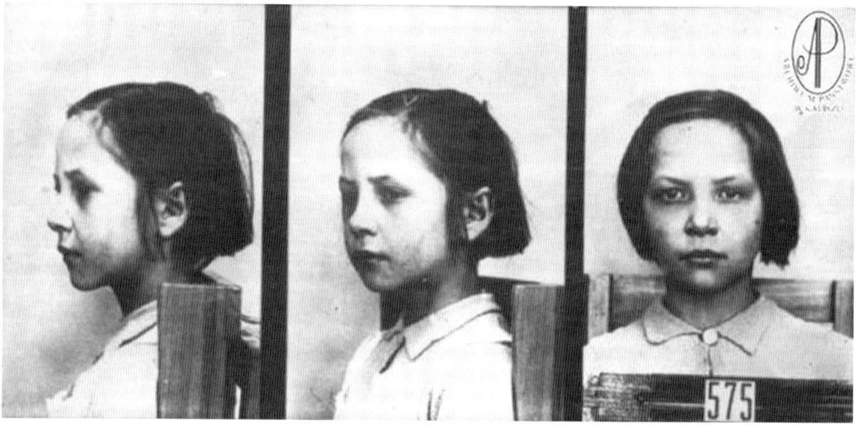

The selected children were extensively examined, with their data being recorded on a so-called Rassenkarte and a series of photographs taken of them. This girl stayed in the Gaukinderheim Kalisch. (*Archiwa Panstwowe Kaliszu*)

the German language. There were three such homes (called Gaukiderheime, because they were under the responsibility of the Gau) in the towns of Brockau (Brochów), Puschkau (Pastuchów) and Kalisch (Kalisz). This last children's home also had its own *polizeiliche Meldestelle* (Police Registration Office). Through this agency, the reporting of the child's whereabouts, which was compulsory in the Third Reich, could be registered, making it impossible for the children's families to find them. In Puschkau there was also a subsection of the Standesamt L, Lebensborn's own registry office, where the children could be provided with a forged birth certificate.

In the children's homes, a psychologist (the very well-known Professor Dr Hildegard Hetzer, who was able to continue her academic career after the war) conducted psychological tests. In addition, the head of the children's home drew up a characterological assessment at the end of the stay. Based on this report and the psychological tests, a final decision was made as to which children were eligible for Germanization. In contrast to the children born in the Lebensborn clinics, the Polish children who had to be Germanized in the three children's homes were treated very harshly. They had to learn German

Staff of the Gaukinderheim Kalisch. In this institution, where the first phase of the Germanization took place, the Polish children were treated very harshly. (*Archiwa Państwowe Kaliszu*)

as quickly as possible and were not allowed to speak Polish. Violations of this prohibition were subject to harsh penalties; the children were denied food, were locked in a cupboard or cage, or were beaten with a cane. An unknown number did not survive the stay and the beatings.

At the end of the stay in the children's home, their future fate depended on age. If they were between 6 and 12 years old, and therefore of compulsory school age, they were initially placed in a *Heimschule* (a National Socialist boarding school) in Germany. This involved a total of about 200 children, the first group of which was transferred to Germany in the summer of 1942. The girls went to the Heimschule in Achern, the boys to Niederalteich. Once again, these boarding schools, officially called *Reichsschule für Volksdeutsche*, followed a very strict regime to Germanize the children as quickly as possible. To this end, the girls also became compulsory members of the Bund Deutscher Mädel and the boys of the Hitlerjugend.

The younger children were sent to a Lebensborn home. The first group arrived in Heim Pommern in Bad Polzin (Połczyn-Zdrój) in the summer of 1942. Later, Polish children also went to Hochland in Steinhöring, Sonnenwiese in Kohren-Sahlis and Moselland in annexed Luxembourg. Although all these children had been extensively examined and selected by the race experts of the RuSHA

The Heimschule in Niederalteich, officially called Reichsschule für Volksdeutsche, was housed in a building of the former Niederaltaich monastery, seen here in an aerial photograph from 1938. (*Private collection*)

and SS doctors, had undergone psychological tests and a characterological assessment, they were not simply admitted to Lebensborn homes without question. The organization only wanted the 'best' offspring, so they were re-examined by Ebner upon arrival. Several children were still rejected by him and sent back to the Warthegau. From September 1943, after Lebensborn had opened Heim Alpenland especially for the 'Ostkinder' in annexed Austria, the 6 to 12-year-old school-age children were housed in this home and therefore no longer attended the Heimschule.

Both at the Heimschule and in the children's homes of Lebensborn, the Polish children were further Germanized. Eventually they were placed with foster parents, preferably SS members or convinced National Socialists, to be adopted later if necessary. In practice, many children also ended up with foster parents who were not fanatical Nazis. Incidentally, it was not the intention that the German foster parents came to know the real origin of the children. One of the last paragraphs of Decree 67/I read: 'Particular attention should be paid to ensure that the expression "racially desirable Polish children" does not become known to the public and thus harm the children. The children are to be called German orphans from the regained eastern territories.'

For this reason, too, all the German institutions involved went to great lengths to hide the children's true identities. Already during the first varietal examination by the RuSHA they were given new, German-sounding names. This was not done at random: if possible, the instructions read, a name should be chosen that closely resembled the Polish in terms of spelling and sound. Thus Kazimierz was henceforth called Klaus and Zygmunt was changed to Sigmund. If it was not possible to transform their real name into German, the variety experts at RuSHA chose a new name. That had to be a generally common German name, and not a specifically Nordic one.[4]

To further obscure the origin of the children, in many cases, when they were placed with a foster family, they were again given a new German name. It was also listed on the brand-new birth certificate issued by Lebensborn's own registry office, Standesamt L in Munich (with the aforementioned sub-section in Puschkau), which had been established in April 1943 with government approval. The Ministry of the Interior had also given Lebensborn permission to declare the Polish children 'foundlings', giving the organization not only the legal right to choose the first and last name, but also the date and place of birth. Posen or Litzmannstadt were often mentioned as places of birth, in many cases the place from where the children had been abducted. The age entered on the new birth certificate was often determined by Ebner because it was unknown. To determine the correct age, an X-ray of a hand was taken if necessary and evaluated by a professor of paediatrics.

Of the many tens of thousands of children abducted from Poland to be Germanized, Lebensborn was involved in several hundred. It concerned the 'racially best' children who were placed under the guardianship of the organization in a Heimschule or ended up in a children's home of Lebensborn in the German Empire. The organization was unable to open its own maternity hospitals or children's homes in Poland and so Lebensborn's branches in this country were therefore limited to the *Kriegsmütter- und Wohnheim Johannistal* in Stettin (Szczecin) and the so-called Heimstätte in Smoszewo. There were also representatives in Posen (Poznań), Krakow (Kraków) and Litzmannstadt (Łodz).

The Krakow office had been opened in the autumn of 1942 and housed with the HSSPF in that city. It was led by Maria Knipp-Merkel who was instructed to establish maternity hospitals on the territory of the Generalgouvernement. This was ultimately unsuccessful. Plans for Lebensborn clinics always failed due to resistance from other German organizations and the army, or were overtaken by military developments. The power struggle between General Governor Hans Frank and Himmler also played an important role.

Several times Lebensborn thought it had found a suitable location, but just as often the plans had to be called off. In Krakow and the surrounding area, Lebensborn's eager eye fell on Wartenberg Castle and the women's clinic in the same city, in Lemberg (Lwów, now Lviv (Ukraine)) on a former children's home, in Otwock on the former Jewish tuberculosis sanatorium Bruijs and in Warsaw on another, unidentified building. Some plans were well advanced before Lebensborn had to abandon them. In July 1943, for example, Ebner announced that the inventory of Heim Friesland, closed shortly before, had to be transferred to Haus Wartenberg and names had already been thought up for the proposed branches in Otwock and Warsaw, with those clinics being called Ostland and Markwald respectively. In the end nothing came of it. Knipp-Merkel was transferred and later put in charge of the children's home Alpenland, which was specially intended for the Germanization of foreign children.

The only branches that Lebensborn did get off the ground in Poland were the Kriegsmütter- und Wohnheim Johannistal and the Heimstätte. The Kriegsmütterheim in Stettin, opened in June 1940, was Lebensborn's first branch in Poland. It could accommodate more than 100 mothers and children and was especially intended for working, single Aryan mothers who wanted to keep their child(ren) with them. It was founded and led for the first two years by SS-Obersturmführer Otto Bachschneider, formerly the administrator of Heim Friesland. The second Lebensborn settlement was in Smoszewo, christened Heimstätte by Himmler. It was opened in the spring of 1944 and was especially

Schloss Wartenberg, near Krakow, was to be the site of a new Lebensborn branch in July 1943, but the plan fell through at the last minute, apparently because it had been seized by the Luftwaffe. (*Private collection*)

intended for single mothers. The complex would consist of several hundred wooden houses, with a school, a childcare centre and its own health service. The Heimstätte not only served to provide shelter for the mothers and children, but also to contribute to the Germanization of the area. The project was never completed, however, because in the summer of 1944, when only a few dozen houses had been built, it was requisitioned by the Luftwaffe.

Slovenia: 'Bandit's Children'

The German army invaded Yugoslavia on 6 April 1941, and eleven days later the regular war was over. Shortly afterwards, the territory of Slovenia, the country's westernmost province, was divided between Italy, Hungary and Germany. Even before Hitler publicly declared that the parts annexed by Nazi Germany – now called Oberkrain and Untersteiermark – should become 'German again', Himmler had already ordered that a large part of the Slovenian population be expelled and the rest be racially screened. Some 80,000 Slovenians were deported, mostly to Germany as forced labourers, and Volksdeutsche from the area annexed by Italy came to the new German territory.

The forced Germanization and repopulation policy encountered increasing resistance among the population and partisan units grew rapidly, partly due to the influx of men who tried to escape forced conscription into the Wehrmacht. The Germans responded with repression and terror and in July 1942, a large-scale operation, dubbed 'Enzian', began to deal with the partisans, or 'bandits' in Nazi terminology. A vague suspicion was sufficient reason for unmerciful

After the occupation of Yugoslavia, Slovenia, the westernmost province of the country, was annexed and divided between Germany, Italy and Hungary. In the German part, ethnic cleansing and Germanization started immediately. 'It is your duty to learn and speak German', reads this placard. (*Public domain*)

The German army cracked down on the resistance. This photograph, taken on 22 June 1941 in the town of Celje, shows the execution of male and female Slovenian hostages. (*Public domain*)

action. On Himmler's orders, eleven villages were completely depopulated and destroyed. The houses were burned down, the male inhabitants executed on the spot and the women taken to a concentration camp.

The fate of the children, separated from their parents and relatives, depended on their appearance. They were taken to the originally German-speaking part of the province at Himmler's behest and examined for their 'racial characteristics'. They had the special interest of the Reichsführer-SS. 'As to the number and pedigree of these children, I expect a separate report', he ordered. According to SS-Obersturmbannführer and RuS-Führer Heinrich Obersteiner, jointly responsible for the kidnapping of the children, this was a necessary action because 'not separating them [from their family] would have meant a great danger for a real Germanization of the children, because the children would naturally learn the truth about their father's death and thus be raised with hatred of the Deutschtum'.

About 1,000 children were 'captured' in this and other operations. They were first brought together in a camp of the VoMi in a former boys' school in the Yugoslav (now Slovenian) city of Celje, where they were racially examined by SS-Hauptsturmführer Rödel of the RuSHA and assigned to one of four racial groups. The children in the highest groups I and II were given a new, German-sounding name. From August 1942 they were then transferred via Passau to camps of the VoMi in the vicinity of Bayreuth. At the beginning of 1943 there were about 600 Slovenian children, half of whom were less than 10 years old. The camps were overcrowded and living conditions were very poor.

Lebensborn was involved in the operation at Himmler's behest from the start, obviously because of the 'racially valuable' children. Inge Viermetz consulted with the

Four Slovenian girls, photographed in the camp of the Volksdeutsche Mittelstelle (VoMi) in Saldenburg, just north of Passau, were among the many hundreds of Slovenian children deported from Western Yugoslavia by the Germans. (*Public domain*)

local leaders of the SS and the VoMi on behalf of the organization in Salzburg. Initially, however, Lebensborn could only provide advice because they had no space available in their own branches. Moreover, Viermetz made it clear that the organization mainly wanted to deal with children born in its own clinics. In the end it was decided that Lebensborn would only take in the children who were no more than 3 years old. For the others, the organization would look for foster parents. However, Lebensborn also received custody of these children.

At the beginning of March 1943, the first Slovenian children were transferred to the recently opened Heim Sonnenwiese in Kohren-Sahlis. This home was mainly used for the reception and Germanization of foreign children. In the following months a small number arrived and by the beginning of 1944 there were about twenty-five Slovenian children in Sonnenwiese.

About half of these children would – highly unusually – return to their families not much later. Surviving family members or relatives of these children, who themselves had also been deported to camps in Germany, had managed to track them down. In addition, the VoMi had started a systematic search for the relatives of the children as the organization considered it desirable to Germanize the Slovenian families in their entirety and not to further arouse the resistance of the population by kidnapping their children. With this action, the VoMi did exactly the opposite of what SS-Obersturmbannführer Obersteiner had deemed necessary; they reunited the families (as much as possible) instead of deliberately separating them. This was certainly neither the first nor the last time that German organizations, in this case both under Himmler's command, energetically opposed each other.

At the end of the war eight Slovenian children were still present in Heim Sonnenwiese in Kohren-Sahlis. A few younger and about 350 older children had been placed with German foster parents by Lebensborn. Three-year-old Vili Gorucan belonged to the latter group. In operation Enzian, practically his entire family was killed by the SS and Vili, then 5 months old, was taken to Germany through the intervention of Lebensborn. He was admitted to Heim Sonnenwiese and later went as a foster child to the Heyder family, of which the head of the household was not only a fanatical Nazi but also Himmler's great-uncle. He had written a letter to the Reichsführer-SS ('Lieber Heinrich') reminding him of the promise he had made in Berchtesgaden to help them have a child. Not much later, Vili Gorucan was renamed Haymo Heinrich Heyder and lived with the family in the Bavarian Abensberg, where Himmler – to whom the child owed its middle name – came to visit them personally. Incidentally, Vili's foster parents also knew nothing about his real background. They had been told by Lebensborn that he was an orphan of murdered Volksdeutsche. It was not until 1969 that Haymo began to suspect something was wrong when he was told by the registry office that the information on his birth certificate was incorrect and that he was adopted. When he confronted his foster parents about this, he was told that his natural parents had been killed in a bombing raid. It would be many years later that the real story finally surfaced.

Czechoslovakia: the Children of Lidice and Ležáky

Lebensborn had no branches in Czechoslovakia and there was no large-scale child robbery there as there was in Poland and Slovenia. Nevertheless, the organization was involved in the fate of a number of children from that country.

Czechoslovakia was the first victim of Nazi Germany's aggressive foreign policy. After having been sacrificed by Britain and France at the Munich Conference in October 1938 for an apparent peace pledge from Hitler, his troops first occupied the Sudetenland – where the population was largely ethnic German – and six months later the rest of the country as well. Slovakia separated itself and continued as a vassal state of Nazi Germany, while Czechoslovakia came under German administration and was called the Reichsprotektorat Böhmen und Mähren by the occupying forces.

In Czechoslovakia, German occupation policy was much more moderate than in Poland. The German Reichsprotektor Konstatin von Neurath was not a fanatical Nazi, and – more importantly – it was of the utmost importance for the German war industry that the Czech armaments factories continued to operate at full capacity. Unrest among the population therefore had to be prevented as much as possible. There were indeed plans to expel a large part of the Czechs in the longer term, a total of about 3.5 million people, and to populate the vacated areas with 'purebred' Germans, but these plans remained on the backburner for the duration of the war. In preparation for this, varietal inspections were already carried out and a resettlement policy had also been developed. Land and goods destined for Aryan emigrants were seized.

The relatively stable situation was disrupted in the spring of 1942 when, on 27 May, SS-Obergruppenführer Reinhard Heydrich, the feared head of the RSHA and the deputy Reich protector, was wounded in an attack by two Czech resistance fighters and died about a week later. He had been appointed to the position in Prague more than eight months earlier because Von Neurath, in Hitler's opinion, was too soft. Hitler was furious after the successful assassination attempt and initially ordered the execution of 10,000 random

Czechs, but was persuaded to limit the reprisal action to avoid major unrest and a disruption of industrial production.

In the following days, over 3,000 people were arrested and more than 1,300 of them killed. The inhabitants of the villages of Lidice and Ležáky, whom the Germans wrongly assumed were connected to the attack, were also among the victims of the revenge attack. On the evening of 9 June, Lidice was surrounded by German police forces and all the inhabitants were rounded up the following night. The women and children were taken to the village school and the male residents over the age of 15 were herded to a farm where they were to be shot the next morning. Before their execution, they had to place mattresses against the wall behind them to prevent members of the firing squad from being hit by ricocheting bullets. The massacre, when it began, lasted more than two hours. There were 173 casualties. Six days later, another twenty-six men, who had escaped on 10 June, would be executed. The 195 female residents and their children were transported to the nearby town of Kladno, where they were separated. The women and girls aged 16 and over were taken to the Ravensbrück concentration camp, where fifty-two of them died.

Lidice, 10 June 1942. Horak farmyard with the bodies of 173 men and boys aged 16 and over. They were executed by the Germans because of the alleged connection between the village and the resistance fighters who had carried out the attack on Heydrich. Their wives and daughters aged 16 and over were deported to Ravensbrück concentration camp. (*USHMM, No. 43164*)

There were now ninety-eight children left, whose fathers had been murdered and their mothers imprisoned in a concentration camp. Only very few of these children would survive the war. One of them was Emilie Frejova, who was 8 years old at the time of the tragedy. She was an orphan and lived with her aunt and uncle in Lidice. Thanks to a statement she made in September 1947 before the Nuremberg tribunal, plus the testimony of a fellow sufferer, the then 12-year-old Maria Hanfova, what happened to the children after the German reprisal action is now understood.[5]

First, they were taken in trucks to the nearby town of Kladno and locked in a hall. They were practically left on their own and the older children had to care for the younger ones, including some babies and infants. Later they were registered and given a card with a number around their neck and ten children, including seven infants, were selected by the Germans and taken away. A few days later, the remaining eight-eight children, aged between 1 and 15, were taken to a train station. After a two-day train journey supervised by German personnel, the children arrived in an overcrowded camp, where conditions were as bad as in Kladno. The children received no care, very little to eat and had to sleep on a bare floor. They were hungry, filthy and covered in lice.

After about a week, a few Germans appeared. They examined the children and selected seven. Through a second camp, these seven children were taken to the Gaukinderheim Puschkau in Poland for the first phase of the 'Germanization', where they arrived in August 1942. The children first and foremost had to learn to speak the language. Czech was strictly forbidden and violations were severely punished. They were beaten for the slightest issue, given no food or had to stand for hours in their underwear in a cold corridor. Since the children only owned the things they wore, the staff of the home repeatedly wrote letters to the Lebensborn Zentrale in Munich asking for clothes and shoes for them.

After more than a year, through the mediation of the Lebensborn-Zentrale, Emilie went to live with the childless Gestapo agent Otto Kuckuck and his wife Frieda in the town of Sassnitz on the island of Rügen in the Baltic Sea. Her surname had meanwhile been Germanized to Frey. Kuckuck generally treated her well, but his wife often beat her and made her work hard. Later this gradually changed. At school she was teased because of her origins, until her foster father stepped in and put an end to it.

Emilie continued to live with the foster family after the German surrender, even when the Russian army entered the territory in April 1946 and the former Gestapo agent Kuckuck fled to the British Zone. Not much later, Czech soldiers appeared who seemed to know that she was from Lidice and were looking for her. They showed her a school photograph of a class in the village and when she recognized the students and teachers, the soldiers saw their suspicions confirmed. The Czechs had tracked her down because Emilie had continued to correspond with one of the other girls from the home until 1944, after she left Puschkau. When that girl returned to Czechoslovakia after the war, she brought with her a letter with Emilie's address.

The 12-year-old Emilie did not want to return to Czechoslovakia; she was afraid of the soldiers and their uniforms. Moreover, she now got along better with her foster mother, who she now called Mum and who wanted to adopt her. She was thankful that she had enough to eat and that someone cared about her. In the end she returned to Kladno, the city near the no longer existing Lidice. There she moved in with her aunt who had returned from the concentration camp seriously ill. Her uncle had been shot dead shortly after the attack.

The girl with whom Emilie had corresponded during the war was Maria Hanfova, one of the other seven children who had been selected shortly after the German action in Lidice and who later testified before the Nuremberg tribunal. After the first phase of Germanization in the Gaukinderheim in Puschkau, she

Maria Hanfova, along with Emilie Frejova and two other girls from Lidice, testified before the US Military Court in Nuremberg during the trial of the perpetrators of race and population politics. This also included the staff of Lebensborn. (*Public domain*)

was placed with the Richter family in Dessau through the mediation of the Lebensborn-Zentrale. After her surname had already been changed to Hanff in Puschkau, she was called Marga Richter from then on. She continued to live with the family, where she was treated badly, until autumn 1945, and returned to Czechoslovakia that November.

Despite the fact their families were killed or imprisoned in a concentration camp and the hardships they endured themselves, Emilie Frejova and Maria Hanfova, together with eight other children (including the three already selected in Kladno), were among the lucky ones. The camp where they had arrived after the train journey from Kladno in Czechoslovakia was under the UWZ in Litzmannstadt (Łodz). There, the eight-eight children were examined by the local RuSHA leader, SS-Sturmbannführer Walter Dongus, who selected the seven children because they were 'considered suitable for Germanization from a racial point of view'.[6] The seven then ended up in the Kinderheim Puschkau via the so-called *Germanisierungslager des Rasseamts*, where they had to be Germanized.

There were now eighty-one other children left in the UWZ camp. On 22 June 1942, the leader of the UWZ, SS-Obersturmbannführer Hermann Krumey, asked the RSHA for instructions on what to do with the other children:

> On 13.6.42, 88 Czech children, who became orphaned by the well-known Aktion from the town of Lidice, arrived in Litzmannstadt.
>
> As no further decision has yet been made on their destination, I request instructions. I have notified Referat IV B4 of the transfer of these children on the assumption that they will receive a Sonderbehandlung. In the meantime, RuS [Rasse- und Siedlungsführer] has selected the seven children suitable for re-Germanization.

The referred Referat IV B4 was a department of Amt IV (Gestapo) of the RSHA, headed by SS-Obersturmbannführer Adolf Eichmann. His Amt was responsible for what was called in concealing language 'Jewish affairs and evacuations', but in reality ran the deportation and mass murder of the Jewish population. Similarly, 'Sonderbehandlung' (special treatment) meant murder; the fate that awaited the remaining eighty-one children. The UWZ handed them over to the Gestapo, who transferred them to the *Vernichtungslager Kulmhof* (Chełmno). There, shortly after arrival, presumably on 2 July, the children were murdered in lorries, the exhaust fumes of which were led into the loading space with the victims. The fact that Krumey was 'under the assumption' that the children would receive a 'Sonderbehandlung' proves that this horrific practice was the rule rather than the exception.

Two weeks after the tragedy in Lidice, a similar reprisal was carried out in the village of Ležáky, also in response to the attack on Heydrich. All thirty-four inhabitants over the age of 15, men and women, were executed. The thirteen children from Ležáky went through the same agony as those from Lidice and eventually ended up in the UWZ camp in Litzmannstadt (Łodz), where SS-Sturmbannführer Walter Dongus judged two children on the basis of their race characteristics as 'suitable for re-Germanization'. The other eleven children suffered the same fate as the eighty-one from Lidice and were shortly afterwards murdered with exhaust fumes in Kulmhof (Chełmno).[7]

Lebensborn was involved in various ways in the fate of the Czech children who would survive the German action because they were 'considered fit for Germanization from a racial point of view'. The organization had custody of the children from the moment they arrived at the children's home in Puschkau and also supplied clothing for them on request. Later, the organization mediated in finding German foster families and, through the branch of the Standesamt 'L', led by Lebensborn employee Erich Schulz, ensured that the children were given a new identity. A small number of Czech children, for whom no foster parents had yet been found, were also taken to Heim Alpenland at the end of 1944.

Almost exactly one year after the massacres in Lidice and Ležáky, Sollmann was ordered

SS-Obersturmbannführer Adolf Eichmann was the head of Referat IV B 4 (Gestapo), responsible for 'Jewish affairs and evacuations'. His department was informed about the Czech children from Lidice, whose parents had been killed or imprisoned in a concentration camp, and who the head of the UWZ assumed would receive 'Sonderbehandlung' (special treatment). (*Public domain*)

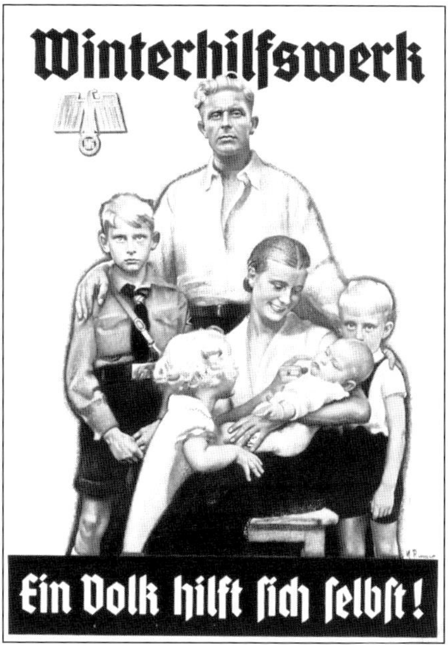

A propaganda poster for the *Winterhilfswerk*, a National Socialist organization closely associated with the NSV. Although the Winterhilfswerk initially had a social purpose – support for the poor – the organization also propagated Nazi ideals, as this depiction of the Aryan family with several children proves. Note also the contrast between the combative, almost intimidating appearance of the man and his sons, and the loving wife and mother of four children; the dream of the Nazis perfectly depicted. (*Public domain*)

by Himmler to consult in Prague with the HSSPF, SS-Obergruppenführer Frank, about the fate of several other Czech children, whose parents had been executed or imprisoned in a concentration camp for membership in a resistance movement. Concerning the children, Himmler remarked: 'The children of a good race, who, of course, could become the most dangerous avengers of their parents, if they were not humane [!] and well brought up …',[8] should reach German families via Lebensborn. After consultation, Lebensborn agreed to take over all children of a 'good race' and arrange adoption through a Lebensbornheim, provided they were no older than 6. At first they counted on 50 to 100, later almost 200 children. The 'bad children' would be transferred to the East, which would most likely mean sending them to their deaths.

Ultimately, this robbery and the presumed murder of a large number of children was abandoned because relatives had learned of their whereabouts. This had caused unrest among the population and to prevent adverse consequences for war production, the action was subsequently called off.

IX

GERMANIC BROTHER PEOPLES

Lebensborn in Western Europe

'As Germans, as brothers, as peoples of the same blood and descent, we adhere to the same ideal ... a Germanic Empire.'
Heinrich Himmler

Beutegermanen (Captured Germans)

The German occupation in Western Europe was of an entirely different nature than in Central and Eastern Europe. The latter was a result of racial ideology and war aims. According to German views, the Slavic lands were inhabited by a predominantly 'inferior race' and therefore had to be exploited and partly annexed. The inhabitants of Northwestern Europe, on the other hand, were considered mainly Nordic and therefore deemed 'worthy' of becoming subjects of the coming Greater Germanic Empire. The inhabitants of Wallonia and France were initially not well received by the racial ideologues, but were later 'promoted' to quasi-Germans after a pseudoscientific study.

The attitude of the occupiers towards the Germanic 'brother peoples' was thus very different from that of the peoples in Eastern and Central Europe. This was especially true in the first years of the occupation, when efforts were still being made to win over the people of Northwestern Europe to the German cause. At the beginning of 1941, for example, Himmler wished Seyss-Inquart, the Reichskommissar of the occupied Netherlands, much success 'with the historically so important task, to re-attach nine million Germanic Dutch people ... with a firm but very gentle hand' to the German-Germanic community.[1]

Himmler's aim was to direct the occupation policy in Northern and Western Europe, which was mainly based on military and economic aspects, more towards the formation of a Greater Germanic state, of which the occupied countries were to become part. He exercised power in the occupied territories through his personal representatives, the Höhere SS und Polizeiführer (Higher

SS and Police Leader; HSSPF). These officials were to bring about the amalgamation of the SS and local police and to represent his interests. Through the HPSSFs he tried to gain as much political influence as possible. Race policy was of great importance in this because the coming empire had to be racially pure, of course. For that purpose, a Rasse- und Siedlungsführer (RuS-Führer) was assigned to each HSSPF, who was responsible for the implementation of the race policy.

In the occupied countries, Lebensborn could contribute to the future Aryan empire by taking care of the children of German soldiers and women from those countries, provided of course they met the racial requirements. As in Germany, this was intended to prevent abortion in order to increase the birth rate of babies with Nordic blood. Moreover, Lebensborn's involvement would contribute to the mother (and later the child) – if necessary – converting to the 'correct' philosophy of life. After all, these children, so the racial ideologues hoped, would form a binding agent between the different nationalities, which nevertheless belonged to the same Germanic race. The babies born in the foreign Lebensborn settlements would thus become the vanguard of the coming Greater Germanic Empire.

In 1941, Lebensborn began to expand its activities into Northwestern Europe, starting in Norway. With the exception of that country, however, it proved difficult for the SS to gain a foothold, because the NSDAP and the German civil and military authorities had their own views and interests, which did not always coincide with those of the Reichsführer-SS. Moreover, opinions were also divided within the SS, even on such an essential subject as racial politics for Himmler.

Norway was also an exception to the rule in terms of time, because Lebensborn's activities in the other Western European countries did not begin until the autumn of 1942, when

This is what Himmler and his fellow race fanatics had in mind with Lebensborn's activities in Northwest Europe: 'racially valuable' children of Germanic women and German soldiers, in this case a Norwegian woman and an SS man. (*Schwert und Wiege*)

Inge Viermetz was sent by Sollmann to Belgium and the Netherlands, among others. Viermetz's mission was in response to a decree issued by Hitler a few months earlier about children fathered by German soldiers in the occupied territories. The issue had been raised by the *Oberkommando der Wehrmacht*, which in early 1941 proposed a settlement of the status of these children and their mothers in Norway, the Netherlands, Belgium, France and the English Channel Islands. Hitler had no objection to such an arrangement, but only for a specific area. 'We want to protect and care for illegitimate Germanic children, we have no interest in French from a racial policy point of view',[2] he said. In the same spirit, a year and a half later Hitler ordered support for Dutch and Norwegian women with children by German soldiers. However, the impact of that regulation varied from country to country. In Norway, Lebensborn received larger financial resources and the exclusive right to care for Norwegian-German children, but in the Netherlands, the NSV came out on top and remained the sole organization responsible for Dutch-German children.

As was so often the case in the Third Reich, the difference in approach between Norway and the Netherlands had very little to do with a well-thought-out plan, but was mainly the result of political machinations, luck, and personal interests. In Norway, for example, both Reichskommissar Terboven and HSSPF Rediess were fanatical supporters of race politics. The latter had already proposed in December 1940, on his own initiative, to call in Lebensborn, and Terboven had immediately declared himself willing to provide the financial means. In the Netherlands it was different. Although the leadership of the SS was committed to the racial doctrine, Reichskommissar Seyss-Inquart distrusted Himmler's Greater Germanic politics and feared that his own powers would be undermined. On the other hand, the NSV, as part of the NSDAP, was established in the Netherlands long before Lebensborn started to develop activities there. At that time the position of the NSV was already so strong that Lebensborn was no longer able to develop into a serious competitor.

The situation was different again in Belgium and France. The former country was inhabited by Walloons and Flemings, the latter of which were and the former not considered to be of Nordic blood, while the French – see Hitler's comment quoted earlier – were initially not regarded as racially valuable at all. Moreover, Belgium and Northern France were controlled by the Wehrmacht during most of the occupation and the military commander was a declared opponent of National Socialism. But in the end a Lebensborn branch was opened in both countries. After a 'scientific' study, a German historian came to the conclusion that the Walloon and Northern French population were mostly

'Romanized Germans'. This meant they now belonged to the Germanic culture and were again in the spotlight from a racial policy point of view.

Lebensborn also opened branches in Luxembourg and Denmark. In the former country, which had already been annexed by Germany, only a children's home was ever built. Denmark was certainly a point of interest in Himmler's eyes because of its Nordic population, but thanks to the political situation in that country, Lebensborn only got a foothold there in early 1944. Just before the end of the war, another maternity hospital with a children's home was opened.

The Norwegian Success Story

After Germany, Norway was the country where Lebensborn achieved the most success when taking into account the number of births.[3] Thanks to the energetic action of the highest local SS officer, supported by the main civilian administrator, Lebensborn was able to register approximately 7,600 babies with a Norwegian mother and a German father in four years. A year after the German invasion, the organization opened the first branch of what would become an entire network. Despite efforts to accommodate as many pregnant women and young mothers with children of the 'correct racial composition', as possible in their own institutions, there was always a shortage of places during the four years that Lebensborn operated in Norway. Therefore, as in the German Empire, public and private clinics and homes were also used.

The Norwegian branch of Lebensborn fell under Himmler's personal staff and received instructions from Germany on the organization and operation of the clinics and on ideological issues and medical matters. Personnel were also sent from Germany and inspections were held in Norway with some regularity. Yet because of the great distance and the excellent relationship between Reichskommissar Terboven and Himmler, who trusted him completely, the Norwegian Lebensborn operated largely independently. The organization was managed from the local headquarters in Oslo, the so-called Zentralstelle, and two regional headquarters.

Establishment

Germany invaded Norway on 9 April 1940 and the Norwegian army was forced to lay down its arms two months later. Hitler appointed his confidant Josef Terboven as Reichskommissar, the highest administrator in the country, and a

Reichskommisar Terboven (left), Generaloberst von Falkenhorst (centre, with sabre) and SS-Gruppenführer Wilhelm Rediess (right), photographed in Oslo harbour around Christmas 1940. Terboven and Rediess played a leading role in the establishment of the Norwegian Lebensborn organization. (*Frihedsmuseet Denmark*)

few months later SS-Gruppenführer Wilhelm Rediess was appointed HSSPF 'Nord'. Mainly due to the initiative and efforts of these men, after Germany Norway became the country where Lebensborn achieved its greatest success.

As early as December 1940 – not coincidentally nine months after the German invasion – Rediess wrote Himmler a letter and initiated talks with Terboven and with Generaloberst von Falkenhorst, the commander of the Wehrmacht in Norway. In his letter, Rediess drew attention to the issue of Norwegian women pregnant by German soldiers. This was a problem because the occupiers were hated and the Norwegian population called such women '*tyske ludder*' (German sluts). If we do nothing, Rediess reasoned, resistance to Germany will only increase and a large amount of 'racially valuable blood for our people will be lost, especially if the children are fathered by members of the SS'.[4] He then made some suggestions for tackling the problem, including opening German-run maternity hospitals modelled on Lebensborn. This seemed the best solution for both the reputation of the occupying forces and the SS racial ideology, and two months later Reichsführer-SS Himmler and Lebensborn leader Sollmann flew to Norway for further talks with Terboven and Rediess.

Given the – in Himmler's eyes – almost ideal racial composition of the Norwegian population, the outcome of this meeting was obvious. It was decided that a branch of Lebensborn would be established, which would be responsible for all issues concerning children of Norwegian women and German soldiers. Incidentally, it was on this trip, in the last days of February or early days of March 1941, during an official meeting in Oslo, that Sollmann became so drunk that he misbehaved in front of Norwegian guests and was ordered by Himmler to abstain from alcohol for a year.

During the consultations it was agreed, among other things, that Himmler would initially provide the appropriate personnel and Reichskommissar Terboven would provide the finance. The day-to-day management of the Norwegian branch of Lebensborn was transferred to Wilhelm Tietgen, who became head of the Lebensborn branch at HSSPF Rediess. SS-Obersturmbannführer Tietgen came from Lebensborn in Germany, where he was still head of a main department in 1938, and was sent to Norway in 1941 to build up the organization there. From June 1944 his position would be taken

During their trip to Norway to discuss the establishment of a Norwegian branch of Lebensborn, Himmler also visited the Ekeberg German military cemetery in Oslo. Walking next to Himmler is the German commander in Norway, Generaloberst von Falkenhorst, with Lebensborn director Sollmann on the far right. (*Moebius, Public Domain*)

over by SS-Hauptsturmführer Ernst Ragaller, formerly chief of several main departments at the headquarters in Munich. SS-Obersturmbannführer Gustav Richert, an officer from the RuSHA and also a racial fanatic, was the head of the department of the Reichskommissariat to which Lebensborn came. Together with Tietgen he was responsible for the establishment of the organization and until the end of 1943 the de facto leader of the Norwegian Lebensborn.

Due to geographical circumstances, the organization was set up differently than in Germany and Austria, where all branches were managed from the headquarters in Munich. In Norway, the head office (the Zentralstelle) was established in Oslo, for the capital and the surrounding area, but two regional headquarters were established in Bergen and Trondheim, with the first representing the organization in West Norway, while the branch in Trondheim was responsible for the north of the country. Later, a number of subdivisions were also added, assigned to the local representatives of the Reichskommissariat, in Kristiansand, Lillehammer, Stavanger, Tromsø, Kirkenes and Narvik.

Between 1941 and 1945, Lebensborn established around fifteen branches in Norway: administrative departments, shelters for pregnant women, boarding houses for pregnant women in transit and staff, maternity clinics and children's homes. The staff of the organization, including the management of the various homes and clinics, employed a few hundred Germans, mainly nurses, midwives and doctors. The latter were usually members of the SS. Presumably there were also two or three times as many Norwegians working in all kinds of support functions.

SS-Gruppenführer Wilhelm Rediess was extremely proud of the success of his initiative and in 1943 had a brochure

In 1943 Rediess published the brochure *Schwert und Wiege* (Sword and Cradle), in which the origin, purpose and results of Lebensborn were recorded. It was intended for internal use by the SS and was steeped in the Nazi worldview. However, post-war research has found the factual data included in it to be mostly correct, thus making it a very useful source. (*Nasjonalbiblioteket Norway*)

Affix stamp here

Pen and Sword Books
c/o Casemate Publishers
1950 Lawrence Road
Havertown, PA 19083

published entitled *SS für ein Grossgermanien: Schwert und Wiege* (SS for a Greater Germania: Sword and Cradle) in which the aim, the origin and the results achieved so far were recorded. The booklet not only contained confidential information about Lebensborn's method and racial selection, but also gave a less than positive picture of the Norwegian population and openly described the danger of enemy propaganda. It was intended for internal use by the SS only and, in addition to providing factual information, also offered valuable insights into the worldview and racial ideology of Himmler's followers. (The Norwegian government-in-exile in London first became aware of Lebensborn's large-scale activities in Norway when the resistance managed to get their hands on a copy of *Schwert und Wiege.*)

The title of the brochure, which translates as 'Sword and Cradle', was actually the core of the SS ideology. The preface explained that Lebensborn's guideline was formed by the words that Hitler had spoken in 1936 on the '*Parteitag der Ehre*'; that he would measure the success of the NSDAP's efforts primarily against the German child and youth. 'If it grows, then I know that my people will not perish and that our efforts have not been in vain.' Finally, SS-Gruppenführer Rediess gave Hitler's words the Germanic interpretation of the SS, adding that they now applied to 'all places where Germans worked and fought', and that nothing beats the experience 'to witness the growing up of healthy children, who will one day be the binding agent between peoples of like blood and race'. The Norse-German babies were to form the vanguard of the coming Greater Germanic Empire.

Norwegian Conditions

For Lebensborn, the situation in Norway was almost ideal. Not only did the majority of the population and thus the expected children meet the racial criteria used by the SS, Terboven and Rediess, the German rulers in the country, were also convinced supporters of the racial policy and gave the organization every possible support. Moreover, unlike later in the Netherlands, the NSV had not yet developed any activities there and there was therefore no competition from that side.

An important factor that also worked in Lebensborn's favour was the social isolation in which the vast majority of Norwegian girls and women found themselves after becoming pregnant by a soldier of the hated occupying army. Once they carried a German soldier's child, unless they lived in a German-friendly environment they were faced with a very difficult choice: either have a dangerous (and illegal) abortion, or ask the Germans for help, meaning they would then go to Lebensborn. There, the mothers-to-be and subsequently their babies received all the necessary support and care at the expense of the occupying forces, all, of course, for the purpose of expanding the Nordic race, and if desired 'until the end of the war', as the wording read. What would happen next, if Norway was planned to become an integral part of the Greater Germanic Empire, was not determined.

To reach the target group and let the Norwegian women know that they could get help from the occupying forces, Lebensborn had to work differently than in Germany. This had to be done discreetly. It was feared that public disclosure would lead to unrest and that enemy propaganda – the Norwegians listened a great deal to English radio – would be 'misused'.[5] That is why first the members of the SS and later also those of the other armed forces were instructed to report it to their unit if a Norwegian was expecting a child from them. This information was then passed on to the Lebensborn regional headquarters. Norwegian doctors, midwives and civil servants were also obliged to report births of Norwegian-German children to Lebensborn. Finally, a *Führerbefehl* gave the occupation authorities control over children of German soldiers and gave them insight into the Norwegian birth registers.

Because of the country's strategic location, Norway, with a population of only about 3 million, was home to a large German force, numbering some 400,000 at its largest. In some regions there were more Germans than Norwegians. An extreme example was Sør-Varanger, a municipality with about 8,000 inhabitants, where around 60,000 German soldiers were stationed, largely billeted with the residents. Partly because of this, the number of births of children by a German father increased very quickly and by the end of 1941, more than 700 Norwegian-German babies had already been registered with Lebensborn. A year later that number had risen to about 2,200 and at the end of the war Lebensborn had 8,000 babies with a Norwegian mother and a German father in the books. The actual number was probably slightly lower, around 7,600, but in addition at least another 3,000 to 4,000 children were born from such relationships, who for various reasons were hidden from the eye of the occupier by the mothers.

Of the 7,600 babies, the vast majority had been born in ordinary Norwegian hospitals or at home, under the supervision or with the help of Lebensborn, but not in the SS's own maternity hospitals. They continued to suffer from a lack of places throughout the war because they could not be built as quickly as they would have liked. A lack of suitable buildings was a particular problem – having often already been requisitioned for other purposes – and once they

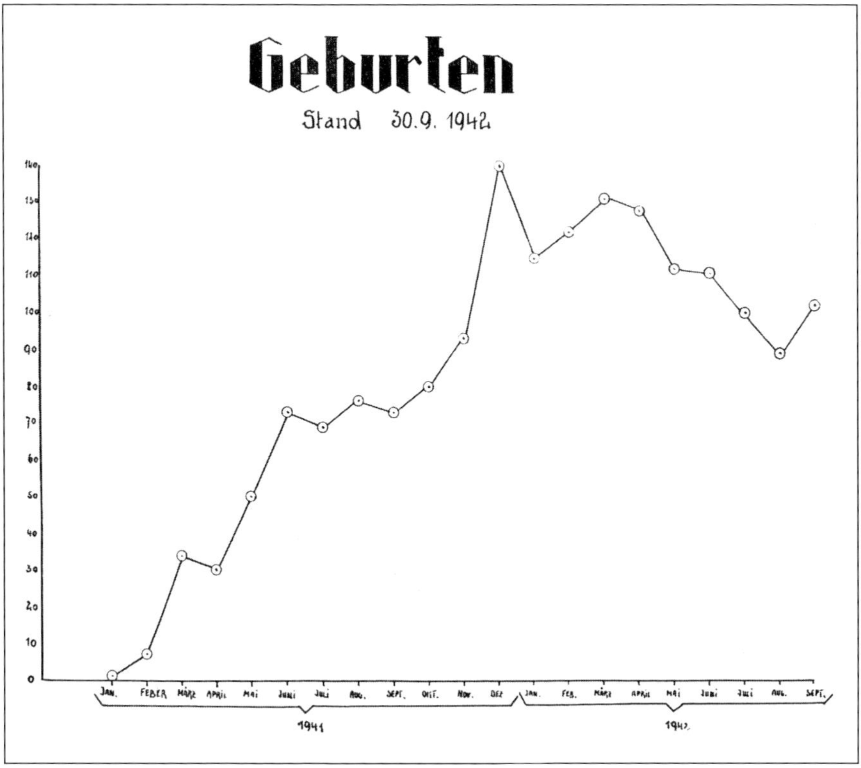

A graph showing the births at Lebensborn in Norway between January 1941 and September 1942, taken from the SS brochure *Schwert und Wiege*. Although from a suspicious source, the figures appear to correspond with post-war research. (*Public domain*)

had been found, the necessary major renovations then took a lot of time. This did not apply to the way in which Lebensborn managed the buildings. These were sometimes rented, but in many cases simply requisitioned by the SD, whereby the residents had to disappear as soon as possible. Nevertheless, there was a shortage of places throughout the war and of the approximately 7,600 Norwegian-German babies registered with Lebensborn, probably no more than 1,200 were born in the own maternity hospitals.

Whether the birth of Lebensborn took place in normal hospitals or at home, the organization paid the costs in all cases and, if desired, provided support, even after the birth. The mother was helped with her new living situation, received a monthly benefit and, if necessary, help in finding suitable work, often with the organization itself. Naturally, Lebensborn also took care of the child's care, because after all, that was what the SS was all about. *Schwert und Wiege* was very

In all Lebensborn locations, children were housed together in a room where only the staff had access. The babies only had contact with their mothers during feeding and changing. It was believed that this was sufficient because mental development would not begin until around their second birthday. This photograph was probably taken in a Norwegian clinic. (*Public domain*)

clear about this: 'It must be absolutely certain that the child is housed correctly and that his education takes place in accordance with our views.'[6]

If the mother returned home with her baby after the birth, the child remained under the control of the organization. The mother was obliged to report regularly on the well-being of her child, and Lebensborn also carried out inspections at her home to check whether the child was growing up under the right conditions. Children's homes were available in case the mother sought temporary or permanent care for her child. Lebensborn was supposed to have enough places in its own institutions, 'to prevent the valuable children from being exposed to the wrong influences', but just like the maternity hospitals, there was a persistent lack of space there too. The children were therefore also placed in ordinary Norwegian children's homes.

If the mother wanted to give up her child definitively and had also given permission for adoption, 'suitable' adoptive parents were sought, based on the child's racial characteristics. Children who met the highest criteria therefore went to Germany, while 'less valuable' children were offered to Norwegian couples. During the war, about 100 children were adopted in this way in Norway and just under 250 children were sent to Germany.[7] The latter group, part of which had been released for adoption but had probably left the country without the mother's consent or knowledge, was flown to Germany in the autumn of 1944. Most of the children, around 150, were taken to the Lebensbornheim Sonnenwiese in Kohren-Sahlis, which was often used for the Germanization of foreign children. The others ended up in Heim Friesland in Hohehorst and Heim Pommern in Bad Polzin.

Selection and Variety Testing

The admission requirements for the Norwegian Lebensborn programme were less strict than those in Germany. This was partly because of the generally 'good racial makeup' of the Norwegian population. In addition, it was not easy to get the papers from both the father and the mother that could prove purebred origin. The main reason for the less strict admission requirements, however, was that the SS wanted to prevent the anxiety and fear among pregnant women and young mothers that the racial examinations, which preceded the admission to the German homes, might cause, and thus scare off potential candidates. This did not mean, of course, that no selection was applied. Both the mothers and their children were medically examined and observed, followed by a racial assessment that was carefully recorded and could have major implications for their future. Everything was done in secret and was part of the following procedure.

When a report came in that a Norwegian woman was pregnant by a German soldier, or when a pregnant woman turned to the occupation authorities with a request for help, a department of Lebensborn went to work to collect the information necessary for the SS. The expectant mother was asked to fill in a questionnaire and submit a passport photograph. In addition, it was decided whether the woman met the requirements to be admitted to a Lebensborn clinic. Therefore, not only was she medically examined to determine the month of pregnancy, but at the same time the SD went to work to investigate the woman's background, mainly looking at her political views and investigating whether she had a criminal record. In addition, the office of the Rasse- und Siedlungs-Führer prepared a so-called 'racial political assessment', which was based on the breed criteria as used in Germany. The physical living conditions and political views in the immediate environment of the expectant mother were also examined. The results of these investigations determined the extent of Lebensborn's involvement and the future of mother and child.

Broadly speaking, there were three options. If the pregnant woman met the criteria of the SD and SS race experts, and therefore had the right political views and no criminal record, as well as the correct race characteristics, then she came under the care of Lebensborn. Depending on the financial situation and the housing and living conditions, the pregnant woman either continued to live at home under the supervision of Lebensborn, or was admitted to a Lebensborn institution. In the latter case, the SS intended to make a distinction according to the racial merit of the mothers, with the 'better' women being placed in one specific clinic. The women in the lower class, the 'lesser', but still judged to be sufficient, went to another Lebensborn clinic, which incidentally still met high requirements. In the third instance, in the case of the 'worst' pregnant women – those who held wrong political views, had a criminal record or had a negative racial assessment – Lebensborn arranged for admission to a normal Norwegian institution, but paid the costs of the stay and childbirth. Not a single Norwegian woman who was pregnant by a German soldier was sent away without help.

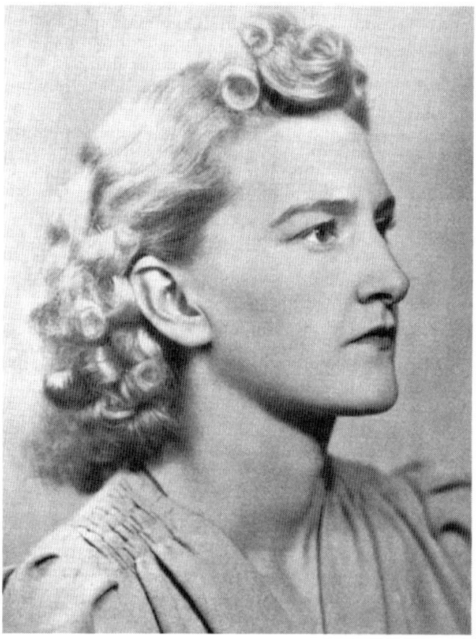

Although *Schwert und Wiege* was very enthusiastic about the racial characteristics of the Norwegian people, it nevertheless considered it necessary to urge the occupying soldiers to remain 'critical'. The blonde lady depicted the ideal; the brunettes were to be avoided. 'German soldiers have also consorted with such women!' reads the warning caption. (*Public domain*)

This had nothing to do with humanity, but rather served to inspire confidence in the intentions of the occupier and to prevent other, possibly more racially valuable, women from being scared off and trying to wrest their baby from Lebensborn's control or, worse still, from having an abortion.

Maternity Clinics

The first Norwegian Lebensborn branch where pregnant women could find shelter was opened in the spring of 1941 in a spacious villa on Kristinelundveien in Oslo. This location was most likely not chosen by chance, as the SS recruitment centre, the SS- und Polizeigericht 'Nord' – where several Norwegian resistance fighters were sentenced to death – and the official residence of Reichskommissar Terboven were located on the same street. It was a temporary solution and the home closed again after the permanent settings were completed. It is not known whether births took place here or whether only pregnant Norwegian women or young mothers with children stayed there.

The first permanent Lebensborn institution in Norway was a maternity hospital called Hurdalsverk, located in the town of the same name, about 80 kilometres northwest of Oslo. This branch officially opened its doors on 14 August 1941 when the first pregnant woman was admitted. Such a remote place was deliberately chosen in order to hide the pregnant women from the attention of their compatriots as much as possible. The maternity hospital was located in a building originally erected in the nineteenth century as the main building of a glass factory. It was later converted into a country house and used as a hotel from 1924.

Heim Hurdalsverk offered the residents an exceptionally luxurious accommodation, being equipped with all modern conveniences and with high, light rooms, colonnades and parquet floors. The maternity hospital had places for forty-five mothers and ninety children, who were cared for exclusively by German personnel: the Heimleiter and doctor, the head nurse, the business director and his secretary, the midwife and the nurses all came from Germany. The other staff, who did not come into contact with the women and children, consisted of Norwegians who worked in the kitchen, the laundry and on the maintenance of the building and the park. The first birth in a Norwegian Lebensborn clinic took place in Hurdalsverk on 24 August 1941, and five more followed within four days, as the leader of the Norwegian branch of Lebensborn, SS-Obersturmbannführer Tietgen, proudly reported to Sollmann on 28 August. In total, around 600 babies were born in Hurdalsverk.

Above and below: Hurdals Verk (called Hurdalsverk in the Lebensborn period) was a luxurious hotel from the 1920s, as these postcards of the exterior and interior show. (*Private collection*)

In 1942 Lebensborn opened two new maternity hospitals with children's homes. The first was located in Hønefoss, about 50 kilometres northeast of Oslo, and was named Klekken, after the former hotel that housed the Lebensborn branch. The building was brand new and equipped with all

Above: The Klekken maternity clinic in Hønefoss was housed in a brand-new hotel and opened on 1 May 1942. The clinic housed thirty-five women and sixty children. Around 350 babies were potentially born there. (*Riksarkivet Norway*)

Entbindungsheim Klekken. Speisesaal.

Right: A page from *Schwert und Wiege* showing the dining room and reception room at ‘Entbindungsheim Klekken’ (Klekken maternity clinic). (*Schwert und Wiege*)

modern conveniences due to the fact the hotel had just been rebuilt after it had been destroyed in fighting during the German invasion. It was taken over by Lebensborn in November 1941 and opened after extensive rebuilding on 1 May 1942 as a maternity hospital with thirty-five places for mothers and sixty for children. Here, too, the women and children only came into contact with German personnel and this clinic was also located in a sparsely populated, remote area.

Because Heim Klekken was more effectively organized than Hurdalsverk, the plan had been conceived 'to include the racially better women in Heim Klekken and the racially lesser women in Heim Hurdalsverk. Naturally, the mothers are not told the reason for being taken into a particular Heim.'[8] Due to problems in the implementation of this intention, this dichotomy does not appear to have been made in practice. A total of around 350 children were born there and after the liberation, Klekken was used for some time by the Norwegian authorities to detain women suspected of having had social and sexual intercourse with Germans.

In December 1942, a Lebensborn branch was opened in Geilo, in the town of the same name on the railway line from Oslo to Bergen. The building in which this maternity hospital was located was initially built as a sanatorium by

Dr Holms Hotel was a favourite residence of the Scandinavian elite before the war but was later requisitioned during the occupation. Submarine crews were housed in one part of the complex, while the Geilo maternity hospital was located in another wing. (*Public domain*)

order of a doctor named Holms. It later became an extremely expensive hotel, called the Dr Holms Hotel, where the Scandinavian elite enjoyed themselves. During the occupation it was requisitioned by the Germans and part of the building was used to house submarine crews between their missions, while another part, the east wing, housed the Lebensborn branch. Geilo was called a Vorheim, and was not only intended to relieve both maternity hospitals, but at the same time remove the pregnant women from the influence of their former environment as early as possible. This would allow them to prepare for a changeover, 'because many of them will later be integrated into the German national community',[9] according to *Schwert und Wiege*. In addition, admission to a Vorheim would facilitate the necessary training, which consisted partly of education and partly of indoctrination. Lebensborn probably intended to set up several such homes, but that was never realised. Vorheim Geilo had room for sixty women and twenty children and was led by a midwife. About 200 children were born there.

In the last months of the war, the organization was busy transferring the location in Geilo to Brumunddal, just north of Hamar, where the Vorheim would be housed in the requisitioned hotel Høsbjør. The hotel had already served as a field hospital in 1940 and was seized by the Germans two years later. Presumably it was already the intention to establish a Lebensborn clinic there, but for unknown reasons this did not happen. In the winter of 1944–1945, the building was adapted to the requirements of Lebensborn and in the spring Heim Høsbjør was still in use for a very short time. In those few weeks, twenty-four babies were born.

Stadtheime (Town Homes)

In addition to the maternity hospitals, in 1942 a number of so-called Stadtheime were established in or near the three largest Norwegian cities. These Stadtheime were intended for short stays and were mainly used for pregnant women or young mothers with children on their way to or from another Lebensborn institution or hospital. In addition, the Stadtheime also had sleeping and living quarters for Lebensborn staff of other institutions located in the countryside, who could use them if they wanted to enjoy city life for a few days during a holiday period.

The first Stadtheim was opened in Oslo on 1 February 1942 at Olav Kyrres Plass and was named Olav. It could accommodate twenty women and six children. The management was in the hands of a midwife, who was supported

Opposite, above and right: In 1942 three so-called Stadtheime were opened for pregnant women and young mothers in transit, but also for Lebensborn personnel on leave in the city. Depicted here are the branches in Oslo, Hop (near Bergen) and Trondheim. (*Schwert und Wiege*)

by Norwegian personnel. A similar institution, Stadtheim Bergen, in the town of Hop, 10 kilometres south of Bergen, opened in the summer of 1942. The home accommodated twenty mothers and six children. It was also run by a midwife and featured a delivery room for emergency births. The third Stadtheim was located in Trondheim on the Nedre Allé and was named Drontheim, the German name for the city. Due to the large number of German troops in and around the city, as in Bergen, there was a great need for a Lebensborn clinic but a chronic lack of suitable buildings. After a long search, Lebensborn found a large, wooden villa on the edge of the built-up area. The house had sixteen rooms, three kitchens, two bathrooms and a large vegetable garden. The owner had bought the house three years earlier and was just completing extensive rebuilding and renovation when the SS caught sight of it. The property was immediately seized with all its contents, while an adjoining house was also seized. After the necessary adjustments, it was opened in the autumn of 1942. Stadtheim Drontheim could accommodate thirty women and ten children.

Kinderheime (Children's Homes)

In addition to the maternity clinics and the Stadtheime, Lebensborn also opened three homes for young children in Norway. These were intended to relieve the maternity hospitals and free up places more quickly for pregnant women and new-born children. After giving birth, many young women preferred to leave their child temporarily or permanently, or needed care when they went back to work, and the capacity of the maternity hospitals was not designed for that. Moreover, Lebensborn 'considered that it was not possible to place children of German soldiers and Norwegian mothers in children's homes of the Norwegian government or similar institutions such as the homes of the Salvation Army, because it could not be avoided that the children would be adversely affected'. Because the SS therefore attached the greatest importance to these children

The first and largest of the three children's homes that Lebensborn set up in Norway was Kinderheim Godthaab, which opened in the summer of 1942 and initially accommodated 165, but later 250 children. This image dates from the early 1930s. (*Public domain*)

being brought up '*in deutschen Sinne*' (in the German spirit), Lebensborn opened three of its own Kinderheime for this purpose.

The first and largest was Godthaab near Oslo, which was commissioned in the summer of 1942. It was housed in a large building that was previously used as an *Erholungsheim* (military convalescent home). When it opened, the children's home could accommodate 165 children, but the need remained high, as evidenced by the fact that the home was soon expanded and in October 1943, no less than 250 children were accommodated there. The ages of the children ranged from 3 months to 4 years. The home was run by a female doctor, assisted by a head nurse.

In the same year, two other children's homes were opened. Kinderheim Stalheim, about 100 kilometres northeast of Bergen, was housed in a former hotel. Initially, Lebensborn planned to establish a maternity hospital here, but because the power supply necessary for such an institution was not reliable and

Godthaab's staff, posing on the steps of the main entrance in the summer of 1942 for a photograph printed in *Schwert und Wiege*. The head nurse is on the left, the (female) doctor in the centre, and an SS officer (probably the Heimleiter) on the right. This company formed the German core of the staff, which consisted of about seventy-five people in total. (*Schwert und Wiege*)

Above and below: The children's home Stalheim was established in a former hotel. It opened in February 1943 and could accommodate 80 to 100 children. Lebensborn originally planned to open a maternity hospital there, but the plan was cancelled because the power supply was unreliable. (*Public domain*)

there was also a need for a children's home in the area, the latter option was chosen. In Stalheim there was room for 80 to 100 children.

At the end of 1942, Lebensborn had access to a vast estate that had already been confiscated by the Sicherheitspolizei in Moldegård.[10] This was about 40 kilometres south of Bergen and belonged to former Norwegian Prime Minister Ludwig Johan Mowinckel, who had fled from the Nazis to Britain. The estate consisted of a large country house with several smaller houses and outbuildings and was surrounded by a park and extensive arable land, situated on a spit of land in a fjord. The country house was adapted to Lebensborn's wishes, including the furnishing of a delivery room, so that children could also be brought into the world in special cases. Kinderheim Moldegård was opened here in the spring of 1943 and could accommodate eighty children. Some sources also mention a Kinderheim Charlottenlund in Trondheim, but it is not certain whether this establishment actually existed.

Ultimately the goal of the SS, to place the Lebensborn children only in their own homes – to prevent the children from being 'adversely influenced' – was not achieved. A large proportion of the children, possibly about half, were placed in ordinary Norwegian children's homes.

The Moldegård estate belonged to the former Norwegian Prime Minister Mowinckel, who fled first to Great Britain and later to the United States after the German invasion. His estate south of Bergen was confiscated by the SS and in 1943, Lebensborn opened the Moldegård children's home in the house. (*Private collection*)

Indoctrination and Marriage

Lebensborn was not only concerned with the health of the mother and child. The organization supervised the pregnancy and childbirth, and also ensured their material well-being afterwards by taking care of the racially desired children and helping the mothers find work. Its work did not stop there, however. As it was assumed that some of the women would marry their child's father and go to Germany – as indeed several hundred young mothers would – Lebensborn considered it necessary to teach them the 'German frame of mind' before then. This was not taken lightly. In *Schwert und Wiege* it is noted:

> One of the most difficult and most necessary tasks is the education of the pregnant woman. The Norwegian women grew up under completely different circumstances than the German women. They know no *'völkische Kampf'* [people's struggle], their view is clouded by one-sided political propaganda, and their outlook on life is influenced by the poison of Anglo-Saxon taste. Therefore, even with good will, they simply cannot follow the German train of thought.[11]

The conclusion was clear: worldview 'education' was an absolute necessity.

In order to teach the expectant mother German-Germanic principles as much as possible, she should preferably be removed from her familiar environment at the earliest moment, after which the 'schooling' should take place in a Vorheim in the fourth to eighth month of pregnancy. So-called *Mütterschulen* (mother schools) were set up there, where lessons were given in all aspects of housekeeping and education, according to the guidelines of the German *Reichsbräuteschulen* (Reich bride schools). An equally large and possibly even more important part of the curriculum consisted of what was called 'philosophical education'. By means of lectures, parties and songs about the – in the view of the SS – shared Germanic history, and by viewing and discussing old German and Norwegian 'cultural goods', the Norwegian women had to develop a feeling for the 'Germanic *Volkstum*'. The third part of the programme consisted of a course in the German language, which was naturally considered very important with a view to the future.

After the birth, the education and indoctrination could be continued at a specially established institution, the Mütterschule Lier in the town of the same name near the city of Drammen, where Reichskommissar Terboven had confiscated the Herredal Hotel for this purpose. There, mothers who had already received training could receive a refresher course, but courses were also given for young mothers who had not given birth in a Lebensborn clinic, and (non-pregnant) brides of members

Mütterschule Lier.

Mütterschule Lier.

Mütterschule Lier.
Ausblick auf die Umgebung.

At the Mütterschule Lier, located in the former Herredal Hotel seized by the SS for this purpose, the young mothers received a six-week course in childcare, household chores, the SS worldview and the German language. This is a page from *Schwert und Wiege*.

of the Wehrmacht, SS and police. At the Mütterschule Lier, all these young women took a six-week course, also according to the guidelines of the German Reichsbräuteschulen, with the same programme components as in the Vorheime: domestic chores, childcare, the Nazi worldview and the German language.

Himmler and his accomplices were thus not only interested in Norwegian-German children who met the correct racial criteria, but were also eager to bring their young mothers and other young Norwegian women to Germany, who could of course produce even more offspring with Nordic blood. Ideally, they went as the bride, after successfully completing a course at the Mütterschule. But it was not that simple, as initially Hitler had explicitly forbidden marriage between German soldiers and foreign women. Later, this prohibition was somewhat relaxed and marriages between members of the Wehrmacht and women from the 'Germanic brother nations' – Denmark, Norway, the Netherlands and Sweden – were allowed, but only after Hitler had given his personal permission. Bormann, Hitler's secretary, noted on 18 February 1942:

> The Führer takes the decision personally. Despite his current workload, he examines every request himself.
>
> The most important condition for the consent is the racial suitability of the bride, because consent is only possible when the bride's inclusion in the German people is desired from a racial policy point of view.

When senior Wehrmacht officers in Norway made the local rules even stricter, Himmler successfully complained to Hitler. Members of the SS continued to be allowed to marry women from 'related Germanic' peoples, because 'the Führer expected that our SS men will marry valuable girls'.[12] However, this was preceded by a long and thorough investigation, mainly into the 'racial characteristics' and philosophy of life of the future bride and her family. The processing of the marriage requests was slow and it could take months or even years before a decision was made. Therefore, only about 500 Norwegian-German marriages took place during the war, while several thousand unmarried women, mostly pregnant, or mothers who had just given birth, moved to Germany with their babies, hoping and expecting to marry the father of their child. Several hundred of them left for Germany in September 1944 with the ship *Monte Rosa*.

The Dutch Connection

The Dutch, together with the inhabitants of Denmark, Norway, Belgium and Sweden, were regarded as members of a Germanic brother nation. In the longer term, those areas would become part of the Greater Germanic Empire, but during the war in the occupied territories – Sweden was a neutral country – volunteers were recruited for the Waffen-SS. In the Netherlands, about 25,000 young men reported to the SS. A considerable part of them would lose their lives on the Eastern Front.

The motives of the Dutch men and boys to join the SS voluntarily were very different. Racial ideology played a role in this for some of them, as the doctrine also had adherents in the Netherlands. A well-known race fanatic was Pieter Emiel Keuchenius, a biologist who developed into the most important Dutch propagandist of racist and anti-Semitic views. From the early 1930s he was a member of various National Socialist and fascist organizations and active as a school leader, board member and 'race advisor'. In addition, he produced a large number of articles, including in the anti-Semitic weekly magazine *De Misthoorn*, which he co-founded (subtitled 'Independent and unpolitical body to fend of Jewish influence') and publications with significant titles such as *Volk en Levensruimte* (People and Living Space). Keuchenius's most important and most successful publication, *Bloed en Mythe als Levenswet* (Blood and Myth as Law of Life), appeared in 1940. It was partly inspired by Chamberlain and Rosenberg and is one of the most vicious anti-Semitic insults ever published in the Netherlands. Despite this, it was reprinted twice and would reach a circulation of more than 10,000 copies. In April 1941, the book also earned him an assignment from the highest SS leadership 'to scientifically work on the material collected during the compulsory registration of Jews and persons of Jewish blood'. According to the National Socialist magazine *Het Nieuwe Volk*, this was of great importance 'for gaining insight into the permeation of our people with Jewish blood for measures to be taken in the future'.[13]

Tens of thousands of Dutch people were attracted to the ideology of the SS and about 25,000 young men volunteered for the Waffen-SS. Among them was the biologist Pieter Emiel Keuchenius, who developed into the most famous Dutch propagandist of racist and anti-Semitic views and produced publications such as *Bloed en Mythe als Levenswet* (Blood and Myth as Law of Life) and *Volk en Levensruimte* (People and Living Space). (*Public domain*)

The leadership of the SS in the Netherlands was in the hands of SS-Obergruppenführer Hanns Albin Rauter. As Generalkommissar für das Sicherheitswesen and HSSPF 'Nordwest', he was responsible for maintaining order and arresting and deporting the Jews and the other enemies of the regime. For racial and population policy, a RuS-Führer was assigned to his staff, SS-Obersturmführer Herbert Aust. In February 1943 Aust was also appointed Lebensborn's representative in the Netherlands. The highest civilian administrator was Arthur Seyss-Inquart, who was appointed Reichskommissar für die besetzten Niederländischen Gebiete by Hitler shortly after the occupation began.

Rauter and Aust were both racial fanatics who carried out their mission with conviction. In doing so, they did not limit themselves to carrying out the tasks imposed on them, but also raised alleged abuses. For example, Rauter had noticed that the nurses of an NSV birth clinic in the Netherlands, 'are

Anton Mussert, leader of the collaborationist NSB (the Dutch National Socialist Party) giving a speech in The Hague on 11 November 1941. Behind him, from left to right, are Generalkommissar für das Sicherheitswesen and Höhere SS- und Polizeiführer SS-Obergruppenführer Hanns Albin Rauter, SS-Obergruppenführer Hendrik Alexander Seyffardt and Reichskommissar für die besetzten Niederländischen Gebiete Arthur Seyss-Inquart. (*Public domain*)

often racially inferior and that it makes a bad impression not to see better nurses in a German NSV home'. He had therefore made agreements with the NSV leadership to attract as many Dutch racial qualified nurses as possible. According to him, this also had the advantage that 'orderly nurses with a pure character and racial value, who also have a good reputation, are also valuable to German soldiers in the homes, that is to say, that if such a person marries a Dutch girl, he gets a racially high-quality wife, which can only be justified for the many hundreds of thousands of German girls who cannot get married because of the war'.[14]

Rauter's subordinate, RuS-Führer Aust, also demonstrated his sacred belief in race ideology. He was deeply offended when his alleged racial superiority as a German was called into question in the Dutch SS-magazine *Storm: blad der Nederlandsche SS*.[15] There, the (Dutch) SS-Untersturmführer Van der Hoeven wrote 'there is a difference in race composition between Germany and the Netherlands, the percentage of Nordic race blood is estimated at 50% in Germany; in the Netherlands this percentage is considerably higher'. From a Dutch point of view, he concluded, it would therefore be a step backwards in terms of race if Dutch people married Germans.

Aust was furious. Less than a week after the publication of the relevant issue of *Storm*, he sent the article, along with an accompanying letter, to his highest boss, SS-Gruppenführer Otto Hofmann, the head of the RuSHA, and called the piece a provocation that also contained untruths. The claim about the percentage of 'Nordic blood' was particularly bothersome to him. Here, however, Aust fell into the pit he himself had helped to dig. By the standards of most German racial experts, there was indeed a greater proportion of 'Nordic blood' among the Dutch people than among the Germans; only the Norwegian people, and possibly also the Danish people, were ranked higher on this point. As far as is known, the article had no negative consequences for Van der Hoeven.

RuS-Führer Aust was responsible, among other things, for the racial selection of the Dutch SS volunteers and their potential brides, who had to meet the same requirements as the German SS recruits, including those of Himmler's betrothal and marriage order. He also propagated Germanic festivals and customs among the volunteers and instructed Dutch doctors about the racial selection of the SS recruits. Aust was also actively involved in the persecution of the Jews and was responsible for the death of many hundreds of people through his racist assessments. He was never convicted.

From the beginning of 1943 SS-Obersturmführer Aust was also the local representative of Lebensborn, first only for the Netherlands and from September of that year also for Belgium. He maintained contact with government and party

Een flinke Stamhouder geboren:

FOLKERT GERHARD

Zoon van

FOLKERT VAN DER POST
SS-Obersturmführer, thans Lazarett Wasserburg a/Inn. (O.B.) en

MIA v. d. POST—SAUREN
tijd. SS-Heim „Hochland"-Steinhöring, (O.B.).

11 Januari 1945.

The announcement of the birth of a baby to a Dutch couple in the Dutch SS magazine *Storm* in Heim Hochland, in Steinhöring, 11 January 1945. Remarkably enough, it says 'SS-Heim' instead of 'Lebensbornheim'. The father, SS-Obersturmführer Folkert van der Post, member of the SS-Grenadier Regiment 1 'Landstorm Nederland', was at that time in a hospital less than 10 kilometres from Hochland. It is not known how many Dutch women gave birth to a child in a Lebensborn clinic. (*Public domain*)

services working in the same field, took care of recruitment and information and had to assist in the preparation of a Lebensborn clinic in the Netherlands. Aust also had the task of selecting Dutch and Flemish women who wanted to give birth at the organization based on their racial characteristics. It is not known how large that number was, but the scant data suggests that it was no more than a few dozen. In any case, it is certain that one or more Dutch women gave birth in the Hochland (Germany), Ardennen (Belgium) and Westwald (France) clinics.

Heim Gelderland

For Lebensborn, the Netherlands was an interesting area where it would be possible to have a large number of babies with the breed characteristics desired by the SS. Moreover, a clinic on Dutch territory, if not too far from the eastern border, could also be used for German women. The foundations for Lebensborn's efforts to establish a clinic in the Netherlands were officially laid on 28 July 1942, when Hitler issued an order for the care of children (and their mothers) of members of the Wehrmacht in Norway and the Netherlands. The purpose of the order was to preserve and promote 'racially valuable Germanic heritage'. Children fathered by German Wehrmacht members and brought into the world by Dutch or Norwegian women were entitled to special care and support. This concerned not only the costs of the delivery and the admission of the mother to a clinic or home, but also an allowance in the period around the delivery and a contribution towards the maintenance of the child. If desired, the child could also be admitted to a home and the mother could be helped to find work.

In the autumn of 1942, Inge Viermetz of the Lebensborn-Zentrale in Munich was sent by Sollmann to The Hague to discuss the establishment of a Lebensbornheim with the leadership of the German occupation forces. In the Netherlands, the relations were different than in Norway. Whereas in the latter country Reichskommissar Josef Terboven was practically the sole ruler and actively cooperated with the HSSPF to put the ideals of Lebensborn into practice, things were not so easy in the Netherlands. In this country, Reichskommissar Arthur Seyss-Inquart held the same position as Terboven in Norway, but here he had to take full account of Fritz Schmidt, Generalkommissar zur besonderen Verwendung. He was (slightly) lower in rank on paper, but just as powerful in practice. Schmidt was, in fact, a confidant of Hitler's right-hand man Martin Bormann, who was himself involved in a permanent power struggle with Himmler. Schmidt represented the NSDAP in the Netherlands and saw the local National Socialist movement NSB and its leader Mussert as useful pawns for his politics. This did not correspond with the Greater Germanic idea of the SS, which was represented in the Netherlands by HSSPF Rauter. But Seyss-Inquart was not particularly enthusiastic about Lebensborn's wishes either, for he regarded Himmler's plans as a threat to his own powers. In his implementing regulation (dated 1 March 1943) of Hitler's aforementioned order, it was therefore only stated about Lebensborn that women in the Netherlands could also give birth in a home belonging to the organization.

The powerful Generalkommissar Schmidt had strong views on birth and population policy. The NSV, a daughter organization of its NSDAP, had been ahead of the SS in that area and had already set up several homes

Reichskommissar Seyss-Inquart (left) with Fritz Schmidt, Generalkommissar zur besonderen Verwendung, who represented the NSDAP in the Netherlands and was a confidant of Bormann. Schmidt successfully opposed Lebensborn's expansion plans in the Netherlands but was mysteriously killed in June 1943. (*Public domain*)

in the Netherlands, where Dutch women who were pregnant by German soldiers could give birth and receive aftercare. By the summer of 1943, 1,000 children had already been born there. During the war, a total of between 5,000 and 6,000 children were born in German NSV clinics in Amsterdam, Rotterdam and The Hague. The NSV had no need for competition and opposed any attempt by Lebensborn to open a birth clinic in the Netherlands as well. In contrast to the situation in Norway, where the SS had more or less a free hand in this area, here they were subsequently dependent on the cooperation of the NSDAP in the person of Schmidt.

However, the odds suddenly seemed to turn. On 20 June 1943, on his way to visit the Atlantic Wall in France, Schmidt fell from a moving train near Chartres and was killed. It has never been clarified whether this was an accident, suicide or murder, but it is significant that in a telephone conversation with the Dutch SS supporter Julia op ten Noort (more on this later), Rauter himself remarked spontaneously 'not being guilty of this'.[16] In any case, the situation seemed to have changed drastically because Schmidt's successor, Generalkommissar Wilhelm Ritterbusch, hardly opposed the aspirations of the SS. The possibilities for Lebensborn now seemed to be open.

Rauter immediately began negotiations with the leader of the NSV in the Netherlands and was soon able to inform Himmler that they had agreed to work closely together. For example, it was agreed that the NSV children 'in cases involving secrecy or cases that are particularly suitable for the SS (racially high quality!), will be handed over to Lebensborn' and that there would be the 'closest cooperation' in biological assessment and reporting between the public health department of the NSV and the RuS-Führer, SS-Obersturmführer Aust. Furthermore, the NSV was to hand over a delivery clinic and a children's home to the SS, which were located in the cities of Hilversum and Baarn, respectively, and were to be opened on 1 September 1943. (The children's home may be later due to a renovation.) Although both institutions would remain the property of the NSV, the mothers and children would be selected in close consultation with the NSV by the Fürsorgeoffizier of the Waffen-SS, who was responsible for the social and financial support of the families of the volunteers. SS-Obergruppenführer Rauter was extremely pleased with the outcome of the talks. 'Whereas before I had asked the NSV dozens of times in vain for the racially valuable children, and Schmidt caused the greatest difficulties and never yielded on any point, everything, I can almost say, went by itself', wrote a delighted Rauter to Himmler on 15 July 1943.[17]

But he had cheered too soon. It is not known whether the NSV leadership had deliberately tricked him, changed its mind later, or whether something else

SS-Obersturmführer Karl Herfurth came to the Netherlands in the spring of 1942 to set up a maternity hospital for Lebensborn in Nijmegen. He not only commandeered and stole movable and immovable property to carry out his mission, but also took the opportunity to enrich himself. (*Private collection*)

happened. In any case, nothing came of the agreements and the NSV in the Netherlands would never hand over children, homes or clinics to the SS.

However, this did not mean the SS regarded the Netherlands as a lost ground for Lebensborn, on the contrary. Because despite all the opposition, preparations for what was to become the first Lebensbornheim in the Netherlands had already started more than a year before the death of the biggest troublemaker, Schmidt. SS-Obersturmführer Karl Herfurth, who had been with Lebensborn for several years and was still working in Heim Kurmark in October 1940, had been ordered to establish the institution and was also designated to become the first Heimleiter.

Herfurth probably arrived in the Netherlands in the spring of 1942, because on 29 May of that year the building where the SS wanted to establish the home, the Jesuit monastery Berchmanianum in the city of Nijmegen, was requisitioned by the occupying authorities. According to the testimony of a priest who was present, the situation unfolded as follows. When they were having breakfast with seventy people in the refectory, a German officer entered, presumably SS-Obersturmführer Herfurth himself, and declared gruffly 'The building is confiscated. You are only allowed to take private properties!'[18] They had to leave immediately.

Confiscating the monastery was the easiest part of Herfurth's task. Heim Gelderland, as the institution was to be called, was to become a maternity hospital with a children's home with room for approximately sixty women and approximately 100 children, making it one of the larger Lebensborn locations. Heim Gelderland, located a short distance from the Dutch-German border, was probably also intended to relieve the German Lebensborn settlements.

SS-Obersturmführer Herfurth, who befriended the collaborating Nijmegen NSB police commissioner Van Dijk, proceeded energetically with the usual SS methods. After the building was confiscated and extensively renovated, it was decorated and furnished with looted items, most of which came from Jewish ownership. Herfurth and Van Dijk took advantage of this and other opportunities to enrich themselves personally. Incidentally, Van Dijk could not enjoy this for long; he was shot by a member of the resistance in July 1943 and died from his wounds a few weeks later.

In early November 1942, Herfurth sent a letter to his boss,[19] SS-Standartenführer Sollmann, in which he explained how he proceeded. The robberies for personal gain, naturally, remained unmentioned. During a short stay in Heim Pommern, according to Herfurth, he took the opportunity to investigate what was needed and drew up lists of all necessary medical resources and materials for an examination room, an operating room, a delivery room etc. He had enlisted the help of the chief physician of the *Befehlshaber der Waffen-SS*, SS-Sturmbannführer Dr Mayer, who, at his request, would assist Herfurth in furnishing and collecting medical supplies. That was no easy matter in wartime. 'Many articles are very difficult to get through the normal route and with long delivery times or maybe not at all. An attempt must therefore be made here in the occupied territory to obtain the necessary equipment from available materials,' Herfurth wrote.

It turned out that he had already succeeded, because in the same letter he reported that the clinic would be furnished with *'beslagnahmtes jüdisches Besitztum'* (confiscated Jewish properties). This concerned material from the Jewish hospital on St Annastraat in Nijmegen, which was closed in December 1942, the household effects of Jewish families who had fled or were deported, and parts of the inventory of the Apeldoornse Bosch. This was a Jewish psychiatric institution that was evacuated in the night of 21-22 January 1943,

The Nijmegen Jesuit monastery Berchmanianum was requisitioned by the SS in May 1942 and converted into a maternity clinic and children's home called Heim Gelderland, with room for about sixty women and 100 children. It was completed in the spring of 1943, but the institution was never opened. (*Private collection*)

after which all patients and a large part of the staff – around 1,300 people – were deported to Auschwitz and murdered.

The renovation and furnishing of the Nijmegen Lebensborn branch was completed in the spring of 1943. The maternity hospital had two delivery rooms, the rooms in the side wing had been converted into children's pavilions with large windows, the building was luxuriously furnished, had a new paint job and everything was spotlessly clean. And because Seyss-Inquart had declared himself willing to take care of the financial exploitation of Heim Gelderland in April of that year, nothing seemed to stand in the way of a speedy commissioning. The opening was initially supposed to take place in the summer of 1943, but was postponed for unknown reasons.

In November of that year, Herfurth received high-ranking visitors in Nijmegen, when Lebensborn director Sollmann, together with SS-Sturmbannführer and Oberstabsarzt Dr Günther Fritze, Lebensborn's representative in France, came to inspect the clinic in Nijmegen. As far as is known, everything was found to be in order and not much later it was announced that Heim Gelderland would open its doors in February 1944. But that date also passed without anything happening, despite the fact everything was ready, including the official stamps. Heimleiter Herfurth, for example, now promoted to SS-Hauptsturmführer, submitted an application to Ebner for pesticides against insects in March on stationery stamped *'LEBENSBORN / Heim Gelderland / Nijmegen - Niederlande'*.

Sometime in June, presumably in connection with the Allied invasion, Himmler finally announced that the facility would not be opened until further notice. The last known report about Heim Gelderland dates from 19 August 1944, when Herfurth reported from Munich that the settlement had still not been taken into use. Four weeks later, all aspirations of Lebensborn and

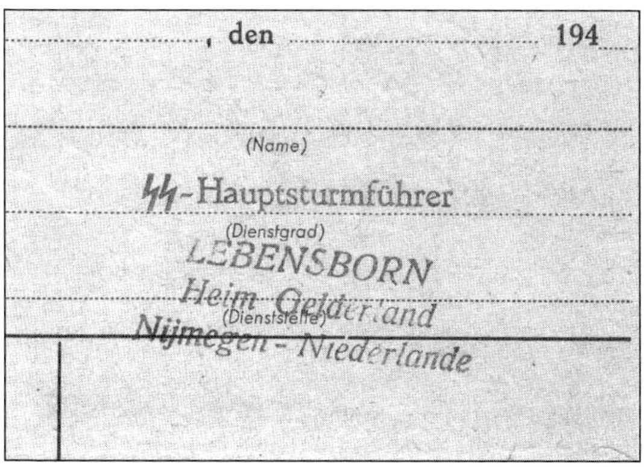

Even the stamp of the Dutch branch had already been made: '*LEBENSBORN / Heim Gelderland / Nijmegen – Niederlande*'. (*Private collection*)

the SS with regard to Heim Gelderland finally came to an end. American paratroopers of the 82nd US Airborne Division landed near Nijmegen as part of Operation Market Garden and liberated the city a short time afterwards. It seems that many American soldiers managed to score a souvenir marked 'Lebensborn'.

It has never been established with certainty why the Dutch branch was never opened. Presumably, Seyss-Inquart wanted to prevent the SS from gaining more influence over his powers than necessary, and through unobtrusive machinations and careful planning of time he managed to postpone the opening until it was finally superseded by military developments. It is possible that Bormann also played a role somewhere in the background, potentially using local NSDAP and NSV representatives to thwart Himmler.

The Op ten Noort Case

On more than one occasion, Lebensborn's childbirth clinics were used to do someone a favour. In many cases these were high-ranking SS officers or other influential figures from Himmler's inner circle who needed a discreet address for the delivery of their girlfriend or mistress. In the later phase of the war, more and more 'official' wives of the Nazi elite also used the Lebensborn facilities. The luxury clinics always remained well-supplied and their location in the safe countryside meant they were not in the centres of the increasingly heavily bombed German cities.

One of the examples of such favours was the case of Julia op ten Noort, who, according to her biographer, was 'the most significant Nazi woman the Netherlands has known'.[20] She came from an influential family who had been ennobled in 1907 by Queen Wilhelmina. Lady Julia Adriana op ten Noort (1910-1994) grew up in an exceptionally well-to-do family and, because of her background and upbringing, felt far superior to the common people. After primary school she went to the gymnasium for three years, and from the age of 15 she mainly enjoyed playing tennis and horse riding and later also dancing, dining and partying.

Around 1930, Op ten Noort became involved in the Oxford Group, which consisted of followers of a Christian doctrine of salvation, preached by the American pastor Frank Buchman, who successfully targeted wealthy Protestant families. Just a year after Julia op ten Noort came into contact with them, she too regarded herself as an 'instrument of God' and a follower of Buchman. The intelligent, attractive and self-confident young woman, unhampered by lack of time and resources, was soon accepted into the leadership of the movement.

Julia op ten Noort (left) with Florrie Heubel, a like-minded friend, at a camp of the (Dutch) National Socialist Women's Organization in the summer of 1940. (*Beeldbank WO2 34249*)

Despite her limited education, she quickly spoke good English and from the age of 21 made several trips abroad to propagate the spiritual renewal, mainly talking to high-ranking and aristocratic figures.

One of those trips took her to Stuttgart in April 1934, to the Germany where the Nazis had taken over power more than a year earlier. National Socialism was certainly not foreign to Op ten Noort. On the contrary, her brother and parents were early members of the Dutch National Socialist movement and she drew a swastika with the dedication she wrote in a book that she gave to her brother in September 1933.[21] She presumably followed developments in Germany with approval, also because Buchman still appreciated the Nazis: in contrast to materialistic communists, in whom he did see a threat, they would adhere to an idealistic ideology. A few years later she would finally break with the Oxford Group, which had gained more and more supporters under the new name of Moral Re-Armament.

After the meeting in Stuttgart, Op ten Noort was invited by a prominent German member of their movement – a friend of the second wife of the former German Kaiser, who had resided in the Netherlands since 1918 – to attend another meeting in Germany, which took place in April 1934. There she and a number of fellow evangelists were invited by Udo von Woyrsch, a Baron and SS-Gruppenführer, for lunch in Breslau, where she met a group that consisted of a large part of high-ranking SS leaders, including the Reichsführer-SS Heinrich Himmler.

Nothing has been recorded about the details of their conversation, but it is certain that Himmler and Op ten Noort spoke for a long time. It is to be expected that the Reichsführer-SS delivered an impassioned speech about his SS as the knights of the coming Greater Germanic Empire, in which the purified blood of the Aryan race would reign supreme etc. The pursuit of unity within the people and the devotion to great ideals, the idea of purification, and especially the elitist character of the SS probably appealed to Op ten Noort, who was very aware of her noble origins. Himmler, for his part, who would later have said several times that he had converted her to National Socialism, was undoubtedly impressed by the attractive, self-confident young woman. In his fantasies about a future class of Germanic noblewomen, he undoubtedly had such a type in mind. (It could be seen as unfortunate that she did not have blonde hair, but Himmler himself did not fit the ideal image of the Nordic warrior either.) So while it is not known exactly what they discussed, it is true that from this meeting, Op ten Noort was certainly won over for the National Socialist cause. Himmler had her all wrapped up: 'He was courteous and a good listener. I especially noticed his modesty. We understood each other.'[22]

From the second half of the 1930s, she radicalized rapidly. Unlike Mussert, the leader of the Dutch National Socialist movement who wanted the country to remain as independent as possible, Op ten Noort supported a movement that would turn the Netherlands into a province (Gau) of the Greater Germanic Empire. Op ten Noort was also completely in line with the SS when it came to views on race and people. She remained in constant contact with Himmler, writing each other letters and meeting on several occasions, including during

Dutch SS volunteer Pieter Schelte Heerema had a short relationship with Julia op ten Noort, but refused to marry her after she became pregnant by him in 1941. A year and a half later, in his black SS uniform, he married Erna Kühnen. Heerema played an important role with in the National Socialist *Nederlandsche Oost Compagnie* (Dutch East Company), which intended to send Dutch settlers to the annexed territories in Eastern Europe. (*Public domain*)

the Reich Party Days in Nuremberg, which she visited several times at his invitation and expense.

Op ten Noort had no problem with the German invasion of the Netherlands on 10 May 1940. Because her Nazi sympathies were well known, she was arrested by the authorities but liberated by German troops after the capitulation of the Dutch army. In 1941 she had an affair with Pieter Schelte Heerema, a Dutchman who had previously joined the SS and was a fanatical supporter of the racial doctrine. Op ten Noort was in love and became pregnant, but he refused to marry her. The pregnancy most likely ended in miscarriage. Later that year she was appointed by Himmler as director of the first Dutch *Reichsschule für Mädel* (Reich School for Girls) where, following the example of the German *Nationalpolitische Erziehunganstalten* (Napolas), the future elite of Germanic women would be educated in 'the right spirit'. The fact that she had no previous education was no problem. The lessons were in German, the girls learned to give the Hitler salute and were thoroughly indoctrinated in every respect, including by Op ten Noort herself, who also taught the staff the correct principles.

In May 1943 she became pregnant again. She was unmarried, had no relationship with the father-to-be, and had no intention of changing that. She kept the man in question, The Hague SS-officer Age Lykle Tromp, at a distance, even when he continued to insist on contact with all SS authorities, including Himmler. Her pregnancy was known to a very small circle – the father's name was hardly known to anyone – and generated the necessary disapproval, including from her German superiors. She herself did not mind becoming an unmarried mother, as long as the progenitor met the correct racial requirements and, according to her, Tromp apparently had the required characteristics. In early September she travelled to Berlin to ask Himmler for advice. This was an ideal scenario for the Reichsführer-SS, who, with his almost unlimited power and means, could provide a quick solution to her problems. A solution in which Lebensborn, which specialized in the discreet delivery of babies of the Aryan race, was of course central.

On 15 September, he explained the plan already discussed orally in a letter to his protégée.[23] Op ten Noort had to travel to Berlin, where SS-Obersturmbannführer Paul Baumert of Himmler's personal staff would meet her and arrange a German passport. She still had to come up with a German name herself. Baumert would then arrange an internship at the colonial Frauenschule in Rendsburg, where she was to stay until one or two months before the birth, in order to be admitted to a Lebensbornheim under her German name and to have the baby. After a few months she would return to the Netherlands and then 'adopt' her own child some time later. Lebensborn would provide the right

Above and below: Two images of Heim Hochland from the Lebensborn brochure. Under the pseudonym Marijke von Weiler-Bock, Op ten Noort gave birth here to her son on 24 February 1944. The baby was appropriately baptized Heinrich.

papers. Himmler would explain her long absence from the Reichsschule für Mädel by informing the relevant authorities that he had sent Op ten Noort to the East on a special assignment.

The plan was executed almost entirely on schedule. The only deviation from the time schedule was that Op ten Noort left for the clinic earlier because she did not particularly like the colonial Frauenschule. She therefore arrived at Heim Hochland in Steinhöring on 8 November, where she was registered under the name Marijke von Weiler-Bock, daughter of a German father and a Dutch mother.

Unbeknown to herself, she was lucky, very lucky. One of the conditions for admission to Lebensborn was that the candidate had to be able to demonstrate with documentary evidence that they had not had any Jewish ancestors for several generations. Op ten Noort could not meet that requirement because her mother's birth certificate had been lost by fire during the German invasion. Further research into her mother's ancestors was also impossible, because she was born in Batavia in the Dutch East Indies, which had been occupied by the Japanese. This twist of fate spared the self-proclaimed 'noble German' Op ten Noort a bitter disappointment, because her mother had Jewish ancestors. An admission by Lebensborn would then probably have been officially impossible, because the obligatory Ahnentafel (genealogical overview) had to go back to the year 1800. Unless, of course, Himmler had turned a blind eye to this shortcoming of his protégée, which would certainly not have been impossible.

She was spared all this, however, and spent a pleasant period in the idyllically situated Heim Hochland. It is an open question whether she knew about the Dutch forced labourers and prisoners from the nearby Dachau concentration camp who were put to work there, but she made no mention of this in her letters. She did not get along well with everyone, but she befriended one of the secretaries of the Reichsführer-SS, who shared a double room with her. According to Op ten Noort, she was 'the wife of Himmler's best friend'.[24]

She gave birth to a baby boy on 24 February 1944, whom she named Heinrich, after both his godfather Himmler and Heinrich I, the latter considered as the founder and first king of Germany (919-936). It was therefore no coincidence that the Nazi-era Heinrich, who in his turn was involved in the creation of the Greater Germanic Empire, considered himself the reincarnation of this monarch. Thanks to the Standesamt L, Lebensborn's own registry office, little Heinrich was registered and provided with the required papers. Mother and child stayed together for a while in Heim Hochland, until a few months later she temporarily placed her son with a foster family in Germany and returned to the Netherlands.

In the summer of 1944 Op ten Noort said goodbye to the Reichsschule für Mädel, returned to Germany and was given a job at the Germanische Leitstelle, part of the SS-Hauptamt in Berlin. Sometime that same summer, she made the important decision to become a German citizen and in November 1944 received her German passport from SS-Obersturmbannführer Baumert. A few months later she was appointed Reichsbeauftragte im SS-Helferinnenkorps by Himmler. That was a very honourable position and one of the highest roles a woman could hold in Nazi Germany. The SS-Helferinnenkorps consisted of about 10,000 women by that time, who mainly served as telegraph operators, telephone operators and secretaries in the concentration camps, with the SD and the Einsatzgruppen in the East. However, for reasons that are unclear, she informed Himmler in January 1945 that she would not accept the position – it may have become too difficult for her in Berlin – and she returned to Bavaria, where she lived for some time with little Heinrich in Heim Hochland and worked in the household there.

About two months before the first American troops reached Steinhöring, she had moved south with her child and ended up in the town of Miesbach. Prisoners of the concentration camp at Dachau had constructed a so-called SS-Berghaus (mountain house), which was first used for vacation and later as an SS-Erholungsheim (convalescent home). The setting suited Op ten Noort well because it was located within the sector of the so-called Alpenfestung,

A picture postcard of the SS-Berghaus in Miesbach, Bavaria. Op ten Noort and her baby spent the last months of the war in this SS-Erholungsheim (convalescent home). (*Private collection*)

the last position the Germans might defend. But this fortress existed mainly in the imagination of the greatest zealots, and on 8 May 1945 the era of the Third Reich was over. A possibly even greater shock for Op ten Noort was Himmler's suicide, more than two weeks later, although it must have taken some time before she heard the news.

Like many other fanatical Nazis, Op ten Noort was only lightly punished after the war. She lied to the American occupation authorities about her membership of the SS and denied knowing anything about the extermination camps, but in February 1947 she was arrested by the Dutch authorities and brought to justice. There she admitted all the charges against her, including her friendship with Himmler, Rauter and membership of the SS. Her sentence was particularly lenient: 2.5 years in prison, of which she would only eventually serve half. In 1952, Op ten Noort, still a convinced Nazi, returned to Germany and lived there in wealth until her death in 1994 at the age of 83. In the last period of her life, she immersed herself in Hinduism.

Things did not end well for young Heinrich. He probably never got to know his father's identity, but he did know that he was born in a Lebensborn clinic that was part of the insane and criminal empire of Himmler, the man whose name he bore and who may have been his father. Although he was in a way privileged compared to most of the other Lebensborn children – he had been raised lovingly by his own mother – he was also the child of at least one fanatical Nazi who lived until decades after the war and, when the monstrous misdeeds of her co-perpetrators could no longer be doubted or denied, still supported the ideas of racial delusion. Heinrich died in 1989, at the age of 45, five years before his mother. He died alone, presumably of cardiac arrest, wrecked by a long-term alcohol addiction combined with chain smoking and drug abuse. He was not found until a few days after his death. It seems that he had suffered greatly from his background.

Belgium: Heim Ardennen

From the second half of 1942, Inge Viermetz carried out various assignments in Western Europe, where Lebensborn wanted to expand its activities and open new maternity hospitals. This operation ultimately yielded no results in the Netherlands, but in Belgium and France, where she bore the title 'Lebensborn-Beauftragten für Belgien und Nordfrankreich' (Lebensborn Representative for Belgium and Northern France), she was more successful. Whereas Lebensborn in the Netherlands mainly encountered resistance from the NSV, in Belgium and France the organization was initially opposed by the army. General der Infanterie Alexander von Falkenhausen, the military commander of Belgium and Northern France, despised the Nazis and tried to limit the SS's influence in his area as much as possible. This was only temporary successful, however, because eventually he, too, had to allow a branch of Lebensborn, and so in 1943 the Lebensborn clinic Heim Ardennen was opened near the town of Ayeneux (municipality of Soumagne) near the city of Liège.

Due to the fact the city is in Wallonia, and the Walloons – in contrast to the Flemish – were not counted among the 'Germanic brother peoples', the chosen location did not seem immediately obvious. The choice was probably determined by the limited number of suitable buildings and its location near the German border. As with the proposed Dutch settlement, it was undoubtedly the intention that German women would also be admitted. In addition, from a racial point of view, the Walloons had gradually become better off with Himmler. Léon Degrelle, the founder and leader of the Légion Wallonie, a SS unit composed of Walloon volunteers, called them 'romanized Germans'. The German historian Petri, who later conducted a 'survey of racial ancestry' in Northeastern France, came to a similar conclusion.

Léon Degrelle, the founder and leader of the Légion Wallonie (later the 28. SS Freiwilligen Panzergrenadier Divison 'Wallonien') awards decorations to his men in Charleroi in 1944. He called these Walloon SS volunteers 'romanized Germans'. (*Public domain*)

Heim Ardennen, opened in March 1943, was located in the castle of Wégimont, near Liège. Around 100 babies were here until the clinic was hastily closed on 1 September 1944 due to the advancing Allied troops. (*Private collection*)

Entirely in the tradition of Lebensborn, Heim Ardennen was housed in a spacious and luxurious accommodation, located in a rural environment. This was the castle of Wégimont, which had been founded in the fifteenth century, subsequently expanded and renovated several times and, after being owned by the d'Oultremont family for a long time, eventually became the property of the province of Liège in 1920. The castle had already been requisitioned by the Germans at the beginning of the war, but a lot still had to be done before Lebensborn could take up residence there. Inge Viermetz conducted the preparatory discussions and led a large part of the practical activities for the establishment of the maternity hospital annex children's home. Not only did the clinic have to be fully equipped – for which 100,000 Reichsmark were made available – staff also had to be selected and hired. Most of the nurses were German, the rest of the staff came from the local area. According to an official letter from the military commander in Belgium and Northern France, the clinic was intended for 'pregnant women of Germanic blood ..., those of Reichsdeutsche Wehrmacht members or foreign members of German aid organizations (Waffen-SS, Walloon legion, Flemish SS, NSKK etc.) who are of Germanic blood ... expecting a child.'[25] After some toing and froing, the Belgian clinic also had its own secret Standesamt (civil registry office), so that births could be kept secret. By March 1943, preparations had progressed to the point where the first women could be admitted, and the work was completed a few months later. Heim Ardennen then accommodated about thirty women and thirty-five children. In July 1943 there were about twenty women and thirty-four children, with around ten births having already been registered.

One of these babies was the son of Clémence F., a girl from Maldegem in East Flanders who had become pregnant in 1942 by an Austrian Wehrmacht soldier. After his commander forbade him to marry her and her request for help was rejected by the ordinary Belgian authorities because she was pregnant out of wedlock, she finally ended up with Lebensborn thanks to the soldier.[26] Clémence first had to undergo a health and racial examination, which presumably took place at the Germanische Leitstelle in Brussels. When she had been approved and had also been able to prove that she had no Jewish ancestors, she was admitted to Heim Ardennen in June 1943. Among the approximately twenty young mothers were Belgian, French and Dutch women and even a Norwegian girl. Pseudonyms were used to protect the identities of her and the other women. The children lived together in a separate room where the mothers were not allowed. They were allowed to take the children for a walk in the park, but not outside, and contact with the local population was prohibited. The young mothers were allowed to choose whether they wanted to keep the children themselves or give them up for adoption. Clémence took her son with her, but said that many young women left their children behind. Usually, they stayed until they were 6 or 7 months old, after which they went to Germany for adoption.

As was customary at Lebensborn, the mothers were helped to find work after giving birth if they wished. For example, Clémence got a job as a waitress in a German army canteen in Brussels while her son was cared for at the clinic. At the end of August 1944, Clémence's was warned that the clinic would be evacuated, meaning she had to hurry to pick up her son. Clémence was well taken care of at home and moved to another place, so no questions about her past were ever asked. She also corresponded for some time with the father of her child, who unsuccessfully asked them to come to his native country. Unlike many other young women, she took her son with her from the clinic and later told him about his origins. Because the boy always stayed with his mother, who later married another man, he had a happy childhood and grew up to be a balanced person. He thus belonged to the minority of the Lebensborn children.

When Viermetz left in the summer of 1943, she would was succeeded as Heimleiter by SS-Obersturmführer Karl Herfurth. He had founded Heim Gelderland in the Netherlands and would also lead that clinic, but the opening was repeatedly postponed. In the end, Herfurth did not come to Belgium and, after a former Lebensborn mother had temporarily held sway, SS-Sturmbannführer Walter Albrecht Lang was appointed as Heimleiter instead. His deputy was the administrator, SS-Hauptsturmführer Pletsch, a war invalid. (His injury did not prevent him from ending up in hospital with syphilis sometime later, after infecting a few other women as well.)

In the first months of its existence, it was very difficult to find suitable personnel. Lebensborn could hardly find nurses and initially there was no permanent doctor on staff. Therefore, two local Belgian general practitioners had to be called upon. At the end of 1943, Ebner sent Heim Schwarzwald's doctor to Belgium, but he probably only stayed temporarily.

The environment was hostile to the staff and patients of the clinic (the village priest called it 'organized immorality') and for this reason a guard unit of the Germanic SS was stationed in Wégimont in the summer of 1943. However, one remained suspicious of the outside world, and when the condition of two babies born to Lebensborn in the Liège university clinic did not improve as expected, they were transferred to the German military hospital in Brussels. When a boy died of suffocation later that year, the Belgian staff came under suspicion, also because he was 'one of the few German children' in the clinic, Ebner wrote to Himmler. However, an investigation showed that a German night nurse had not performed the tasks assigned to her in accordance with the rules. Nevertheless, drastic measures were taken. All the Belgian care staff, including the midwife Fanny Montulet, were dismissed and replaced by German staff and quite a few braune Schwestern from the NSV appeared in the castle.

On 1 September 1944, Heim Ardennen was hastily closed after the Allies had advanced dangerously close. The pregnant women, the young mothers with children and the staff were taken to Heim Taunus near Wiesbaden, where twenty children and five mothers from Belgium and France were staying at the time. SS-Sturmbannführer Lang was transferred to Hohehorst near Bremen, where he was now in charge of Heim Friesland. That home was closed in the course of 1941 due to the increasing air danger, but the lack of space at Lebensborn had become so great in the course of 1944 that it was reopened.

Heim Ardennen was in use for less than a year and a half, and because the SS allegedly burned the entire administration of the Belgian clinic during the evacuation, it cannot be known for certain how many children were born, but it is likely that there were about 100.

Luxembourg: Heim Moselland

Luxembourg was annexed by Germany in August 1942 and then became part of the Gau Moselland. In July 1943, Lebensborn opened a children's home with the same name: Heim Moselland. It was housed in Bofferding Castle,

The only tangible remnant of the children's home Moselland in annexed Luxembourg is this soup tureen, which illustrates that little was lacking in the furnishing of the establishments and that they even had specially made crockery. Moselland was located in the former castle of Bofferding. (*Public domain*)

whose pro-French owner Marcel Noppeney had already been arrested. He was eventually imprisoned in Dachau but would survive the war.

The castle was converted into a modern and luxurious children's home by Bauleiter Diehl under the supervision of SS-Sturmbannführer Damm. The required labour force was supplied by forced labourers and concentration camp prisoners, including Jehovah's Witnesses, who were also put to work in the home. Heim Moselland was mainly used to receive children from other Lebensborn locations, and in August 1943 it received children from the evacuated Mütterwohnstätten in Munich. In addition, it was used to 'Germanize' Polish children. The home could accommodate several dozen children and was headed by Oberschwester Margarethe Petroswka, who previously held that position at the Ardennes in Belgium.

With the Allied armies approaching, on 9 September 1944 the staff of the home received orders to evacuate Heim Moselland immediately and to take as much of its contents as possible to the train station in Luxembourg. However, upon arrival at the station, the train was already overcrowded and so they were ordered to evacuate to Trier by horse and carriage. As a result, the goods taken with them were left behind at the train station: a soup tureen is the only object that has been preserved. The children were transferred first to Heim Franken I and II and then to Hochland in Steinhöring.

France: Heim Westwald

As in Belgium, Lebensborn had only one branch in France, which opened in February 1944.[27] This maternity hospital with a children's home was initially to be called Heim Westland, but the name was changed to Westwald for unexplained reasons before it opened. It was located near the town of Lamorlaye, 40 kilometres north of Paris, and was housed in a beautiful country house on the Bois-Larris estate of the same name, deep in the Chantilly Forest. The residence was built between 1912 and 1919 for the Menier family, the (still) famous chocolate manufacturers. The accommodation met the most important requirements for a Lebensborn location: spacious and luxurious accommodation on a large estate, located in the countryside, with good connections to and a short distance from a large city.

Although the presence of Lebensborn in France was not obvious at first – in contrast to the population of Northwestern Europe, the French were not counted among the 'Germanic brother peoples' – Himmler gradually changed his mind in the first half of 1942. He was concerned both with strengthening

Heim Westwald, in operation from February to August 1944, was housed in a large country house in the town of Lamorlaye, 40 kilometres north of Paris. It is seen here in a pre-war postcard. (*Private collection*)

his own ranks and with weakening the opponent. The Reichsführer-SS had in mind the same method he used in the occupied East: by abducting the 'Germanic' children to Germany, he thought he would deprive those countries of their future leaders. In April of that year, he proposed to Hitler that a large number of children from the 'Germanic' part of France be transferred annually to German boarding schools at a young age in order to 'distract them from their accidental French nationality and point them to their Germanic blood and the fact that they belonged to the great Germanic people'. Hitler liked the idea and declared 'that it would be a severe blow to France if its leading upper class were to be withdrawn from the Germanic youth.'[28] However, the plans were not immediately put into action, probably because at that stage it was still hoped to seduce the French Vichy government into closer (military) cooperation and their collaboration was needed for the deportation of the Jews in France. Things changed definitively in November 1942, when the Germans occupied Vichy France after the Allied landings in North Africa and the French navy blew up its own ships in Toulon to prevent them from falling into German hands.

Six months earlier, in May 1942, Himmler had been alerted to the problem of the children of German soldiers and French mothers by the Reichsgesundheitsführer, SS-Gruppenführer Leonardo Conti. Up to that point, Conti wrote, 'some 50,000 children had been born to French women who are generally no worse than those born to Norwegian women'.[29] If the current situation did not change, Conti feared that those children would remain in France and 'be lost to Germany'. Not much later, Himmler had the historian Franz Petri conduct an investigation into the nature and origin of the French population, and the expert came to the conclusion that Northeastern France largely belonged to the Germanic culture. This argument apparently convinced the Reichsführer-SS, for shortly afterwards he ordered Sollmann to contact SS-Brigadeführer Oberg, the HSSPF in Paris, and not much later SS-Sturmbannführer Tesch, Lebensborn's chief jurist, travelled to the French capital for consultations on the issue.

The negotiations and discussions took many months and the 'problem' of the Franco-German soldier's children had apparently faded into the background when Himmler announced in January 1943 that he wanted to establish a Lebensborn maternity clinic near Paris. As far as is known, he also did not return to the proposal to Hitler about the transfer of French 'Germanic' children to German boarding schools. Presumably he had come to the conclusion that transferring thousands of French children to Germany would cause major problems in many respects. The situation here was different from Eastern Europe, where such practices could be carried out with impunity.

As far as the Lebensborn branch was concerned, HSSPF Oberg was able to report in the spring of 1943 that he had found suitable accommodation. Viermetz was then sent to France in the summer to prepare for the opening of the clinic. On Himmler's instructions, only French women were allowed to be admitted, but it is certain that Belgian and even Dutch women also gave birth to a child. Heim Westwald was officially opened on 6 February 1944. It was a relatively small institution by Lebensborn standards, with only a few dozen places for mothers and children. As in Belgium, the French Lebensborn site was guarded by an SS unit because it was in occupied territory. SS-Sturmbannführer and Oberstabsarzt Dr Günther Fritze, Lebensborn's representative in France, who had his office in Paris, was responsible for medical care and had to visit several times a week. This did not happen often, and when he visited the clinic he was usually a heavy drinker and often brought guests.[30] At the end of June, Ebner wrote to Sollmann that medical care by Fritze was not guaranteed, but that an Oberfeldarzt of the Wehrmacht, named Finke, could be called up from Chantilly for medical emergencies.

Ebner had personally inspected the facility a month earlier and prepared a report on his findings. The buildings and entourage had made a good impression,

Left and below: The country house of Bois-Larris was located on a large estate and was built in 1911 by order of the wealthy Menier family, the famous chocolate manufacturers, and was luxuriously furnished. (*Private collection*)

but Ebner was dissatisfied with the quality of the furnishings. Moreover, there were not enough medicines and medical instruments available. He would have it brought over from Steinhöring. A big problem was the lack of a Heimleiter thanks to a fierce rivalry, meaning the personnel was divided into two camps. On one side stood SS-Unterscharführer Grünwald, who managed it together with his wife. The other party was formed by Oberschwester Josefa Kroll, who had previously worked in Sonnenwiese and Ardennen, and midwife Christel Höhe. According to the latter, Grünwald was particularly attached to his position in Westwald because it would allow him to escape service at the front. Furthermore, they had reason to believe that Grünwald had deliberately delayed the completion of the Lebensborn site in order to make himself indispensable. It is not known how the feud between the two groups ended.

No more than twenty to twenty-five children were born in Heim Westwald, mainly because the clinic was not in use for more than seven months. On 10 August 1944, shortly after the Allies had succeeded in breaking out of their beachheads in Normandy and Brittany and into the French interior, the clinic was closed. The women and children present were transferred to Heim Taunus near Wiesbaden, where the mothers and children from the Belgian branch would also arrive a few weeks later. A number of children from Westwald were taken to Germany during the evacuation without the knowledge or consent of their mothers.

Denmark: Just or Not?

Denmark was an interesting country for the SS because children of German soldiers and Danish women would mostly meet the racial characteristics required by Lebensborn. However, the political situation differed greatly from that in the other Western European countries, which limited the freedom of action of the SS and Lebensborn. The Danish army had put up virtually no resistance to the German invasion on 9 April 1940 and had laid down its weapons after just two hours. This had a major influence on the occupation policy, with the Danish government and the king being allowed to remain in office. For much of the war, the country was a de facto German protectorate with significant control over domestic politics. The situation changed in August 1943, however, and the country was placed under German military administration.

The SS had been present in Denmark from the beginning of the war to recruit volunteers, just as they had in other Northwestern European countries, but it was not until the end of 1943 that a Höhere SS und Polizeiführer was appointed and the influence of the SS in the country increased. Other legal measures regarding the status of German-Danish children also came into force around that time. These events had gradually changed Himmler's mind, who had made it known only a year earlier that he had no plans for Lebensborn in Denmark.

In January 1944 he ordered the establishment of a branch of Lebensborn in Denmark. Ebner toured the country a month later and reported that the local German authorities were very interested in the Lebensborn plans. In practice, however, preparations proceeded very slowly. It was not until December 1944 that SS-Hauptsturmführer Willi Ziesmer, until then the head of the main department 'Arbeit' of the Zentrale in Munich, was sent to Copenhagen by Sollmann and in February 1945 he reported that he had found some suitable locations.

It seems that the intention was to open four Danish Lebensborn branches, and that two were worked on in the last months of the war: one in Copenhagen and the other in Tønder, near the Danish-German border. Only the clinic in the latter town, which supposedly housed forty children, seems to have been in operation for a very short time, while the one in Copenhagen was completed almost simultaneously with the German surrender. The latter was then used for some time as a clinic for female refugees from East Germany in consultation with the Red Cross.

X

PERPETRATORS AND VICTIMS

The End and the Aftermath

'"Super Babies"
Illegitimate children of SS men are housed in a German castle.'
Life Magazine

Evacuation

In the last phase of the war, as the Allied armies approached from all sides, one Lebensborn house after another had to be evacuated, starting with the foreign settlements. The women, children and staff – and often also some of the buildings' contents – were taken to places considered safer. Sometimes they had to move three or four times within a few months.

Forced to do so by the military situation, Hitler issued the order for the *Rückführung deutscher Frauen und Kinder in die Heimat* (Repatriation of German Women and Children to the Fatherland) on 25 August 1944. But Heim Westwald, near Lamorlaye, 40 kilometres north of Paris, had been hastily evacuated before that date. On 10 August 1944, shortly after the Allies succeeded in breaking out of their beachheads, the clinic was closed. The women and children present were taken to Heim Taunus near Wiesbaden. A number of children, whose mothers worked outside Westwald, were taken to Germany without their mothers' knowledge or consent. The cause of this was probably great haste in the evacuation, and not a conscious attempt to withdraw the children from their mothers' authority.

There was also a long wait with the evacuation of Heim Ardennen near Liège. It was not until 1 September 1944, when the Allies had come dangerously close, that the Belgian Lebensborn branch was hastily closed. The pregnant women, the young mothers with their children and the staff were also transferred to Heim Taunus. Heim Moselland in annexed Luxembourg was next eight days later. On the approach of the Allied armies, the staff were ordered to evacuate the children's home immediately on the morning of 9 September 1944. The children were transferred first to Heim Franken I and II and then to Hochland.

German Clinics and Children's Homes

After the foreign settlements, a number of clinics and homes on the territory of the Third Reich were also evacuated. For example, the inhabitants of Pommern were first transferred to Taunus, and from there to Hochland via Franken in March 1945. In this place, where it all started in 1936, evacuees from various locations arrived in the last months of the war. When American units of the US 86th Infantry Division entered the village on 3 May 1945 and reached the maternity hospital, they found 163 babies and small children,[1] young mothers and pregnant women, plus a number of nurses and twenty-four Jehovah's Witnesses who were used as domestic servants.

According to an eyewitness, in the last days of the war there had been enormous chaos. There were many more pregnant women and children than places in the clinic, the SS men still present were nervously preparing their flight and burning papers – a convoy of documents had left for an unknown destination just before – and a few braune Schwestern of the NSV were apparently so desperate that they committed suicide. When the Americans arrived, it seems that all male personnel had fled and only SS-Oberführer Gregor Ebner remained behind. He was arrested and imprisoned; the other members of the staff followed soon. From mid-May, the home was led by the Wehrmacht doctor Josef Kleinle on the instructions of the US Army.

The braune Schwestern of the NSV were first replaced by Catholic sisters and not much later the children of Hochland were taken to the convent of Indersdorf, which had been set up by the United Nations Relief and Rehabilitation Administration (UNRRA) as a relief camp for displaced and orphaned children. In September 1945 there were about 200 children. They were cared for by the nuns and by the staff of UNRRA Relief Team 182 and came from a wide variety of backgrounds: Jewish children from concentration camps, Eastern European children who had been used as forced labourers, children of former forced labourers, children from Hochland and other Lebensborn settlements, and orphans from very different backgrounds.

In addition to Hochland, Sonnenwiese in Kohren-Sahlis and Friesland in Hohehorst near Bremen also remained in operation until the end of the war and children and mothers from evacuated maternity hospitals and homes were taken in. A large number of refugees had also been given shelter in Heim Friesland in

The children were taken care of in the Indersdorf monastery, which had been set up by UNRRA as a reception camp for displaced and orphaned children. Here they are cared for by a local nun and the Dutch UNRRA Medical Welfare Officer Annemarie de Waal Malefijt (right), who later left for the United States and became a famous anthropologist. (*UNRRA*)

Another group of toddlers in Indersdorf being fed by UNRRA employee Greta Fischer. It is said that these children came from Hochland. (*UNRRA*)

the last weeks. The women and children could do nothing but await the arrival of the enemy troops. The staff under SS-Sturmbannführer Walter Albrecht Lang used the time to pack Friesland's records into crates, bury them on the estate, and give the children other names to conceal their origins. Shortly afterwards Lang changed his mind – why is not known – and the crates were dug up again. Not much later he abandoned his patients and staff and fled the clinic.

On 5 May, British soldiers arrived in Hohehorst to find only women and children left. The British units took possession of the basement and ground floor and the staff and children were allowed to continue to use the rest of the building. A few weeks later, the area was taken over by American troops. In the meantime, the braune Schwestern had been replaced by nurses from the German Red Cross.

Heim Friesland became widely known after the famous American photographer Robert Capa visited the clinic more than a month after Germany surrendered. He took a series of photographs that were printed in *Life Magazine* of 13 August 1945. The photographic article was titled *'"Super Babies" Illegitimate children of SS men are housed in a German castle'* and consisted of a short introductory text and fifteen images with captions. The whole piece (in which Hohehorst was incorrectly written as Hohenhorst) still strongly exuded the atmosphere of the war and the deep hatred of the Nazis and the SS; it was only months after the Allies encountered the horrors of the concentration and extermination camps. The letters to the editor, published in the magazine a month later, took a different tone and emphasized that the children were innocent. It was also asked if they could be adopted.

The vast majority of the German children who remained in Hochland, Sonnenwiese and Friesland at the end of the war – if not picked up and taken away by their mothers – were adopted in the summer and autumn of 1945, mostly by people living in the area. The children in Sonnenwiese in Kohren-Sahlis, which was first occupied by the Americans but later included in the Soviet Zone, had to gather in the hall of the home at one point, after which residents of the surrounding villages could choose one or more foster children.

Among the approximately fifty small children the Allies found in Heim Friesland in May 1945 was group of thirty-two babies and infants who had been brought there six months earlier from Norwegian Lebensborn homes. These were the children of Norwegian mothers and German fathers who met the highest 'racial criteria' of the SS and in most cases had been given up for adoption. In total, just under 250 Norwegian-German children were transferred to Germany in this way. The thirty-two babies and infants in Heim Friesland were waiting for their German foster parents, but this would turn out differently.

After the US Army, which had taken over responsibility for the area two weeks after the arrival of the British, had become aware of the situation in the home and that of the Norwegian babies, they contacted the Norwegian government. They sent a Norwegian-Swedish delegation to repatriate the children, with thirty of them being taken by bus to Lübeck at the end of July, from where they were taken by ship to Malmö, Sweden. (One baby was in hospital and another would remain with foster parents in Germany.) In Malmö, however, at the insistence of the Norwegians, it was suddenly decided to leave the children in Sweden because, it was argued, due to their background they would have a greater chance of adoption and a normal future in that country. They were placed in a children's home and at the same time a newspaper article appeared stating that these children came from Buchenwald concentration camp and that their origin was unknown. This was almost certainly a deliberate deception because when most of the children were adopted shortly afterwards, the authorities appeared to have erased their identities.

The reason behind this curious turn of events was that the Norwegian government simply did not want the children back. They were descendants of the hated occupier and were living proof of the warm relationship that quite a few Norwegian women had had with German soldiers. A committee was therefore formed that looked for other destinations for the Norwegian-German children, and the 'Swedish variant' was one of those alternatives. It was also investigated whether they could be transferred to Australia. Another alternative was to leave as many children as possible in Germany and have them adopted there.

Of the other Norwegian children who were in Heim Sonnenwiese and Pommern at the time of the German capitulation, about fifty would return to Norway between 1947 and 1949. However, this only happened after the country, following repeated insistence from the Allies and UNRRA, had declared itself willing to take back those children who received insufficient care in Germany. But even the repatriation of these children by UNRRA did not always follow the rules, and in some cases they were abruptly and traumatically snatched from their German foster families. The children who eventually returned to Norway, all between the ages of 5 and 9, usually ended up in orphanages awaiting adoption. Because of their background and the fact they only spoke German, their stay there would often be very long. Some even spent their entire childhood in institutions.

More than eighty Norwegian-German children remained in Germany because they were left with German adoptive families, or because they could not be traced, were reported dead, or because they lived in East Germany, which was now behind the Iron Curtain. The Stasi, the East German secret service, took advantage of the situation in 1962 by using the identity of a number of children raised in East Germany. The service sought out the real war children – who were officially Norwegian citizens – and banned them from ever making contact with the Norwegian authorities, as well as using their identities for agents who were taken in as 'lost children' in Norway and received a Norwegian passport. A 'real' war child who grew up in East Germany also used his right to Norwegian citizenship as a Stasi agent.[2] The fate of about seventy-five Norwegian-German children who were in Germany in the spring of 1945 is uncertain.

As far as is known, most of the other foreign children who stayed in Lebensborn homes, about 1,000 in total, eventually returned to their own countries. This was mainly due to the efforts of the various international organizations (UNRRA, IRO, ITS and the Red Cross) who tracked down and repatriated them. A smaller group remained in Germany after the war. These children were either not found by the investigative organizations or wanted to stay with their German foster parents. In the latter case, it often concerned children who had already been living in Polish orphanages before the German invasion.

An unknown number of the children who were placed with foster parents at a very young age never knew they came from abroad. They were perhaps better off than those who did know or found out later in life and embarked on an often-fruitless search for their origins. These were often impossible to trace, especially because they had been given a new identity at Lebensborn and many of the files in which their real names and backgrounds were recorded had disappeared around the time of Germany's surrender. Doubts about their origins persisted throughout their lives.

The Norwegian Institutions

The approximately 500 children who were in the Norwegian settlements of Lebensborn at the end of the war often fared little better than the Norwegian-German children in Germany. The hatred of the Germans and the Norwegian women who had relations with them also affected their children. Moreover, there was also fear among part of the Norwegian population that the Lebensborn children could form a future 'Fifth Column' of Nazis in Norway. Apparently, the Norwegians who harboured such fears believed in the views of the 'Germanic blood' as much as the racial ideologues of the SS.

As was the case with their mothers, the children were not only looked down upon by the population, but also by the Norwegian government. This began immediately following Germany's surrender. Although the Norwegian government was responsible for them from then on and should have taken over the care of the infants and young children, practically nothing happened. In Moldegård and Stalheim, where there was a total of more than 200 children and several dozen young mothers, it turned out that the German personnel had fled and left the infants and women to fend for themselves. The situation was so serious that local branches of the Red Cross had to intervene immediately. Despite repeated requests, the Red Cross initially received no support from the government and local volunteers had to provide the financial resources themselves. Only throughout the month of June, about a month and a half later, did the Norwegian government take any action, but the Red Cross remained responsible for food and care until the closure of both homes.

In the Kinderheim Godthaab and Heim Høsbjør, both the German and the Norwegian staff had remained at their posts after the capitulation. Heim Høsbjør closed two weeks later when all the mothers and their children had

A group photograph of children, young mothers and nurses in an unidentified Lebensborn Norwegian children's home, possibly Godthaab, in (for them) better times; before the German capitulation and the chaotic situation that followed. (*Nasjonalbiblioteket Norway*)

left the clinic, but Godthaab, where some 160 children were present, would continue to function much longer. There, the staff of seventy-five, forty of whom were Germans under the leadership of the braune Oberschwester Berta Betz, remained responsible for the children for almost half a year. She received help in this from the leader of the Norwegian branch of Lebensborn, the (former) SS-Hauptsturmführer Ernst Ragaller, who was not arrested after the German surrender but continued to run the organization's headquarters in Oslo for several weeks. He wanted to finish his work and then hand over the administration to the Norwegian government. When the police closed the office at the end of May, Ragaller remained at large and travelled to Godthaab. There he continued the administrative settlement and arranged the supply of the children's home by organizing food from former Wehrmacht depots. The Norwegian authorities refused to take over the home or provide support and only after much deliberation and insistence did the Norwegian Red Cross send help. In the end, Oberschwester Betz, her German nurses and SS-Hauptsturmführer Ragaller left Godthaab in October 1945.[3]

In the next six months, the majority of the children went to their mothers, other relatives, foster families or a children's home. Of the latter group, a number of children were subjected to a psychiatric examination after some Norwegian experts in the field were convinced that the children in the former Lebensborn homes were mentally underdeveloped. Although living in large groups and the relatively limited personal attention was certainly not conducive to development, hardly any indications were found for this. But the fact that such an investigation was carried out gave the population even more reason to think that something was wrong with the children themselves. Partly because of this, a number of them were never adopted and spent a large part or even the rest of their lives in homes.

Their mothers also suffered a sad fate. After five years of oppression and terror, the Norwegian population was extremely hostile to the Germans and all their compatriots who had associated themselves with the occupiers. This was especially true for Norwegian women who had had friendly or even sexual relations with German soldiers. As in most other countries after the German occupation, these women were labelled 'Jerry's whores', mistreated by the population and, in many cases, had their hair cut off. And although they had not broken any Norwegian law, they were also punished by the government. Thousands of women lost their jobs, were rounded up and imprisoned for shorter or longer periods of time or made to work as forced labourers. The former maternity hospital of Lebensborn Klekken was also used for this purpose.

Some women, such as the mother of the most famous Norwegian Lebensborn child, Anni-Frid Lyngstad, the brunette[!] singer of ABBA, fled abroad. After a

The Norwegian women who had had relationships with German soldiers suffered heavily after the war, just as they did in all other former occupied countries. They were mistreated and discriminated against by the population and punished by the Norwegian government, even though they had not broken any laws. Many women were imprisoned, some of them in the former Lebensborn establishment of Klekken, as seen here. (*Private collection*)

short relationship with the German NCO Alfred Haase, Synni Lyngstad became pregnant and Anni-Frid was born on 15 November 1945 in Ballangen near Narvik. Lebensborn did not have its own clinics there, but there was a sub-department of the organization in Narvik where Anni-Frid's mother probably asked for help. As a result of the poor treatment the women received after the war, her grandmother went to Sweden with Anni-Frid, followed shortly by her mother.

A large number of Norwegian women, with or without a child, were able to marry their German boyfriends at the end of the occupation, but had to pay a high price for it, just like those who had earlier married soldiers of the occupying forces. These women immediately lost their nationality and were subsequently detained, awaiting deportation to Germany.

Justice?

From the end of 1945 to the spring of 1949, trials were held in Nuremberg against the leading figures of the Nazi regime and the most important war criminals. First, the twenty-four highest leaders were brought before an international tribunal. There Göring, Hess, Keitel, Ribbentrop, Speer and a number of others had to answer for their actions. In October 1946, a second series of trials began before a US military court to convict those who had committed the actual war crimes. These 'Nuremberg Military Trials' concerned twelve different cases in which, among others, doctors, lawyers, industrialists and bankers, senior civil servants, staff officers, SS leaders and the executors of race and population policy were brought to court.

The latter group consisted of the leaders of the RuSHA, RKFDV, VoMi and Lebensborn. According to the prosecutors, these SS organizations existed 'for one primary purpose in effecting the ideology and programme of Hitler, which may be summed up in one phrase – the two-fold objective of weakening and eventually destroying other nations while at the same time strengthening Germany, territorially and biologically, at the expense of conquered nations.'

The lawsuit against the operatives of race and population policy (officially 'United States of America vs. Ulrich Greifelt et al.', but commonly referred to as the 'RuSHA Case') had thirteen men and one woman on trial: the leader of the RKFDV, SS-Obergruppenführer Ulrich Greifelt and some of his subordinates; senior officers of the VoMi and RuSHA; and Max Sollmann, Gregor Ebner, Günther Tesch and Inge Viermetz from Lebensborn. Viermetz was the only woman to be charged with war crimes at Nuremberg.

The accused – all SS officers except Viermetz – stood trial for crimes against humanity, war crimes and membership in criminal organization. According to the prosecutors, to achieve their goals they had kidnapped foreign children and selected them for Germanization on their racial value; forced Eastern European workers to have abortions or taken their children away; executed Eastern Europeans who had a sexual relationship with Germans; carried out ethnic cleansing of enemy populations to settle ethnic Germans; looted public and private property in Germany and the occupied territories, and participated in the persecution and mass murder of the Jews.

The trial lasted approximately eight months, from the initial indictment on 7 July 1947 to 10 March 1948. The leader of the RKFDV, SS-Obergruppenführer Greifelt was sentenced to life and his subordinates between two and twenty years in prison; the RuSHA officers were sentenced to between ten and twenty years. One of them, SS-Obergruppenführer Hildebrandt, was then extradited to Poland, tried again, and executed.

The fourteen defendants of the trial against the executors of the race and population policy that took place in Nuremberg between 20 October 1947 and 10 March 1948. Among them are Lebensborn's Max Sollmann (front row, far right), Günther Tesch (back row, left), Gregor Ebner (back row, centre), and Inge Viermetz (back row, right). (*USHMM No. 16809*)

SS-Obersturmbannführer Sollmann was also threatened with possible extradition to Poland, Czechoslovakia, or the Soviet Union during his interrogation, but in the end, like the other Lebensborn defendants, he escaped severe reprimand. Both Sollmann and Ebner were convicted to two years and eight months in prison; Tesch two years and ten months. However, they were not punished because of their role at Lebensborn and the associated charges, but because of their membership in the SS, which had been declared a criminal organization in its entirety a few years earlier. Because the men had already been detained for this amount of time, they were immediately released. Viermetz was also acquitted.

The acquittal of Lebensborn's staff was explained by the presiding judge, Lee B. Wyatt, as follows:

> It is quite clear from the evidence that the Lebensborn Society, which existed long prior to the war, was a welfare institution, and primarily a maternity home. From the beginning, it cared

The US Military Tribunal. From left to right are judges Daniel T. O'Connell, Lee B. Wyatt (Chairman), and Johnson Tal Crawford. (*USHMM No. 07350*)

for mothers, both married and unmarried, and children, both legitimate and illegitimate. The prosecution has failed to prove with the requisite certainty the participation of Lebensborn, and the defendants connected therewith, in the kidnaping programme conducted by the Nazis. While the evidence has disclosed that thousands upon thousands of children were unquestionably kidnaped by other agencies or organizations and brought into Germany, the evidence has further disclosed that only a small percentage of the total number ever found their way into Lebensborn. And of this number only in isolated instances did Lebensborn take children who had a living parent. The majority of those children in any way connected with Lebensborn were orphans of ethnic Germans. As a matter of fact, it is quite clear from the evidence that Lebensborn sought to avoid taking into its homes, children who had family ties; and Lebensborn went to the extent of making extensive investigations where the records

> were inadequate, to establish the identity of a child and, whether it had family ties. When it was discovered that the child had a living parent, Lebensborn did not proceed with an adoption, as in the case of orphans, but simply allowed the child to be placed in a German home after an investigation of the German family for the purpose of determining the good character of the family and the suitability of the family to care for and raise the child. Lebensborn made no practice of selecting and examining foreign children. In all instances where foreign children were handed over to Lebensborn by other organizations after a selection and examination, the children were given the best of care and never illtreated in any manner. It is quite clear from the evidence that of the numerous organizations operating in Germany who were connected with foreign children brought into Germany, Lebensborn was the one organization which did everything in its power to adequately provide for the children and protect the legal interests of the children placed in its care.

The acquittal of Lebensborn's leaders did not cause much controversy at the time. The main executors of the race and population policy, the leaders of the RuSHA, had received relatively long prison sentences. Among their acts, murder and kidnapping, Lebensborn's conduct, as far as was known, compared favourably. Circumstances had also changed. The war had already ended four years ago and people preferred to look ahead. More importantly, the Cold War was in full swing and western countries viewed West Germany as an important ally in containing communism. The highest American administrator in occupied German territory therefore pursued a policy aimed at propitiating German public opinion towards the United States. German soldiers who had committed even more serious war crimes than the leaders of Lebensborn therefore usually got off with very mild sentences.

The defenders of Sollmann, Ebner, Tesch and Viermetz could be satisfied. They had managed to convince the judges that Lebensborn had played little part in the main charge against the organization; the kidnapping of foreign children. According to them, the children from other countries who came to Lebensborn were almost all orphans of ethnic Germans. Therefore, there would be no question of Germanization, but rather of re-Germanization; after all, they were already Germans, according to the defence. Furthermore, Lebensborn would not have known anything about the kidnappings, and if there were kidnappings at all, the organization was not involved because they only received children who were sent to their homes. The defence also found a number of witnesses, including children and forced prisoners, who told the court they had been treated well. And it could truthfully be argued that many of the children had been placed with loving foster parents who in many, if not most cases, had not belonged to the SS.

However, the truth was widely violated in the statements of the accused, which were characterized by forgetfulness and lies. They denied any allegations unless they were presented with hard evidence. For example, Ebner, the avowed racial fanatic, stated that 'when I finally went to Lebensborn, I did that prompted by my love of the medical profession and prompted by my compassion with mothers and children who, because of wrong moral conceptions, were not or could not be cared for by their own people and were covered with shame'. According to him, race played no role whatsoever. A former employee of Lebensborn confirmed those lies. She testified that Ebner would have selected pregnant women for admission based on social and health criteria, not race. Moreover, as she knew from personal conversations, 'he would have regarded the doctrine of the primacy of the Nordic race as an infancy of racial doctrine'. Lebensborn's medical director said during his interrogation the prosecutors also misinterpreted those terms; 'racially valuable' did not mean that someone belonged to a particularly valuable race, but referred to a mentally and physically healthy person from whom similar offspring could be expected. We came to use that expression through the language of the time, which was 'created by National Socialism and above all by Himmler,' added the former friend and general practitioner of the Reichsführer-SS.

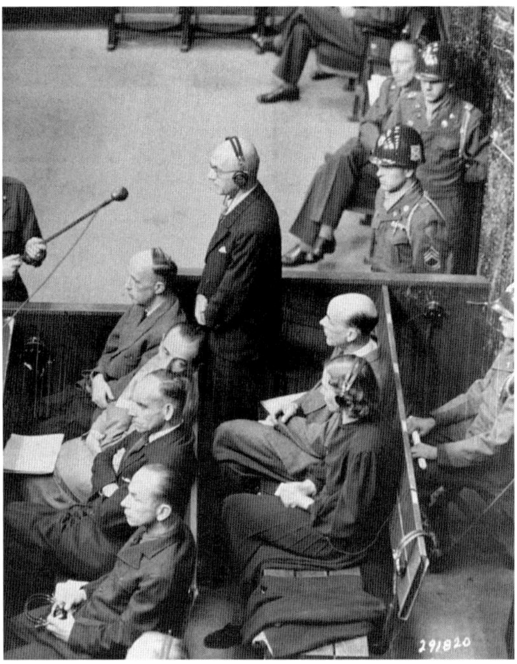

The former medical chief of Lebensborn, SS-Oberführer Gregor Ebner, claimed that the concept of 'race' had played no role in his organization and pleaded not guilty to all charges. (*USHMM No. 43044*)

Sollmann, for his part, claimed that he welcomed the trial to refute the prosecutors' 'unimaginable claims', which he 'would never understand'. During his interrogation he had used the same tactics as most other Germans on trial for war crimes; some of the incriminating facts he had never known about, he claimed, and others he had very little recollection of. He had only 'strongly suspected' that racial tests were taking place and the fact that children were taken from abroad only became clear to him after the surrender. For the answer to such questions, he often referred to Viermetz, who had regularly been on foreign missions for such matters. He first claimed to know nothing about the presence of Czech children in a Lebensborn home, only to declare a little later – after being confronted with evidence – that he had accidentally discovered there were some but had no idea how they got there. When he was subsequently shown a letter in which he promised Himmler to take Czech children into Lebensborn, he stated that he had not really intended to do so and that he had lied to Himmler.

Sollmann maintained that all foreign children who came to Lebensborn were Volksdeutsche orphans placed there by the RKF. The accusation that they had illegally and deliberately tried to conceal their identity was completely wrong; the children were given the names of the adoptive or foster parents on Himmler's orders and, because he was chief of the German police, this practice was therefore lawful. Moreover, he added, the children had an easier time in Germany because their foreign origins were hidden. On the use of buildings belonging to Jewish individuals and institutions by Lebensborn, Sollmann argued that those buildings were already

Like Ebner, Lebensborn director SS-Obersturmbannführer Max Sollmann, seen here in 1950, claimed to be unaware of any wrongdoing. According to his testimony, he had known nothing about foreign children, had lied to Himmler about Czech children and had only suspected that racial examinations were being carried out at Lebensborn. (*Private collection*)

empty because they had been evacuated by the city council due to the aerial threats. Moreover, he added, Lebensborn had officially bought the buildings from the owners, and the fact they had not received their money was due to a change in the law that left it in a blocked account. Sollmann was very angry when he found out, he claimed.

Günter Tesch, Sollmann's deputy and Lebensborn's chief lawyer, stated that Lebensborn was all about caring for people. He declared:

> The activity of Lebensborn, however one may understand it, consisted of care for other people. Mistakes may have occurred, errors which one may only be able to judge today in retrospect. The basic motives, however, the basic motive for helping and assisting other people was predominant in every case.
>
> I personally never had any other motive or other intentions.

Inge Viermetz also denied any charges and claimed to know nothing unless the prosecutors could prove otherwise. She had held only a subordinate position, knew nothing of plans and programmes about genocide and child kidnapping or about racial assessments. She also made use of her gender: 'I am a woman, so I have to make sure that the children are doing well ...' And, her lawyer added: 'Whoever knows the power relations in the Third Reich, who especially knows the views of the SS about man and woman, he knows that a woman had nothing to say in public life and in politics …'

However, the release of Ebner, Sollmann and Viermetz

Inge Viermetz claimed that because of her subordinate position she had not known about child abduction and racial selection. Her sole concern would have been for the well-being of the children. Her lawyer added that, as a woman in the Third Reich and part of the SS, she naturally had had no say in her actions. (*Public domain*)

at the end of the American military trial did not mean that they could resume their place in society undisturbed. A short time later, they were arrested again and at the end of 1949 were back in court, this time appearing before the Munich *Hauptspruchkammer* as part of the denazification process.

Viermetz was again acquitted, but Ebner and Sollmann were found guilty thanks to their criminal activities under the Nazi regime. The punishments were nevertheless relatively mild. Ebner, who had since reopened his general practice, received a hefty fine, sixty days' community service and a professional ban for five years. Not much later, however, the fine was reduced and after a request for leniency, in which he promised to make an effort to be 'a loyal servant of the young democratic state', he was allowed to return to work immediately as a GP. The support of the municipality of Kirchseon, where his practice was located, and of the local doctors' association were of decisive importance in this amnesty. Sollmann's sentence was even lighter, if that were possible. He stated in court that he had 'always been a convinced National Socialist' and that he 'believed in the cause of National Socialism and in the possibility of a successful outcome of the war until 1 May 1945'.[4] Despite this, he received no

Not long after the end of the Nuremberg trial, four staff members of Lebensborn had to answer again, this time before the Hauptspruchkammer in Munich in the context of the denazification. Sitting here awaiting the verdict are (from left to right) Max Sollmann, Wolfgang Überschaar (Sollmann's former adjutant), Gregor Ebner and Inge Viermetz. Sollmann and Ebner were found guilty, but only received very light sentences. (*Private collection*)

more than thirty days' community service less pre-trial detention and a fine of 30% of his assets. The fine was reduced to 50 Deutschmarks after his appeal.

In the early 1970s, Sollmann, then living in a flat on the outskirts of Munich, was tracked down by the French journalist Marc Hillel and his wife Clarissa Henry, who were working on a book about Lebensborn and had easily found Sollmann in the Munich telephone directory. After Clarissa Henry had posed on the phone as a Lebensborn child who had been born in the French clinic in Lamorlaye, Sollmann was willing to meet them.

A particular detail that immediately caught the eye of the French couple was a deluxe edition of *Mein Kampf* displayed on Sollmann's bookcase. During the meeting, the former SS-Obersturmbannführer was particularly indignant about the way he had been treated after the war and the stories that were circulating about Lebensborn at the time. He declared that Lebensborn was 'a good thing' and they had 'unfortunately not taken advantage of the opportunities offered by it'. He also claimed to have known nothing about the existence of concentration camps – 'hardly anyone knew anything about them' – and thus forgot about his own KZ-Aussenlager 'Lebensborn'. Sollmann clearly still believed in his old ideals and especially in those of Lebensborn. He showed great interest in the fortunes of Clarissa Henry, the alleged Lebensborn child, and offered her all possible help. Sollman still had a job at the time, but what exactly he did is unknown. He would die eight years later, on 27 May 1978.

After Sollmann, the French duo also tracked down Gregor Ebner, who was living in the village of Wolfratshausen, about 30 kilometres south of Munich. Ebner's wife let them in after Clarissa Henry again pretended to be a Lebensborn child and received a warm reception. Ebner, who had run his family practice until the 1960s, had become paralyzed a year earlier and could no longer speak, but his wife did the honours brilliantly. Like Sollmann, she was disgraced that Lebensborn was portrayed as a breeding farm and an SS brothel. She explained Lebensborn's preference for blonde women with blue eyes as fashionable at the time. She complained about the many 'illegitimate children of Americans and Negroes' who were born in Germany after the war, and whose children were left unattended. 'In the homes of Lebensborn, such girls were at least helped and their children cared for.' When asked by the French whether this also applied to Jewish and Slavic girls, she replied: 'Certainly, everyone was helped'. She then reminisced about Himmler and how he would often come to their house before the war with his daughter Gudrun and play with their children. 'He was a good and honest man who was always willing to help others. Unfortunately, we rarely saw him during the war, because he was so busy with all those prisoners in those camps.'[5]

Gregor Ebner, the former SS-Oberführer, died on 22 March 1974, not long after Hillel and Henry's visit.

The other employees of Lebensborn also got off lightly and at most were only punished with a fine. Like virtually all the other SS race experts, who were both theorists and implementers of the ruthless race policy, they were never held accountable for their actions. After the war, many built up a fine career in which their past endeavours presented no obstacle.

Just like Sollmann and Ebner, Inge Viermetz had to appear before the Hauptspruchkammer München, but she was acquitted. She married for the third time in 1957, to a man who had worked for the VoMi and who had made a – presumably false – exculpatory statement for her before the court in Nuremberg. After that she lived an inconspicuous life and refused to speak further about Lebensborn, not even to Clarissa Henry, the so-called Lebensborn child. Viermetz died on 23 April 1997.

The former SS-Sturmbannführer Günther Tesch, Lebensborn's chief legal man and Sollmann's deputy, was a free man after the Nuremberg trial and was no longer prosecuted. He returned to Dortmund and had a successful career there as a lawyer and civil-law notary until the 1970s. Tesch died on 7 March 1989.

Hans-Hilmar Staudte (1911-1979), the second man and deputy head of the legal department, was not charged despite his high position in the organization, but was called as a witness in Nuremberg, where he gave false testimony that Lebensborn had nothing to do with the race and population policy of the SS. He stated the organization only served to improve the social position of mother and child. After the war, the former SS-Obersturmbannführer reached a high

Former SS-Obersturmbannführer Hans-Hilmar Staudte, the deputy head of the important Rechtswesen (legal) department, was not charged at Nuremberg but called as a witness. He falsely testified to Lebensborn's purpose and methods and had a fine career in the following decades with the West German Ministry of Finance. (*Public domain*)

official position in the West German Ministry of Finance. Staudte was an excellent chess player and competed for West Germany in the Chess Olympiad. He passed away on 1 January 1979.

Erich Schulz headed Lebenborn's own registry office (Standesamt L) and was responsible for a large number of false birth certificates. He managed to evade prosecution and resumed his career as a lawyer in Minden. In 1964 he gave false testimony to prevent a child with an identity forged by his department from returning to her Polish family.[6] The former SS officer was a prominent member of the political party FDP for a long time. He passed away on 1 June 1979.

SS-Sturmbannführer Ernst Ragaller headed several main departments at the Zentrale and later the Lebensborn department at the Reichskommissariat in Norway, where he remained active until October 1945. He was then detained in Norway and transferred to Germany two years later, where he acted as a witness at the military trial in Nuremberg and stated, among other things, that he 'cannot remember that there were children at Lebensborn who were not born there'. After a lengthy legal procedure, in 1950 the Hauptspruchkammer München sentenced him to pay court costs of 6,000 Deutschmarks. He died on 10 June 1951.

A few individuals associated with the organization paid with their lives for their war crimes, though not for their part in Lebensborn. The first director, Guntram Pflaum, came to an end in style. He was most likely murdered around the end of the war by recently released prisoners of concentration camp Ebensee, near Mauthausen.

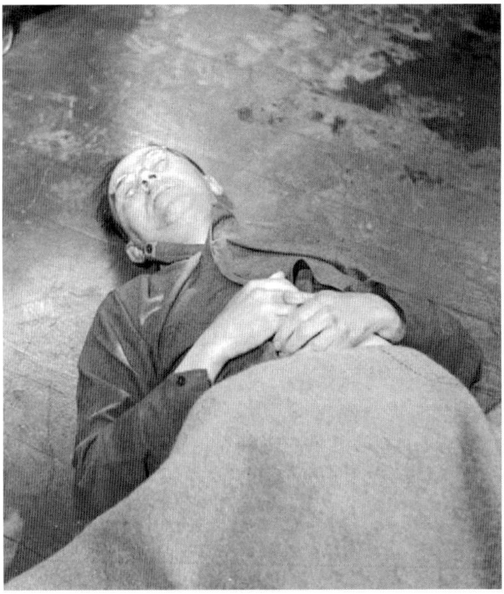

The former founder, spiritual leader and chairman of Lebensborn, Heinrich Himmler, after his suicide at the headquarters of the British 2nd Army on 23 May 1945. (*L. Sutton, Public domain*)

The duo responsible for establishing and operating the Norwegian branch of Lebensborn, SS-Obergruppenführer Wilhelm Rediess and Reichskommissar Terboven, committed suicide on 8 May 1945. After Rediess first shot himself in the head, Terboven blew up his body and himself by detonating 50 kilograms of dynamite in a bunker.

The creator, founder and leader of Lebensborn, Reichsführer-SS Heinrich Himmler, was still on the run at the time of Germany's surrender and tried to escape arrest with forged papers and a false identity. A few days after he was arrested at a checkpoint on 21 May, he revealed his identity. Three days later, he committed suicide by biting down on a capsule of cyanide hidden in his mouth.

Half a Century Later

In 1999, over half a century after the end of the war, a group of Norwegian children born in Lebensborn clinics founded the organization *Krigsbarnforbundet Lebensborn*. Its aim was to obtain reparation and compensation from the Norwegian government for the ill-treatment and discrimination they – mothers and children – had suffered after the war. The women were treated as criminals, excluded by society and often mistreated. Many were imprisoned in special camps, and those who had married German soldiers had their nationalities stripped before being transferred to Germany.

Many of the Norwegian-German children who remained in Norway were so scarred by long stays in homes and psychiatric institutions or poor treatment by foster parents that they could never lead a normal life again. After several proceedings in Norway, a lawsuit was filed with the European Court of Human Rights in 2007, but it deemed the case time-barred. It was not until 2018 that the Norwegian government officially apologized to the women and children.

In Germany, the association *Lebensspuren* was founded in 2005 by children who were born in Lebensborn clinics or were transferred from abroad to a home of the organization. The association provides information about Lebensborn to propagate that it was not a charity nor an SS brothel – two misconceptions that still seem to exist. Furthermore, Lebensspuren aims to promote mutual communication between the Lebensborn children and to help them in their search for their own roots. The lack of love and security in their early childhood and the uncertainty about their origins in later years has marked the lives of the Lebensborn children.

In the words of Lebensspuren:

> Part of the children born at Lebensborn and those abducted from occupied foreign countries lacked the necessary security and warmth of a family during their formative first years of life. They were sent from home to home or had to change foster homes frequently. Their origin was often concealed from them even at a later age. Even when they grew up with their own mothers, they often did not learn the truth about their birth. The children experienced the separation of the mother or parents, the lack of a trusted caregiver or the lies of the mother as a basic breach of trust. It shaped them for the rest of their lives.
>
> Because the records of the Lebensborn civil registry were lost at the end of the war, some of the children born in the clinics are still looking for their natural parents. This also applies to foreign children abducted to Germany. Because of their Germanized names and the deliberate destruction of documents, not all of them could be identified and returned to their own countries after the war. It is not known how many of them still live in Germany today without knowing who their parents are or what their real nationality is.

Appendix I

SUMMARY OF ALL LEBENSBORN BRANCHES

(See map on p.78)

Hochland, Steinhöring, Germany, maternity hospital & children's home

Acquisition	Purchased from the Bavarian government for approximately 5% of market value.
Open from/to	August 1936 – May 1945.
Capacity	First 30 women and 45 children; from 1940 onward 51 women and 106 children.
Number of births	1,438.
Heimleiter(s)	SS-Oberführer Gregor Ebner.
Oberschwester	Else Oventrop; Leni von Radziewski and others.
Details	The first branch and model clinic. Had its own KZ-Aussenlager 'Lebensborn'. From the autumn of 1943, the largest part of the Zentrale was gradually established here. On 3 May 1945, American troops found 163 babies and toddlers.

Harz, Wernigerode, Germany, maternity hospital & children's home

Acquisition	Donated to Lebensborn by the NSV.
Open from/to	June 1937 – May 1945.
Capacity	First 14 women and 5 children; later 30 women and 48 children.
Number of births	1,103.
Heimleiter(s)	SS-Untersturmführer and Dr Fritz Wohlfahrt; Dr Lindemann; SS Hauptsturmführer Dr Baatz.
Oberschwester	Ida Matthiesen; Ella Blank; Anna Dickel; Luise W.
Details	A private nurse in this town regularly received payments from Lebensborn, which she registered as 'Kind Himmler'.

Kurmark, Klosterheide, Germany, maternity hospital & children's home

Acquisition	Rented from the Wehrmacht, later possibly donated.
Open from/to	September 1937 – end of 1944.
Capacity	First 28 women and 30 children; later 23 women and 86 children.
Number of births	Approximately 1,000.
Heimleiter(s)	SS-Hauptsturmführer Werner Laumann; SS-Hauptsturmführer Heinz Westermann.
Oberschwester	Johanna Veiel; Erika Wittmann; Else Bertram.
Details	According to some sources, the home was led in 1943–1944 by SS-Standartenführer Guntram Pflaum, who was chairman of Lebensborn until 1940.

Pommern, Bad Polzin (Połczyn-Zdrój), Poland, maternity hospital & children's home

Acquisition	Donated by Hitler to Lebensborn.
Open from/to	May 1938 – February 1945.
Capacity	60 women and 75 children.
Number of births	Unknown.
Heimleiter(s)	SS-Untersturmführer Dr Robert Düker; SS-Obersturmführer Dr August Hagemeijer; SS Hauptsturmführer Dr Norbert Schwab.
Oberschwester	Paula Hessler(?).
Details	In a later phase also used for the Germanization of foreign children.

Friesland, Hohehorst, Germany, first maternity hospital & children's home; later children's home

Acquisition	Purchased from the German government for approximately 8% of market value.
Open from/to	May 1938 – May 1945.
Capacity	First 34 women and 45 children; from 1940 40 women and 64 children.
Number of births	217.
Verwalter(s)	SS-Untersturmführer Otto Bachschneider; SS-Anwärter Ernst Günther Häusing; SS-Untersturmführer Fritz Meyer-Schmidt; Franz Langer (rank unknown); SS-Untersturmführer Walter Decker.

Heimleiter(s) SS-Sturmbannführer Walter Albrecht Lang.
Oberschwester Margot Holm; Anna Holzer; Leni von Radziewski; Helen Lehrke; Else Bertram; Else Schwartman.
Details Closed early 1941 due to air danger; reopened in the autumn of 1944 and then mainly used for the care of mothers and children from evacuated homes. 32 Norwegian babies were also brought there.

Wienerwald, Feichtenbach, Austria, maternity hospital & children's home

Acquisition Looted Jewish property.
Open from/to November 1938 – April 1945.
Capacity 49 women and 83 children.
Number of births Between 1,200 and 1,700.
Heimleiter(s) Dr Karl Sernetz; SS-Hauptsturmführer Dr Norbert Schwab; SS Hauptsturmführer Dr Bissing; Dr August Hagemeijer.
Oberschwester Unknown.
Details The first branch in annexed Austria. The property was personally seized by the then director SS-Obersturmbannführer Guntram Pflaum. Initially called Heim Ostmark for a short time.

Taunus, Wiesbaden, Germany, first only a children's home; later also a maternity hospital

Acquisition Leased by the church to Lebensborn under heavy pressure from the SS.
Open from/to November 1938 – March 1945.
Capacity Initially 55 children, later unknown number of women and children.
Number of births Approximately 500.
Heimleiter(s) From autumn 1943 SS-Untersturmführer and Dr Robert Wilhelm Düker; in the first period Verwalter Müller and female physician Dr Mader.
Oberschwester Anna Dickel; Else Krauss.
Details Opened as a children's home but closed in November 1941 due to poor condition and reopened after a renovation in autumn 1943, then also as a maternity hospital.

Schwarzwald, Nordrach, Germany, maternity hospital & children's home

Acquisition	Looted Jewish property.
Open from/to	November 1942 – April 1945.
Capacity	Unknown.
Number of births	Approximately 250.
Heimleiter(s)	SS-Obersturmführer and Dr August Hagemeijer.
Oberschwester	Unknown.
Details	After the war, used by the French occupation forces to investigate German-French children.

Sonnenwiese, Kohren-Sahlis, Germany, children's home

Acquisition	Sold by the city council under duress from SS to Lebensborn.
Open from/to	November 1942 – April 1945.
Capacity	170 children.
Heimleiter(s)	Ullrich.
Oberschwester	Erika Wittmann.
Details	Children may have been admitted a year before the official opening. The (male) Heimleiter was not a doctor, but two female doctors were employed. First Herma Hermengild, then Hildegard Feith. Widely used for Germanizing foreign children.

Alpenland, Laakirchen, Austria, children's home

Acquisition	Stolen property from owner with 'hostile disposition'.
Open from/to	September 1943 – Spring 1945.
Capacity	About 50 children.
Heimleiter(s)	Maria Plate; Hedwig Ridder; Maria Knipp-Merkel.
Oberschwester	Unknown.
Details	Specially founded and used exclusively for the Germanization of foreign children. From September 1944, Maria Knipp-Merkel was not only Heimleiter here, but also headed the department of the Lebensborn Zentrale from the home, which was responsible for the mediation of the foreign children.

Franken I & II, Ansbach, Germany, children's homes

Acquisition	Unknown.
Open from/to	June 1944 – April 1945.
Capacity	Probably about 50 children.
Details	Specially established due to evacuation of other locations due to increasing air danger and the advancing enemy. Franken II was established in a former care and nursing home, whose original inhabitants had been murdered as part of Aktion T4.

Kristinelund, Oslo, Norway, guest house

Acquisition	Seized.
Open from/to	March 1941 – August 1941(?).
Capacity	15 women.
Number of births	Unknown.
Details	First branch in Norway, intended for temporary care of pregnant Norwegian women until the first maternity hospital opened.

Hurdalsverk, Hurdalsverk, Norway, maternity hospital & children's home

Acquisition	Seized.
Open from/to	August 1941 – May 1945.
Capacity	About 45 women and 69 children.
Number of births	Approximately 600.
Details	Lebensborn's first maternity hospital in Norway. (Also called Hurdal Verk or Hurdalverk.)

Klekken, Hønefoss, Norway, maternity hospital & children's home

Acquisition	Seized.
Open from/to	May 1942 – May 1945.
Capacity	35 women, 60 children.
Number of births	Approximately 360.
Details	After the war used by the Norwegian government to detain women suspected of social and/or sexual intercourse with Germans.

Geilo, Geilo, Norway, maternity hospital & children's home

Acquisition	Seized.
Open from/to	December 1942 – April/May 1945.
Capacity	60 women and 20 children.
Number of births	Approximately 200.
Details	As 'Vorheim' also intended to remove women from their environment earlier and thus bring them under German influence more quickly. Would close in the spring of 1945 to be replaced by Høsbjør.

Høsbjør, Brumunddal, Norway, maternity hospital & children's home

Acquisition	Aeized.
Open from/to	April – May 1945.
Capacity	100 women, unknown number of children.
Number of births	24.
Details	Would open in the spring of 1945 and take over the function of Geilo.

Godthaab, Oslo, Norway, children's home

Acquisition	Seized.
Open from/to	February 1942 – Spring 1946.
Capacity	160 children.
Oberschwester	Berta Betz.
Details	Godthaab remained under German rule for almost six months after the capitulation.

Stalheim, Voss, Norway, children's home

Acquisition	Seized.
Open from/to	February 1943 – May 1945.
Capacity	80 to 100 children.

Moldegård, Os (Bjørnafjorden), Norway, children's home

Acquisition	Seized.
Open from/to	April 1943 – May 1945.
Capacity	80 children.

Olav, Oslo, Norway, boarding house

Acquisition	Seized.
Open from/to	February 1942 – May 1945.
Capacity	20 women and 6 children.
Number of births	Unknown.
Details	The first of three Stadtheime, which were intended for (expectant) mothers and Lebensborn staff.

Bergen, Hop, Norway, boarding house

Acquisition	Seized.
Open from/to	June 1942 – May 1945.
Capacity	20 women and 6 children.
Number of births	Unknown.
Details	Stadtheim: boarding house for (future) mothers and Lebensborn staff.

Drontheim, Trondheim, Norway, boarding house

Acquisition	Seized.
Open from/to	Autumn 1942 – May 1945.
Capacity	30 women and 10 children.
Number of births	Unknown.
Details	Stadtheim: boarding house for (future) mothers and Lebensborn staff.

Ardennen, Ayeneux, Belgium, maternity hospital & children's home

Acquisition	Seized.
Open from/to	March 1943 – 1 September 1944.
Capacity	About 30 women and 35 children.
Number of births	Approximately 100.
Heimleiter(s)	SS-Sturmbannführer Walter Albrecht Lang.
Oberschwester	Margarethe Petrowska, Lydia Vorsatz and Josefa Kroll(?).
Details	Founded and led in the first months by Inge Viermetz.

Moselland, Luxembourg, children's home

Acquisition	Seized.
Open from/to	July 1943 – 9 September 1944.
Capacity	Several dozen children.

Oberschwester	Margarethe Petrowska.
Details	Luxembourg was annexed by Nazi Germany.

Westwald, Lamorlaye, France, maternity hospital & children's home

Acquisition	Seized.
Open from/to	February 1944 – 10 August 1944.
Capacity	Several dozen women and children.
Number of births	About 20 to 25.
Heimleiter(s)	SS-Unterscharführer Grünwald.
Oberschwester	Josefa Kroll.

Tønder, Tønder, Denmark, maternity hospital & children's home

Acquisition	Presumably seized.
Open from/to	April – May 1945.
Capacity	Probably several dozen women and children.
Number of births	Unknown.
Details	Opened in the last weeks of the war; the name of the establishment is not known with certainty.

Kriegsmütter- und Wohnheim Johannistal, Szczecin, Poland, guesthouse

Acquisition	Seized.
Open from/to	June 1940 – mid 1944.
Capacity	About 100 mothers and children.
Heimleiter(s)	SS-Obersturmführer Otto Bachschneider.
Details	Intended for working, single 'Aryan' mothers who wanted to keep their child(ren) with them. Founded and led for the first two years by SS-Obersturmführer Otto Bachschneider, formerly the administrator of Heim Friesland.

Heimstätte, Smoszewo, Poland, guesthouses

Acquisition	Unknown.
Open from/to	April 1944 – Summer 1944.
Capacity	About 22 women and 22 children.
Specifics	Never completed project which, according to the plan, should have provided approximately ten times as many places. In addition to sheltering women and children, it also served to Germanize the region.

Gelderland, Nijmegen, the Netherlands, maternity hospital & children's home

Acquisition	Seized.
Capacity	About 60 women and 100 children.
Details	The building was confiscated in the spring of 1942 and after an extensive and costly renovation, was ready in the spring of 1943. Its opening was repeatedly postponed and in the end was never commissioned.

Appendix II

GLOSSARY

BDM / Bund Deutscher Mädel
League of German Girls

EWZ / Einwandererzentralstelle
Central Bureau for Immigration

HSSPF / Höhere SS- und Polizeiführer
Higher SS and Police Leader

KZ / Konzentrationslager
Concentration camp

NSDAP / Nationalsozialistische Deutsche Arbeiterpartei
National Socialist German Worker's Party

NSV / Nationalsozialistische Volkswohlfahrt
National Socialist Public Welfare Association

RKFDV / RKF / Reichskommissariat für die Festigung deutschen Volkstums
Reich Commission for the Strengthening of Germanism

RSHA / Reichssicherheitshauptamt
Reich Security Main Office

RuS-Führer / Rasse- und Siedlungsführer
Race and Settlement Leader

RuSHA / Rasse- und Siedlungshauptamt
SS Race and Settlement Main Office

SS-Eignungsprüfer
SS Racial examiner

Standesamt
Civil Registry Office

UWZ / Umwandererzentralstelle
Central Bureau for Resettlement

VoMi / Volksdeutsche Mittelstelle
Repatriation Office for Ethnic Germans

WVHA / Wirtschafts- und Verwaltungshauptamt
SS Economic and Administrative Main Office

Appendix III

RANKS OF THE SS

Reichsführer-SS	Field Marshal
SS-Oberstgruppenführer	General
SS-Obergruppenführer	Lieutenant General
SS-Gruppenführer	Major General
SS-Brigadeführer	Brigadier
SS-Oberführer	Senior Colonel
SS-Standartenführer	Colonel
SS-Obersturmbannführer	Lieutenant Colonel
SS-Sturmbannführer	Major
SS-Hauptsturmführer	Captain
SS-Obersturmführer	First Lieutenant
SS-Untersturmführer	Second Lieutenant
SS-Junker	Officer Aspirant
SS-Sturmscharführer	Sergeant Major, regimental
SS-Hauptscharführer	Sergeant Major
SS-Oberscharführer	Staff Sergeant
SS-Scharführer	Sergeant
SS-Unterscharführer	Corporal
SS-Rottenführer	Lance Corporal
SS-Sturmmann	Private First class
SS-Schütze	Private
SS-Anwärter	Recruit

ENDNOTES

Foreword

1. G. Lilienthal, *Der 'Lebensborn e.V.' Ein Instrument nationalsozialistischer Rassenpolitik* (Frankfurt 2003).

I Racial Delusion

1. The book by Will Berthold, *Lebensborn e.v:. Tatsachen-Roman* (Munich 1958), was the first to appear about the organization. Although the title suggested otherwise, it was almost entirely based on fantasy.
2. In 1985, the German historian Georg Lilienthal published *Der Lebensborn e.V. Ein Instrument nationalsozialistischer Rassenpolitik*, which is still the standard work on this subject. He was also the first to consign the rumours of an SS brothel or human breeding to the realm of fables.
3. W. Schallmayer, *Vererbung und Auslese im Lebenslauf der Völker* (Jena 1903).
4. *The Archiv für Rassen- und Gesellschaftsbiologie and the Deutschen Gesellschaft für Rassenhygiene.*
5. T.W. Ryback, *Hitler's Private Library*, 69.
6. Ryback, 71.

II Himmler's Obsessions

1. P. Padfield, *Himmler, Reichsfuhrer-SS*, 99.
2. The standard work on Nazi racial politics is: I. Heinemann, *Rasse, Siedlung, deutsches Blut: Das Rasse- und Siedlungshauptamt der SS und die rassenpolitische Neuordnung Europas* (Göttingen 2003). Much of the information about the SS race experts and their activities is taken from this book.
3. Heinemann, 11-12.
4. G. Lilienthal, *Der Lebensborn e.V. Ein Instrument nationalsozialistischer Rassenpolitik*, 203.

III The Racially Pure Greater-German Reich

1. M. Mazower, *Hitler's Empire: Nazi Rule in Occupied Europe*, 181.
2. Ibid., 80.

3. J. Ackermann, *Heinrich Himmler as Ideologe*, 298-300.
4. F. Kersten, *The Kersten Memoirs*, 132.

IV The New Nobility

1. Lilienthal, 43.
2. Ibid., 48.
3. Ibid., 54.
4. See: A. Baumann & A. Heusler (eds), *Kinder für den 'Führer': Der Lebensborn in Munich.*
5. D. Schmitz-Köster, *Deutsche Mutter bist du bereit - Alltag im Lebensborn*, 367.
6. Lilienthal, 124.
7. V. Koop, *Dem Führer ein Kind schenken. Die SS-Organization Lebensborn e.V.*, 72.

V Baby Machines?

1. Schmitz-Köster, 190-1.
2. Ackerman, 117-19.
3. Ibid., 127.
4. F. Kersten, *Klerk en Beul. Himmler van nabij*, 52.
5. Ibid., 52-3.
6. Ackermann, Document No. 3.
7. Ibid., 92.
8. Ibid., 93.
9. Ibid., 95-7.
10. Schmitz-Köster, 158.
11. Ibid., 179.
12. Baumann & Heusler, *Kinder für den 'Führer'*, 102.
13. T. Bryant, *Himmler's Kinder. Zur Geschichte der SS-Organization 'Lebensborn e.V.'*, 221.
14. Lilienthal, 75.
15. Schmitz-Köster, 201.
16. Koop, 266-267.

VI Himmler's Henchmen

1. Baumann & Heusler, 109.
2. Heinemann, 513.
3. Baumann & Heusler, 110.
4. Lilienthal, 212.
5. Ibid., 51.
6. Ackermann, 129.
7. Baumann & Heusler, 113.
8. Bräsel, 114.
9. Koop, 243.
10. Schmitz-Köster, 243 ff.

11. See A. Böltken, *Führerinnen im 'Führerstaat*, 105-25, for a short biographical sketch of Inge Viermetz.
12. Lilienthal, 211.
13. Koop, 247.
14. Lilienthal, 223.
15. Koop, 4.
16. Lilienthal, 67.

VII Aryan Babys

1. Baumann & Heusler, 101.
2. Ibid., 136.
3. M. Hillel & C. Henry, *In naam van het ras*, 286.
4. D. Schmitz-Köster, *Deutsche Mutter bist du bereit - Alltag im Lebensborn* is devoted almost entirely to the history of Heim Friesland: all information presented here is derived from this book.
5. Lilienthal, 57.
6. Ibid., 103.
7. Hillel, 288.
8. The information about Heim Alpenland is mainly taken from: I. Hopfer, *Geraubte Identität. Die gewaltsame 'Eindeutschung' von polnischen Kinder in der NS-Zeit*, 163 ff.

VIII Child Abduction

1. Ackerman, 181.
2. Ibid., 298-300.
3. Hopfer, *Geraubte Identitat*, 44-46.
4. Ibid., 55.
5. *Trials of War Criminals before the Nuernberg Military Tribunals under Control Council Law* No. 10, Vol. IV *'The Einsatzgruppen Case' 'The RuSHA Case'*, 1033-8.
6. *Trials of War Criminals*, 1064.
7. Heinemann, 516-17.
8. Koop, 156.

IX Germanic Brother People

1. Ackerman, 274.
2. Lilienthal, 163.
3. For the best survey work on the Norwegian Lebensborn, see: K. Olsen, *Vater: Deutscher: Das Schicksal der norwegischen Lebensbornkinder und Ihrer Mütter von 1940 bis heute* (Frankfurt 2002).
4. Koop, 192.
5. *Schwert und Wiege*, 29.
6. Ibid., 51.

7. K. Olsen, 'Under the Care of Lebensborn', in: Ericsson, K. & E. Simonson (eds), *Children of World War II, the Hidden Enemy Legacy* (Bloomsbury 2005), 22.
8. *Schwert und Wiege*, 41.
9. Ibid., 42.
10. For those who wish to consult the map, the name 'Os' has disappeared. This area is now called Bjørnafjorden.
11. *Schwert und Wiege*, 55.
12. Koop, 197-8.
13. Olsen, 'Under the Care of Lebensborn', 24.
14. N.K.C.A. In 't Veld, *De SS en Nederland*, Vol. 2 (The Hague 1976), 1150-1.
15. In 't Veld, Vol. 1, 836.
16. R. van Duijn, *Een zoon voor de Führer: De Nazi-utopie van Julia Op ten Noort*, 107.
17. In 't Veld Vol. 2, 1148-51.
18. Most of the information about Herfurth is taken from www.oorloginnijmegen.nl, consulted in August 2022.
19. www.oorloginnijmegen.nl.
20. Most of the information about Julia op ten Noort is derived from the aforementioned book by Roel van Duijn: *Een zoon voor de Führer: De Nazi-utopie van Julia Op ten Noort* (Amsterdam 2018).
21. Van Duijn, 46.
22. Ibid., 53.
23. Koop, 19.
24. Van Duijn, 158.
25. Koop, 203.
26. L. Sioen, 'Hitler's kindercrèche in the Ardennen', *De Standaard*, 26 September 2009.
27. Most of the information on Heim Westwald is taken from: B. Thiolay, *Lebensborn: La fabrique des enfants parfaits* (Paris 2012).
28. Lilienthal, 189.
29. Ibid., 190.
30. Hillel, 155.

X Perpetrators and Victims

1. Koop, 211.
2. Ibid., 234-6.
3. Olsen, *Vater: Deutscher*, 315.
4. Baumann & Heusler, 113.
5. Hillel, 16.
6. A. Fasel, 'Von Nazis der Identität und Kindheit beraubt'. *Welt Nordrhein-Westfalen*, 7 March 2016.

SELECT BIBLIOGRAPHY & ILLUSTRATIONS

Ackermann, J., *Heinrich Himmler als Ideologe* (Göttingen, Zürich, Frankfurt 1970).

Bakker, G., *Duitse Geopolitiek* (Assen 1967).

Baumann, A. & A. Heusler (ed.), *Kinder für den 'Führer' Der Lebensborn in München* (München 2013).

Biesecke, K., *Der Lebensborn: Frauen zwischen Myhtos und Macht* (Norderstedt 2009).

Böltken, A., *Führerinnen im Führerstaat: Gertrud Scholtz-Klink, Trude Mohr, Jutta Rüdiger und Inge Viermetz (*Pfaffenweiler 1995).

Bryant, T., *Himmlers Kinder: Zur Geschichte der SS-Organisation 'Lebensborn e.V.' 1935-1945* (Wiesbaden 2011).

Clay, C. & M. Leapman, *Master Race: The Lebensborn Experiment in Nazi Germany* (London 1995).

Duijn, R. van, *Een zoon voor de Führer: De Nazi-utopie van Julia Op ten Noort* (Amsterdam 2018).

Fasel, A., 'Von Nazis der Identität und Kindheit beraubt', *Welt Nordrhein-Westfalen*, 7 March 2016.

Heinemann, I., *Rasse, Siedlung, deutsches Blut: Das Rasse- und Siedlungshauptamt der SS und die rassenpolitische Neuordnung Europas* (Göttingen 2003).

Helbing, I., *Polens verlorene Kinder: Die Suche und Repatriierung verschleppter polnischer Kinder nach 1945* (Frankfurt 2017).

Hillel, M. & C. Henry, *In naam van het ras* (Den Haag 1977).

Hillel, M. & C. Henry, *Of Pure Blood* (New York 1978).

Hitler, A. *Mijn kamp* (Amsterdam 1939).

Höhne, H., *The Order of the Death's Head: The Story of Hitler's SS* (London 1969).

Hopfer, I., *Geraubte Identität: Die gewaltsame 'Eindeutschung' von polnischen Kinder in der NS-Zeit* (Wien 2010).

Huxley, J., *'Ras' in Europa* (Oxford 1944).

Karpińska-Morek, E., & e.a., *Als wäre ich allein auf der Welt: Der nationalsozialistische Kinderraub in Polen* (Freiburg 2020).

Kershaw, I., *Hitler 1889-1936: hoogmoed* (Utrecht 2008)

Kershaw, I., *Hitler 1936-1945: vergelding* (Utrecht 2008).

Kersten, F., *The Kersten Memoirs* (New York 2011).

Kersten, F., *Klerk en beul: Himmler van nabij* (Amsterdam 1948).
Koop, V., *Dem Führer ein Kind schenken: Die SS-Organisation Lebensborn e.V.* (Wien & Köln 2007).
Königseder, A. (ed), *Der Ort des Terrors: Geschichte der nationalsozialistischen Konzentrationslager. Band II Frühe Lager Dachau Emslandlager* (München 2005).
Krul, A., & e.a., *Het Berchmanianum: Van studiehuis tot academiegebouw* (Nijmegen 2019).
Krumwiede, D., *Der Lebensborn – Lebenshilfe als Rassepolitik: Das Beispiel des Heims 'Friesland'* (München 2013).
Lenhart, A.M., *Eine Darstellung der Organisation 'Lebensborn e.V.'* (Hamburg 2013).
Lilienthal, G., *Der Lebensborn e.V. Ein Instrument nationalsozialistischer Rassenpolitik* (Frankfurt 2003).
Lilienthal, G. & M. Pohl, 'Das 'Lebensborn' Heim 'Taunus' in Wiesbaden (1939-1945), *Nassauische Annalen* 103 (1992), 295-310.
Lilienthal, G., 'Kinder als Beute des Rassenkrieges, Der "Lebensborn e.V." und die Eindeutschung von Kindern aus Polen, der Tschechoslowakei und Jugoslawien', *Dachauer Hefte* 9 (1993), 181-196.
Mazower, M., *Hitler's Empire: Nazi Rule in Occupied Europe* (London 2009).
Neumaier, D., *Das Lebensbornheim 'Schwarzwald' in Nordrach* (Marburg 2017).
Nuernberg Military Tribunals, *Trials of War Criminals before the Nuernberg Military Tribunals under Control Council Law No. 10*, Vol. IV '*The Einsatzgruppen Case*' '*The RuSHA Case*' (Washington N.Y.).
Oelhafen, I. von & T. Tate, *Niemands kind* (Amsterdam 2015).
Olsen, K., *Vater: Deutscher: Das Schicksal der Norwegischen Lebensbornkinder und ihrer Mütter von 1940 bis heute* (Frankfurt 2002).
Olsen, K., 'Under the Care of Lebensborn', in: Ericsson, K. & E. Simonson (eds), *Children of World War II, the Hidden Enemy Legacy* (Bloomsbury 2005), 15-34.
Padfield, P., *Himmler Reichsführer SS* (London 2001).
Rediess, W., *SS für ein Grossgermanien – Schwert und Wiege* (Oslo 1942).
Rehberg, S., 'Die deutsche Besatzung in Norwegen und das Schicksal der "Kriegskinder"', in: G. Heidenreich (ed.), *Born of War – Vom Krieg geboren* (Berlin 2017), 173-190.
Reich, P., *Lebensborn e.V. in Wernigerode: Auswirkungen nationalsozialistischer Geburten- und Rassenpolitik im Harz* (München 2014).
Ryback, T.W., *Hitler's Private Library* (London 2010).
Sandke, C., *Der Lebensborn e.V.. Eine Darstellung der Aktivitäten des Lebensborn e.V. im Kontext der nationalsozialistischen Rassenideologie* (Saarbrücken 2008).
Schmitz-Köster, D., *Deutsche Mutter bist du bereit - Alltag im Lebensborn* (Berlin 1997).
Schmitz-Köster, D., *Lebenslang Lebensborn* (München 2012).
Schwarz, C., 'Das geraubte Baby', *Müncher Merkur*, *Bayern & Region*, Nr. 21, 27 January 2021, 11.
Silke, J., 'Lebensborn in Wernigerode. Auf der Suche nach der wahren Geschichte', in: *Magdeburger Volksstimme*, Nr. 263 (Magdeburg 2002), p.3.
Sioen, L., 'Hitlers kindercrèche in de Ardennen', *De Standaard*, 26 September 2009.

Strippel, A., *NS-Volkstumspolitik und die Neuordnung Europas: Rassenpolitische Selektion der Einwandererzentralstelle des Chefs der Sicherheitspolizei und des SD 1939-1945* (Paderborn/München/Wenen 2011).

Thiolay, B., *Lebensborn. La fabrique des enfants parfaits: Enquête sur ces Français nés dans les maternités SS* (Paris 2012).

Thompson, L.V., 'Lebensborn and the Eugenics Policy of the Reichsführer-SS', *Central European History* 4 (1971), 54-77.

Veld, N.K.C.A., In 't, *De SS en Nederland* 2 dln (Den Haag 1976).

Wältermann, D, 'The Functions and Activities of the Lebensborn Organisation within the SS, the Nazi Regime, and Nazi Ideology', *The Honours Journal II* (1985), 5-23.

Weissteiner, E., *Blonde Kinder für Himmler: Der Lebensborn e.V. im Dritten Reich* (Saarbrücken 2008).

Ziegler, H.F., Fight Against the Empty Cradle: Nazi Pronatal Policies and the SS-Führerkorps, *Historical Social Research* (1986), 11(2), 25-40.

Illustrations

The sources of the illustrations are mentioned after the captions. The following abbreviations are used:

UNRRA	United Nations Relief and Rehabilitation Administration
USHMM	United States Holocaust Memorial Museum
USNA	United States National Archives

INDEX